SPIRITUAL LIVES

General Editor
Timothy Larsen

SPIRITUAL LIVES

General Editor
Timothy Larsen

The *Spiritual Lives* series features biographies of prominent men and women whose eminence is not primarily based on a specifically religious contribution. Each volume provides a general account of the figure's life and thought, while giving special attention to his or her religious contexts, convictions, doubts, objections, ideas, and actions. Many leading politicians, writers, musicians, philosophers, and scientists have engaged deeply with religion in significant and resonant ways that have often been overlooked or underexplored. Some of the volumes will even focus on men and women who were lifelong unbelievers, attending to how they navigated and resisted religious questions, assumptions, and settings. The books in this series will therefore recast important figures in fresh and thought-provoking ways.

Mark Twain

Preacher, Prophet, and Social Philosopher

GARY SCOTT SMITH

OXFORD
UNIVERSITY PRESS

OXFORD
UNIVERSITY PRESS

Great Clarendon Street, Oxford, OX2 6DP,
United Kingdom

Oxford University Press is a department of the University of Oxford.
It furthers the University's objective of excellence in research, scholarship,
and education by publishing worldwide. Oxford is a registered trade mark of
Oxford University Press in the UK and in certain other countries

First Edition published in 2021

Impression: 1

Published in the United States of America by Oxford University Press
198 Madison Avenue, New York, NY 10016, United States of America

British Library Cataloguing in Publication Data
Data available

Library of Congress Control Number: 2021931808

ISBN 978-0-19-289492-2

Printed and bound by
CPI Group (UK) Ltd, Croydon, CR0 4YY

To my wife Jane. As Mark Twain's wife Livy was for him,
Jane is the love of my life, and, as Livy was for Mark,
she has been over many years, my inspiration and best editor.

Preface

Mark Twain regularly attended church and Sunday school as a child and adolescent. As an adult, he discussed religious themes extensively in his novels, short stories, articles, autobiography, speeches, and personal correspondence and conversations. Through these varied venues, Twain frequently expressed views of God, Jesus, Christianity, other religions, the Bible, human nature, providence, prayer, salvation, and the afterlife.

Although many scholars have ignored the impact of Christianity on Twain as well as his views of religious topics and issues, others have written extensively (and often insightfully) about his religious perspectives. The mountain of information provided by Twain and commentators on his views, coupled with the prescribed length of books in the Spiritual Lives series, has required me to be very selective in what I include, thereby restricting somewhat the analysis, context, and related material about Twain's religious views I provide. To explain what Twain believed about theological topics, I have used statements from his letters, speeches, stories, essays, and autobiography that were written during different periods of his life. Because Twain's religious views changed significantly over time, deciphering what he believed is problematic.

He frequently used hyperbole and humor, making it hard to determine when he was being sarcastic and when he was expressing his own perspective. Often it is impossible to know whether a statement presents Twain's own view or only that of a character in a novel or short story. Twain, like Thomas Jefferson, who also held heterodox beliefs, kept many of his religious perspectives private until after his death, fearful that their revelation would harm his public image and discourage Americans from buying his novels. During the Gilded Age, many Americans were deeply concerned about theological issues, and although significant numbers of people began to question Christian orthodoxy privately, very few did so publicly.

Twain's life and writings offer conflicting evidence about whether he believed or disbelieved in Christianity. Consider these two illustrative statements. In 1869, he wrote to his future mother-in-law, "I now claim that I am a Christian" and "my [forthcoming] bearing shall show that I am justly entitled to so name myself."[1] In 1905, however, he asserted that the doubts planted about Christianity when he was a youth had grown over fifty years to convince him that it and "all other religions are lies & swindles."[2]

Twain's declaration that "all men are liars" and "half tellers of truths" necessitates caution about accepting everything he says as "gospel truth."[3] Anticipating Postmodernism, Twain offered a moral in his short story "The Fable": "You can find in a text whatever you bring, if you will stand between it and the mirror of your imagination." Moreover, he declared, "It is only by keeping steadily in my mind that my Autobiography is not to be published until I am dead, that I am enabled to force myself to say the things I think, instead of merely saying the things which I wish the reader to *think* I think."[4] Adapting lyrics from the musical group Peter, Paul, and Mary to describe Twain's situation, one could imagine him thinking that "if I really say it," it won't play with my wife Livy and my potential readers, so "I must lay it between the lines." Despite these challenges, I have endeavored to explain accurately what Twain believed about religious issues and how Christianity affected his life and writings.

This book is aimed at general readers, not Twain scholars. I have therefore provided historical background on Twain's life in addition to an analysis of his key religious views and an assessment of major religious themes in several of his best-known novels.

Notes

1. SLC to Olivia Lewis Langdon, February 13, 1869, MTP, 90.
2. Autobiographical Fragment #146, MTP, AMT, 2:545.
3. MTN, May 1, 1885, 181.
4. Mark Twain, "A Fable," *Harper's* (December 1909), 71; AMT, January 15, 1907, 2:374.

Acknowledgments

To adapt a phrase from Isaac Newton, my analysis of Mark Twain's faith has benefited greatly from "standing on the shoulders of Giants"—the many gifted scholars who have dissected, debated, and delineated the life, work, and religious convictions of the celebrated author. I would like to thank two anonymous readers who reviewed my book for Oxford University Press (one who did so twice). Bruce Barron applied his amazing editorial skills to my book before the final product was submitted to the publisher and helped improve its prose and argument immensely. I owe a large debt to Timothy Larsen, the editor for Oxford University Press's Spiritual Lives series. He made numerous helpful comments and suggestions on both my original proposal and my manuscript and provided excellent guidance through the entire process. I also want to thank Tom Perridge, my editor at OUP, Karen Raith, Senior Assistant Commissioning Editor, Religion at OUP, Bhavani Govindasamy, the OUP project manager, and copy editor Joanna North for her meticulous work. Sue Macffray, a retired history professor, helped me obtain numerous books I needed from the UNCW library, which I could not access myself because of COVID-19 restrictions.

Contents

Contents

Abbreviations of Frequently Cited Persons and Works

People:

JHT	Joseph Hopkins Twichell
MMF	Mary Mason Fairbanks
OL	Olivia Langdon
OLC	Olivia Langdon Clemens
SLC	Samuel Langhorne Clemens
WDH	William Dean Howells

Books, Articles, and Archives:

AMT   *Autobiography of Mark Twain*. 3 vols. Berkeley: University of California Press, 2012–2015.

BA   Stanley Brodwin, "The Theology of Mark Twain: Banished Adam and the Bible." *Mississippi Quarterly* 29 (1976), 167–89.

CAR   Tracy Fessenden, *Culture and Redemption: Religion, the Secular and American Literature*. Princeton, NJ: Princeton University Press 2012.

CS   Mark Twain, *Christian Science*. New York: Harper, 1907.

CSS   Charles Neider, ed., *Complete Short Stories of Mark Twain*. New York: Bantam Books, 1981.

CT 1   Mark Twain, *Collected Tales, Sketches, Speeches, and Essays*, Volume 1: *1852–1890*. Ed. Louis Budd. New York: Library of America, 1992.

CT 2   Mark Twain, *Collected Tales, Sketches, Speeches, and Essays*, Volume 2: *1891–1910*. Ed. Louis Budd. New York: Library of America, 1992.

E&E   Mark Twain, *Europe and Elsewhere*. New York: Harper and Brothers, 1923.

FE   Mark Twain, *Following the Equator*. Hartford, CT: American Publishing, 1897.

IA   Mark Twain, *The Innocents Abroad: or the New Pilgrim's Progress Being Some Account of the Steamship Quaker City's Pleasure Excursion to Europe and the Holy Land*. Hartford, CT: American Publishing, 1869.

ILR   Dwayne Eutsey, "The Influence of Liberal Religion on Mark Twain."https://www.meadville.edu/files/resources/v1-n2-eutsey-the-influence-of-liberal-religion-on-.pdf.

LLMT   Dixon Wecter, ed., *Love Letters of Mark Twain.* New York: Harper, 1949.

LMT   Mary Lawton, *A Lifetime with Mark Twain: Katy Leary, for Thirty Years His Faithful and Devoted Servant.* New York: Harcourt, Brace, 1925.

LTR   *Mark Twain's Letters.* 6 vols. Berkeley: University of California Press. vol. 1: 1853–1866; vol. 2: 1867–1868; vol. 3: 1869; vol. 4: 1870–1871; vol. 5: 1872–1873; vol. 6: 1874–1875.

MF   Clara Clemens, *My Father, Mark Twain.* New York: Harper, 1931.

MIW   Michael Shelden, *Mark Twain: Man in White. The Grand Adventure of His Final Years.* New York: Random House, 2010.

MMT   William Dean Howells, *My Mark Twain.* New York: Harper, 1910.

MTA   Albert Bigelow Paine, ed., *Mark Twain's Autobiography.* 2 vols. New York: Harper, 1924.

MTAP   Maxwell Geismar, *Mark Twain: An American Prophet.* Boston: Houghton Mifflin, 1970.

MTAS   Sherwood Cummings, *Mark Twain and Science.* Baton Rouge: Louisiana State University Press, 1988.

MTATB   Allison Ensor, *Mark Twain and the Bible.* Lexington: University of Kentucky Press, 1969.

MTB   Albert Bigelow Paine, *Mark Twain, a Biography.* New York: Harper, 1912.

MTC   Paul Boller, "Mark Twain's Credo." *Southwest Review* 63 (Spring 1978), 150–62.

MTE   Bernard DeVoto, ed., *Mark Twain in Eruption.* New York: Harper, 1922.

MTFM   John Tuckey, Kenneth Sanderson, and Bernard Stein, eds., *Mark Twain's Fables of Man.* Berkeley: University of California Press, 2000.

MTFP   Leah Strong, *Joseph Hopkins Twichell: Mark Twain's Friend and Pastor.* Athens: University of Georgia Press, 1966.

MTHL   Henry Nash Smith and William Gibson, eds., *Mark Twain–Howells Letters.* 2 vols. Cambridge, MA: Harvard University Press, 1960.

MTL   Albert Bigelow Paine, ed., *Mark Twain's Letters.* 2 vols. New York: Harper, 1917.

MTLE   *Mark Twain's Letters,* Electronic Volumes 1–5: 1876–1880. Mark Twain Project.

MTMF   Dixon Wecter, ed., *Mark Twain to Mrs. Fairbanks.* San Marino, CA: Huntington Library, 1949.

MTMS   William Gibson, ed., *Mark Twain's Mysterious Stranger Manuscripts.* Berkeley: University of California Press, 1969.

MTMW   Edward Wagenknecht, *Mark Twain: The Man and His Work.*
        Norman: University of Oklahoma Press, 1967.

MTN   Albert Bigelow Paine, ed., *Mark Twain's Notebook.* New York:
        Harper, 1935.

MTP   Mark Twain Papers, The Mark Twain Collection, Bancroft
        Library, University of California, Berkeley.

MTR   William Phipps, *Mark Twain's Religion.* Macon, GA: Mercer
        University Press, 2003.

MTS   Paul Fatout, ed., *Mark Twain Speaking.* Iowa City: University of
        Iowa Press, 1976.

MTSC   Harold K. Bush, *Mark Twain and the Spiritual Crisis of His Age.*
        Tuscaloosa: University of Alabama Press, 2007.

MTT   Stanley Brodwin, "Mark Twain's Theology: The Gods of a Brevet
        Presbyterian." In *The Cambridge Companion to Mark Twain*, ed.
        Forrest Robinson, 220–48. New York: Cambridge University
        Press, 1995.

MTUF   Joe Fulton, *Mark Twain Under Fire: Reception and Reputation, Criticism
        and Controversy, 1851–2015.* Rochester, NY: Camden House, 2016.

NF   Kenneth Andrews, *Nook Farm: Mark Twain's Hartford Circle.*
        Cambridge, MA: Harvard University Press, 1950.

N&J   *Mark Twain's Notebook and Journals*, 3 vols. Berkeley: University of
        California Press, 1975–1979; vol. 1: 1855–1873, ed. Frederick
        Anderson, Michael Frank, and Kenneth Sanderson; vol. 2:
        1877–1883, ed. Frederick Anderson, Lin Salamo, and Bernard
        Stein; vol. 3: 1883–1891, ed. Robert Pack Browning, Michael
        Frank, and Lin Salamo.

PW   Mark Twain, *The Tragedy of Pudd'nhead Wilson.* Hartford, CT:
        Charles L. Webster, 1894.

REV   James Wilson, "Religious and Esthetic Vision in Mark Twain's
        Early Career." *Canadian Review of American Studies* 17 (Summer
        1986), 155–72.

RI   Mark Twain, *Roughing It.* Hartford, CT: American Publishing,
        1872.

RMT   Joe Fulton, *Reverend Mark Twain: Theological Burlesque, Form, and
        Content.* Columbus: Ohio State University Press, 2006.

RV   James Wilson, "In Quest of Redemptive Vision: Mark Twain's
        Joan of Arc." *Texas Studies in Literature and Language* 20 (Summer
        1978), 181–98.

SMT   Fred Kaplan, *The Singular Mark Twain.* New York: Anchor Books,
        2003.

TS   Mark Twain, *The Adventures of Tom Sawyer*. Hartford, CT: American Publishing, 1885.

WM   Mark Twain, *What Is Man? and Other Philosophical Writings*. Ed. Paul Baender. Berkeley: University of California Press, 1973.

Writings   Writings Albert Bigelow Paine, ed., *Writings of Mark Twain*. 35 vols. New York: Gabriel Wells, 1922–1925.

1
Introduction

The Importance of Mark Twain

Few figures in American history are as fascinating as Mark Twain. His literary works have intrigued, illuminated, inspired, and irritated millions from the late 1860s to the present. Despite being born in an obscure village in Missouri and having little formal education, Twain was arguably America's greatest writer from 1870 to 1910.

The most highly esteemed works of Washington Irving (1783–1859), Nathaniel Hawthorne (1804–1864), Henry David Thoreau (1817–1862), and Herman Melville (1819–1891) were all written before 1865. Ralph Waldo Emerson (1803–1882), Henry Wadsworth Longfellow (1807–1882), Harriet Beecher Stowe (1811–1896), Walt Whitman (1819–1892), Emily Dickinson (1830–1886), Louisa May Alcott (1832–1888), and Oliver Wendell Holmes, Sr. (1809–1894) penned important and influential works between 1870 and 1890. Theodore Dreiser (1871–1945), Jack London (1876–1916), and Upton Sinclair (1878–1968) began publishing notable books in the first decade of the twentieth century. Twain's greatest American rivals for literary and popular acclaim over his entire forty-year period of productivity were William Dean Howells (1837–1920) and Henry James (1843–1916). Howells published many more novels than Twain, but they did not achieve sales comparable to those of Twain's books and have not had as much lasting approbation or impact. James's numerous novels were not as highly regarded during these years as those of Twain.

Mark Twain, Edward Wagenknecht asserts, is "incomparably the dominating personality in American literature, the mightiest figure in our American mythology." Howells insisted that Twain was "sole, incomparable, the Lincoln of our literature." "His name," Fred

Kaplan claims, "is inseparable from issues so important that they have helped shape our view of ourselves and our national identity."[1]

In an era of mostly lackluster presidents and before the advent of cinema, radio, television, or sports stars, Mark Twain was the most popular person in America during the 1890s and competed with only Theodore Roosevelt for the title during the 1900s. His celebrity status exceeded that of other American presidents and European kings. Only Roosevelt, steel magnate Andrew Carnegie, and Standard Oil founder John D. Rockefeller had similar name recognition. During the first decade of the twentieth century, Michael Shelden contends, Twain was "the most beloved person in America." His novels were classics and "occupied a place of honor in many American homes."[2] Twain's magnetic personality, striking appearance, national and world speaking tours, stage presence, and genius for publicity made him widely known and respected. He was a friend of some of the nation's most prominent intellectuals, business leaders, and shapers of culture including Howells, Carnegie, President Ulysses S. Grant, showman P. T. Barnum, activist Frederick Douglass, educator Booker T. Washington, labor leader Samuel Gompers, and Henry Rogers, the vice president of Standard Oil. By the time of his death, Twain's likeness, photographed and drawn, was probably "the most frequently reproduced of any person in all of human history."[3] His image was used to advertise everything from kitchen stoves to cigars.[4]

Among Americans, perhaps only Benjamin Franklin and Abraham Lincoln have been quoted as often as Mark Twain. Among his best-known quips are "The rumors of my death are greatly exaggerated"; "A lie can travel halfway around the world while the truth is putting on its shoes"; and "It's not the size of the dog in the fight, it's the size of the fight in the dog." In addition, numerous quotations have been attributed to him that he never said, including "The coldest winter I ever spent was a summer in San Francisco" and "Golf is a good walk spoiled."

Born two weeks after the perihelion of Halley's Comet in 1835 and dying one day after its perihelion in 1910, Twain was a perceptive and provocative penman who flashed across the skies of America and the world for forty-five years, entertaining, challenging, and inspiring millions of readers. His varied experiences as a journeyman printer, riverboat pilot, prospector, miner, journalist, novelist, humorist, businessman, and world traveler, combined with his incredible imagination and astonishing creativity, enabled him to devise some of American literature's most memorable characters and enthralling stories.

Initially named Samuel Clemens, at age thirty-three Twain adopted the pseudonym by which he soon became known around the world. Derived from his days as a riverboat pilot, "mark twain" means a depth of twelve feet, the point at which a steamboat had entered safe water in a river. Ironically, few aspects of American society would find similar safety from Twain's scathing and satirical analysis.

Twain tackled universal themes with penetrating insight and wit including the character of God, the nature of humanity, providence, sin, corruption, greed, hypocrisy, poverty, racism, and imperialism. He denounced discrimination against African Americans, Asian Americans, Jews, women, and blue-collar workers. Twain's lectures and prose, Karen Lystra asserts, expressed "a quintessentially American spirit, a mix of sly humor, cynicism, affirmation, and plain speech that felt both unique and universal and that captivated audiences in the United States and Europe."[5] Although widely viewed as the archetypal American author, humorist, and public figure, Twain traveled extensively throughout the world and lived in Europe for many years, exposing him to numerous ethnic groups, diverse cultural practices, and competing versions of truth and helping him develop a global, comparative perspective.

Twain was mesmerized, perplexed, frustrated, infuriated, and inspired by Christianity. As much as any public figure of his era, he strove to understand, critique, and occasionally even promote various theological ideas and insights. He referred to himself, sometimes in jest, as a theologian, missionary, prophet, and saint, and as Holy Samuel or the Reverend Mark Twain. On the other hand, he was called a skeptic, an agnostic, an unbeliever, an atheist, an apostate, a heretic, a "Profaner of Divinity," and "a son of the devil."

Twain's Religious Perspective

Twain's religious perspective was complex, inconsistent, sometimes contradictory, and constantly changing. Much evidence supports his assertion that he was harried and haunted by his "trained Presbyterian conscience." Describing his religious journey, he declared, "No man *remains* the same sort of Presbyterian he was at *first*—the thing is *impossible*; time and various *influences modify* his Presbyterianism; it *narrows* or it *broadens*; grows *deeper* or *shallower*, but does not stand *still*." Wagenknecht argues that Twain "was almost consistently inconsistent"; on many religious subjects he took both or multiple sides. Twain embodied Ralph Waldo Emerson's claim that "a foolish consistency is the hobgoblin of little minds."[6]

The diversity of Twain's religious convictions has led scholars to disagree sharply about the core of his philosophical vision. Because Twain "was neither systematic nor dogmatic about most theological issues," Harold Bush, Jr. maintains, "conclusions about Twain's faith" have been intensely debated. Samuel Clemens/Mark Twain not only had two names, Victor Strandberg argues, but he was a "double-minded, divided man." On one hand, Twain railed against Christianity and seemed to be an unbeliever, while on the other hand, he appeared to remain "open to orthodox, supernaturalist Christian belief."[7] Twain's views were eclectic; he did not have a *weltbild*, a comprehensive outlook on the world.

Determining what Twain truly believed about religious matters is further complicated by the difficulty in determining which characters in his novels and short stories express his perspective and which ones function as devil's advocates. Moreover, Twain often did not reveal what he actually believed because he did not want to irritate his wife Olivia (Livy) Langdon (who frequently asked him not to publish works critical of Christian orthodoxy), damage his reputation, or reduce the sale of his books. Twain insisted that "only dead men can tell the truth," and these concerns led him to state his true religious convictions primarily in works published after Livy died in 1904 and even more so after his own death. While alive, Twain wanted to avoid the public verdict that he was a fanatic who sought "to destroy the illusions and tradition and conclusions of mankind."[8]

In the slightly more than a century since Twain's death, many people skeptical of Christianity have cited Twain for support. Christopher Hitchens, for example, includes some of Twain's writings in *The Portable Atheist* (2007), and atheist websites often feature Twain quotations. To some, Twain's ridicule of missionaries in *Roughing It*, his lampooning of camp meeting revivals in *Adventures of Huckleberry Finn*, his skewering of Christian concepts of the afterlife in *Extract from Captain Stormfield's Visit to Heaven*, and his attack on major Christian doctrines in *What Is Man?* clearly demonstrate his anti-Christian perspective.[9]

In some ways, Twain's assault on religious orthodoxy is as scathing as those of leading twenty-first-century detractors or as the attacks lodged by Robert Ingersoll, America's best-known late nineteenth-century critic of Christianity.[10] Twain criticized the character of God, predestination, the Calvinist concept of election, infant damnation, Christ's "invention" of hell, and God's alleged admission of only a small percentage of people to heaven. He protested that Adam's trial in the Garden of Eden was unfair because Adam lacked a moral sense. Twain denied the divinity and virgin birth of Christ, asserted that God did not answer prayer, and complained that God unfairly punished families or nations because of the sins of individuals.

These assertions have led numerous scholars to portray Twain as a secularist, an atheist, or an agnostic who rejected Christianity.[11] Some refer to Twain's relationship with God and the Bible as a "lover's quarrel."[12] Biographer Ron Powers insists that Twain "had a constant, life-long sort of jilted love affair with the Bible. He wanted to believe, but he couldn't."[13] Justin Kaplan confidently states that Twain "never became a *Christian*," while Allison Ensor claims that he abandoned Christian orthodoxy by the early 1870s. James Wilson contends that scholarly analysis of Twain's theological position usually focuses on his deterministic cosmic view, his savage attacks on a callous deity, and the relentless despair he experienced during his last fifteen years of life. Although "the preponderance of evidence favors" viewing Twain as an unbeliever, declares Victor Strandberg, Twain "remained open to orthodox, supernaturalist Christian belief."[14] Much of Twain's censure of Christianity, however, occurred either in private letters, was published after his death, or was delivered by characters in his books and short stories whose views could be construed as not representing Twain's personal perspective.

Preacher

Twain was an entertainer, a novelist, and a satirist, but during his literary career he also functioned as a preacher, prophet, and social philosopher. He told his brother Orion in 1865 that he had had only "two powerful ambitions" in life. "One was to be a [riverboat] pilot, & the other was a preacher of the gospel. I accomplished the one & failed at the other because I could not supply myself with the necessary stock in trade—i.e. religion." However, he had a "call" to write humorous literature: "It is nothing to be proud of, but it is my strongest suit." If he had listened "to that maxim of stern *duty* which says that to do right you must multiply the two or three talents which the Almighty entrusts to your keeping," he wrote, he would have much earlier "turned my attention to seriously scribbling to excite the laughter of God's creatures."[15]

Twain hoped that another member of his family would become a pastor. He urged Orion to answer "the voice of God" calling his brother to be a minister. A person should do "what his Creator intended" for him. Twain exhorted Orion to "Go forth & preach," arguing that he "would tower head & shoulders above any of the small-fry preachers of my experience!" Twain assured Orion that he "would be great & useful as a minister of the gospel" and would "never be any better lawyer"—the career Orion was contemplating— than many others. "I would rather be a shining light" in the ministry, Twain declared, "than the greatest lawyer that ever trod the earth." Saving a widow's property or a murderer's life scarcely compared with "snatching an immortal soul in mercy from the jaws of hell." The former, he proclaimed, is the feeble "glitter of the firefly" while the latter is "the regal glory of the sun."[16]

Similarly, Twain told a boyhood friend, Frank Walden, who had become a Methodist minister, "I am glad that you are in the ministry, and hope that your career may be long and useful. It is the highest dignity to which a man may aspire in this life." Medicine, Twain asserted, was the most noble profession because it reduced pain and saved lives. "Next comes the pulpit, which solaces mental distress" and "soothes the sorrows of the soul." The gap between these two "great professions" and all others, he insisted, is "an abyss."[17]

"I wanted to be a minister myself," Twain wrote in 1866; "it was the only genuine ambition I ever had—but somehow I never had any [other] qualification."[18] Later in his life, Twain called becoming a minister "the most earnest ambition I ever had."[19] In 1873, a Brooklyn *Daily Herald* columnist declared that nature had designed

Twain to be "a Methodist circuit preacher, but forgot to endow him with a particle of reverence," which had also happened to François Rabelais, Jonathan Swift, and Sydney Smith.[20] Twain insisted that humor "must not *professedly* teach" or "professedly preach," but that to "live forever," it must do both indirectly. He had lasted thirty years as a humorist, Twain avowed in 1906, because "I have always preached."[21]

Twain was disappointed that in sixty years Hannibal had not produced "a solitary preacher" and that no one in his immediate family had been a minister. To some extent, Twain tried to atone for this by befriending pastors and serving as "a moralist in disguise."[22] He believed that his "preaching" was frequently better than that of the ordained clergy.[23] On a visit to Hannibal in 1902, during his most antireligious period, Twain was invited to speak at a Baptist church, "not to preach a sermon but to say a few words." He responded: "What I say will be preaching. I am a preacher. We all are preachers. If we do not preach by words, we preach by deeds . . . . Words perish, print burns up, men die, but our preaching lives on."[24] Twain saw himself, like his clergy friends, as rousing people from their religious complacency and motivating them to alleviate deplorable social ills.

Twain informed another audience in 1902 that he "wanted to preach a sermon, since he was as reverend as anyone" else. He then told a story about how St. Francis took one of his brothers with him to a village to preach. As they walked, they rejoiced in the soft spring sunlight and discussed the love of God. When they returned to their monastery, the brother asked, "But are we not going to preach today?" Twain then provided the punchline: "'We have preached,' said Francis. 'We have been happy in the love of God and the glory of His sunlight—that is our sermon for the day.'"[25]

Echoing Twain's self-assessment, Donald Mackay, pastor of the Collegiate (Presbyterian) Church of St. Nicholas in New York City, claimed in 1900 that Twain "is as much a preacher of righteousness in this world today as any consecrated bishop, priest, or minister." Brander Matthews, a Columbia University English professor, asserted four years later that Twain and renowned British author Rudyard Kipling were both moralists and preachers. In a 1911 article titled "Mark Twain as Preacher," a Methodist clergyman called him "a fearless knight of righteousness" who had ministered to many people.[26]

Prophet

Twain, Harold Bush, Jr. argues, was "a raving Jeremiah," "a profoundly religious and spiritual" force who denounced his era's social and ethical injustices. Like those of Frederick Douglass and Harriet Beecher Stowe, Twain's jeremiads are written from within, not outside, the church and contrasted the true gospel with a corrupted version.[27] Arguably, no other American literary figure wrote so persistently, passionately, provocatively, and prophetically about religious issues and social ills during the Gilded Age.

When Yale awarded him an honorary degree in 1888, Twain asserted that humor's "one serious purpose" was deriding shams and laughing "stupid superstitions out of existence." Whoever "engaged in this sort of warfare," Twain added, "is the natural friend of human rights."[28] Displaying "the moral earnestness" of a minister, Paul Fatout writes, Twain exhorted Americans to provide honest government and improve the lives of the poor, the blind, blacks, and other maltreated groups. Twain's social criticism, Maxwell Geismar contends, was "bold, brilliant, satirical, and prophetic."[29] Twain, like earlier American Christian prophets, used the jeremiad to deplore the moral failures of society.[30] As Martin Luther King, Jr. would do later, Twain attacked the religious establishment and status quo.[31] The literary lion used the prophetic form to "startle, stun, and shock" his readers, particularly religious ones.[32] Like many proponents of the Social Gospel during the years from 1870 to 1910, Twain denounced social injustice, greed, political corruption, and moral debauchery. Twain, according to his contemporary Joel Chandler Harris, was "the friend and champion of all who are poor and oppressed."[33]

Social Philosopher

Finally, Twain was a social philosopher.[34] Twain was not professionally trained as a philosopher or theologian, and "his forays into the field of metaphysical speculation were sporadic and unsystematic."[35] Nevertheless, he spent much of his life ruminating about religious and philosophical questions including the structure of the universe, the nature of God and human beings, the basis for knowledge, and the purpose of life. "He was a seeker and a searcher all his life" who lived "without the support of a traditional religious faith" and continually searched for meaning, purpose, and truth. Despite his satirical deconstruction of Christian theology and practice and "his irreverent persona," Twain's "personal and literary struggles," Dwayne Eutsey argues, reveal a sincere and strong "spiritual search for meaning amid a tumultuous life." One of his contemporaries, journalist Edward Sandford Martin, declared that Twain understood the plain truth, delighted to utter it, and did so without cant.[36]

Twain and Religion

Religion was extremely important to Twain in his personal life and his prose. The humorist was raised and spent his adult life in two principal eras—the antebellum period and the Gilded Age—during which most Americans took theology seriously. Twain was reared and lived most of his life in social and cultural milieus that were deeply impacted by specific varieties of Protestant faith. "The quasi-religious ethos of Twain's adult life—particularly in Hartford, Connecticut and Elmira, New York," Bush argues, "was dominated by orthodox Christianity, much of which was a response to the spiritual crises of the Gilded Age." Joe Fulton avows that Twain "infused his work with religious and theological concerns"; among major nineteenth-century American authors, only Nathaniel Hawthorne and Harriet Beecher Stowe were as influenced by religion as Twain. His collected works contain more references to the Bible than to any other literary work and are saturated with religious imagery and allusions. Many elements of Twain's work, including his characters, plots, themes, and settings, reveal a fascination with religion. Even the language Twain employed to communicate his core commitments was "biblical and theological rather than secular."[37]

Twain's courtship letters to Livy are peppered with religious discussions. He enjoyed amiable friendships with numerous ministers, most notably Joseph Twichell. Twain's first biographer, Albert Bigelow Paine, insisted that "his heart always warmed toward any laborer" in God's vineyard. He preferred preachers as companions, Kenneth Andrews maintained, because they were not devoted to accumulating money.[38] Twain attended church frequently at various times in his life, gave Christian organizations substantial monetary gifts, and read many religious books. He loved hymns and African American spirituals and supported numerous Social Gospel causes with his pocketbook and pen. Twain discussed theological issues with many individuals, including several pastors, Livy, his brother Orion and sister-in-law Molly, his sister Pamela, his sister-in-law Susan Langdon Crane, William Dean Howells, Henry Rogers, and Charles Stoddard. He analyzed such theological themes as the character of God, human nature, providence, the problem of evil, and the conditions of heaven in many literary works. Nevertheless, many biographers have paid scant attention to Twain's preoccupation with religious matters.[39]

Since the 1970s several academics have helped elucidate Twain's religious views, but most scholars have continued to ignore or underplay the spiritual dimensions of both Twain's literary works and life.[40] Literature professors have especially paid little attention to the place of religion in Twain's life or fiction. The claim of many Twain scholars that he "was ignorant of, or disinterested in, the Christian doctrines and creeds," Joe Fulton insists, is patently false.[41] The theologically liberal Christianity Twain encountered in Hartford and in Elmira, New York, significantly affected his worldview and "his work as a social critic and moral storyteller." In his books, short stories, and essays, Twain participated in cultural discussions about many biblical concepts, sometimes accepting but also often questioning, lampooning, and revolting against them.[42]

Twain's life provides a window into the principal trends and developments in American religion from 1865 to 1910. His religious pilgrimage took him from theologically conservative Presbyterianism through theologically liberal Congregationalism and deism to a worldview largely based on new developments in the natural and social sciences. In the course of his journey, he encountered Calvinism, revivalism, Millerism, Mormonism, freemasonry, Christian Science, spiritualism, the occult, Unitarianism, Transcendentalism, determinism, positivism, scientific theories, biblical criticism, and the deistic or agnostic works of such leading religious skeptics as Thomas Paine and Robert Ingersoll.[43]

Twain was not a scholar; he did not attend college or read systematically. He did, however, read widely, experience many aspects of human life, and reflect deeply about many matters. Examining Twain's spiritual life from cradle to coffin helps illuminate the religious issues and developments of his era and sheds light on many issues in our own time.

Notes

1. Edward Wagenknecht, *Cavalcade of the American Novel* (New York: Henry Holt, 1952), 114; MMT, 84; SMT, 3.
2. MIW, xx.
3. MTSC, 274–5.
4. MIW, xxxiv.
5. Karen Lystra, *Dangerous Intimacy: The Untold Story of Mark Twain's Final Years* (Berkeley: University of California Press, 2004), 1.
6. Writings 31:411 (first quotation); Mark Twain, "Consistency," December 2, 1887, CT, 1:910 (second quotation); MTMW, 152; Harold Bush, Jr. and Joe Webb, "Transfigured by Oratory," *The Mark Twain Annual* 7 (November 2009), 92.
7. MTT, 220; MTSC, 277; Victor Strandberg, review of MTSC, *Christianity and Literature* 57 (Winter 2008), 322.
8. MTB, 1234.
9. Charles Martin, review of MTSC, *Journal of the Midwest Modern Language Association* 40 (Fall 2007), 130.
10. Twain regularly read *The Truth Seeker*, which expressed Ingersoll's views, and he often expressed admiration for the nation's leading freethinker. See Gregg Camfield, *The Oxford Companion to Mark Twain* (New York: Oxford University Press, 2003), 288; and Thomas Schwartz, "Mark Twain and Robert Ingersoll: The Freethought Connection," *American Literature* 48 (1976), 183–93. On Ingersoll, see Mark Plummer, *Robert G. Ingersoll: Peoria's Pagan Politician* (Macomb: Western Illinois University, 1984); and Susan Jacoby, *The Great Infidel: Robert Ingersoll and American Freethought* (New Haven, CT: Yale University Press, 2013).
11. See, for example, Hamlin Hill, *Mark Twain: God's Fool* (New York: Harper & Row, 1975), 272, 274, and passim. Maxwell Geismar labeled Twain "an eloquent and outraged atheist" (MTAP, 384). Max Eastman, *Harper's Magazine*, May 5, 1938, 621, called Twain "the great infidel." For similar appraisals, see Bernard De Voto, "The Symbols of Despair," in *Mark Twain's The Mysterious Stranger and the Critics*, ed. John S. Tuckey (Belmont, CA: Wadsworth, 1968), 92–108; Roger Saloman, "Escape as Nihilism: The Mysterious Stranger," in ibid., 174–82; SMT, 135, 145: Twain "had

no belief in Christian theological claims," 190, 369–70; Kenneth Andersen, "Mark Twain, W. D. Howells, and Henry James: Three Agnostics in Search of Salvation," *Mark Twain Journal* 15 (1970), 13–16; Van Wyck Brooks, *The Ordeal of Mark Twain* (New York: Dutton, 1920); William MacNaughton, *Mark Twain's Last Years as a Writer* (Columbia: University of Missouri Press, 1979); Guy Cardwell, *The Man Who Was Mark Twain* (New Haven, CT: Yale University Press, 1991); and Camfield, *Mark Twain*, 156. Wesley Britton, argues that throughout his adult life Twain had no "faith or belief in any deity or religion, orthodox or 'wildcat'" ("Mark Twain: 'Cradle Skeptic,'" September 1997, http://www.twainweb.net/filelist/skeptic.html). Other scholars conclude that Twain ultimately accepted deism. See, for example, J. Harold Smith, *Mark Twain: Rebel Pilgrim* (New York: Heath Cote, 1973), 157; and MTT, 228, 244.

12. MTR, 262. See also Everett Emerson, "Mark Twain's Quarrel with God," in *Order in Variety*, ed. R. W. Crump (Newark: University of Delaware Press, 1991), 32–48.

13. Quoted in Kimberly Winston, "New Film on Mark Twain Highlights His Religious Doubts," https://religionnews.com/2017/10/16/new-film-on-mark-twain-highlights-his-religious-doubts/.

14. Justin Kaplan, *Mr. Clemens and Mark Twain* (New York: Simon & Schuster, 1966), 80; MTATB, 40; REV, 155; Strandberg, review, 322.

15. SLC to Orion and Mollie Clements, October 19, 1865, LTR, 1:322–3.

16. SLC to Clements, LTR, 1:322–3.

17. SLC to Frank Walden, March 4, 1870, LTR, 4:86 (first quotation); MTN, October 4, 1895, 252 (second and third quotations).

18. SLC to Sammy Moffett, November 2(?), 1866, LTR, 1:367.

19. MTB, 84. See also C. J. Armstrong, "Sam Clemens Considered Becoming a Preacher," *The Twainian* (May 1945), 1.

20. Walter Francis Frear, *Mark Twain and Hawaii* (Chicago: Lakeside Press, 1947), 445.

21. AMT, July 31, 1906, 2:153.

22. Mark Twain, "Villagers of 1840–3," in *Hannibal, Huck and Tom*, ed. Walter Blair (Berkeley: University of California Press, 1969), 33; SLC to Helene Picard, February 22, 1902, MTL, 2:719; quotations in that order.

23. Jeffrey Holland, "Soul-Butter and Hogwash: Mark Twain and Frontier Religion," March 8, 1977, https://speeches.byu.edu/talks/jeffrey-r-holland/soul-butter-hogwash-mark-twain-frontier-religion/.

24. *St. Louis Post-Dispatch*, June 2, 1902, 5. See also Armstrong, "Sam Clemens," 1.

25. Allison Ensor, "A Clergyman Recalls Hearing Mark Twain," *Mark Twain Journal* 15 (1970), 6.

26. "Banquet of the St. Nicholas Society, *New York Times*, December 7, 1900, 3; Brander Matthews, "Literature in the New Century," *North American Review* 179 (October 1904), 520; Fred Adams, "Mark Twain as Preacher," *Methodist Review* (July 1911), 565.

27. MTSC, 82 (quotation), 139.

28. As quoted in the *Hartford Courant*, June 29, 1888, 5.

29. MTS, xxvi–xxvii; MTAP, 6.

30. Harold Bush, Jr., "'A Moralist in Disguise': Mark Twain and American Religion," in *The Oxford Historical Guide to Mark Twain*, ed. Shelley Fisher Fishkin (New York: Oxford University Press, 2002), 66.

31. MTR, 4.

32. RMT, 188; Joe Fulton, "Mark Twain's New Jerusalem: Prophecy in the Unpublished Essay 'About Cities in the Sun,'" *Christianity and Literature* 55 (Winter 2006), 189 (quotation).

33. "Mark Twain 70th Birthday Supplement," *Harper's Weekly Magazine*, December 23, 1905, https://twain.lib.virginia.edu/sc_as_mt/70birthday/harpers02.html.

34. See Louis J. Budd, *Mark Twain: Social Philosopher* (Columbia: University of Missouri Press, 2001) and Philip Foner, *Mark Twain: Social Critic* (New York: International Publishers, 1958).

35. MTC, 151.

36. MTMW, 179 (first quotation); MTT, 232 (second quotation); MTSC, 47; Dwayne Eutsey, "God's 'Real' Message: 'No. 44, The Mysterious Stranger' and the Influence of Liberal Religion on Mark Twain," *Mark Twain Annual* 3 (September 2005), 55 (third quotation); Dwayne Eutsey, "Mark Twain's Attitudes toward Religion: Sympathy for the Devil or Radical Christianity?" *Religion & Literature* 31 (Summer 1999), 45 (fourth quotation); Martin, as quoted in Albert Paine, "Introduction," E&E, xxxiv.

37. MTSC, 2 (quotation), 66–7; MTUF, 148 (quotation), 183; BA 173; Jeanne Campbell Reesman, "Mark Twain vs. God: The Story of a Relationship," *Mark Twain Journal* 52 (Fall 2014), 121; BA, 171 (final quotation).

38. MTB, 371; NF, 71.

39. MTSC, 6.

40. MTSC, 276. The most important have been Stanley Brodwin, Lawrence
    Howe, Duane Eutsey, Harold K. Bush Jr., Lawrence Berkove, Joseph
    Csicisila, Susan K. Harris, Joe Fulton, and William Phipps.

41. RMT, 28.

42. MTSC, 66–7.

43. Bush, "Moralist in Disguise," 56; MTR, 313.

2

1835–1860

Life along and on the Mississippi

When Samuel Clemens was about six years old, his schoolteacher, Elizabeth Horr, read Jesus' statement, "Ask and it shall be given to you," to her class. She promised her pupils that God would answer people's heartfelt prayers. In response, Clemens prayed fervently that he would receive a slice of the gingerbread a baker's daughter brought to school every day. As Clemens later explained, "I did as much praying in the next two or three days as anyone in that town, I suppose, and I was very sincere and earnest about it too, but nothing came of it." Frustrated, Clemens took a piece of gingerbread when his teacher was not looking. His subsequent prayers for more gingerbread also produced no results. "I found that not even the most powerful prayer" brought more gingerbread, he concluded. He deduced that if a person faithfully kept his eyes on the gingerbread, prayer was unnecessary.[1]

Writing in his autobiography in 1905, Clemens declared, "Why should one laugh at my praying for ginger-bread when I was a Child? What *would* a child naturally pray for?—and a child who had been lied to by teachers & preachers & a lying Bible-text? My prayer failed. It was 65 years ago. I remember the shock yet. I was astonished as if I had caught my own mother breaking a promise to me. Was the doubt planted then, which in fifty years grew to a certainty" that Christianity and all other religions "are lies & swindles"?[2]

Clemens later tearfully told his mother Jane that he had "ceased to be a Christian." Shamefully, he had tried to use religion to achieve his own selfish desires. "I found out that I was a Christian for revenue only and I could not bear" this very ignoble thought, he explained. This gingerbread episode must have profoundly affected Clemens because he discussed it twice in his autobiographical dictations and portrayed Huckleberry Finn as similarly concluding that prayer did not work for him.[3] As we will see, however, Clemens's religious views and experiences as a child were diverse and had a much more mixed impact than his recollections at age seventy suggest.

Religion in Hannibal and the Clemens Household

Presbyterians organized their first presbytery in Missouri in St. Louis in December 1817, three years before Missouri became a state. When Clemens was born in 1835, the frontier had just recently moved west beyond Missouri to other locales. Hannibal, nearby Missouri towns, and the adjacent countryside along the Mississippi River were a colorful mixture of trappers, boatmen, entrepreneurs, traders, farmers, Native Americans, and adventurers of all sorts. Illiteracy, spiritual apathy, and religious diversity characterized the region.[4] In addition to Presbyterian, Methodist, Baptist, Episcopal, Christian, and Catholic churches, Hannibal had followers of William Miller, a herald of Christ's imminent Second Coming. Mormons, phrenologists, and palm readers all passed through the town. Residents flocked to camp meetings and revivals outside the town for spiritual enlightenment and enrichment and entertainment.

As a youth, Clemens interacted with Alexander Campbell and Barton Stone, who founded movements seeking to restore first-century Christianity. Campbell visited Hannibal when Clemens was eleven, and a few years later some of Campbell's sermons were printed in a shop where Clemens worked. Clemens had several personal experiences with Stone, who was the grandfather of Will Bowen, Clemens's best friend, and who lived for a short period with Bowen's family in Hannibal. Clemens was attracted to Campbell's Disciples of Christ movement, which challenged "narrow creedal statements," rejected the doctrine that God elected some people to salvation and others to damnation, and tried to unify all Christians.[5]

Religious diversity also characterized Clemens's family. His mother, Jane Lampton Clemens, who had the strongest influence on Sam's religious and moral views, was a Presbyterian. Sam's father, John Marshall Clemens, was a freethinker who, influenced by Enlightenment deism, questioned Christ's divinity. Sam's uncle, John

Quarles, a farmer who lived near Florida, Missouri (27 miles from Hannibal), and with whom Sam spent several summers, was a Universalist.

Despite this religious variety, the Reformed worldview was predominant in Hannibal and the Clemens family. Jane took Sam and her other children to the Sunday school and church services at a small Methodist church called the "Old Ship of Zion" for about three years after the family moved to Hannibal in 1839. Influenced by a sermon by Ezra Stiles Ely, who came to the Hannibal area to teach theology and Bible courses at Marion College (recently established by David Nelson), Jane joined First Presbyterian Church in 1842 by professing her faith in Christ.[6] Thereafter, she required her children to attend the church's Sunday morning services and Sunday school. She also sometimes forced Sam to attend the Sunday evening services as a punishment for his misdeeds and to help reform his mischievous behavior.

Some Twain biographers describe Jane as a staunch Calvinist and a strict disciplinarian. Her religion, Albert Bigelow Paine argued, was a "clean-cut, strenuous kind" that regarded Satan and hell as necessary instruments. Other scholars contend that Jane was a rigid Calvinist more in the mind of her young rebel son than in fact. Her granddaughter, who lived with Jane for twenty-five years, did not remember her ever referring "to the retribution of a stern Calvinistic God" or similar statements that many Twain biographers attribute to her.[7] Jane smoked a pipe, danced, and had rather eclectic religious views, especially in later life.[8] Her grandson maintained that she took an interest in all religions, "the livelier the better."[9]

Clemens's mother is often seen as the prototype for Aunt Polly in *The Adventures of Tom Sawyer*. The novel depicts Polly as leading family worship by beginning "with a prayer built" on "scriptural quotations, welded together with a thin mortar of originality"; from this summit "she delivered a grim chapter of the Mosaic Law, as from Sinai." Nevertheless, Sam's sister Pamela, a devout Christian who was eight years older than him, rather than their mother, supervised his nightly prayers. More tenderly, Polly agonized over Tom's wayward behavior and prayed for him "so touchingly, so appealingly, and with such measureless love" that Tom cried. Clemens similarly insisted that his mother had "a fine and striking and lovable" character. Her heart was "so large that everybody's grief and everybody's joys found welcome in it, and hospitable accommodations."[10]

Named for the prominent Supreme Court justice, John Marshall Clemens was a religious skeptic who prized reason and science. Sam respected his father's religious views, which may have contributed to the author's later doubts about Christianity. "My father," Clemens declared, was "a sternly just and upright man, albeit he attended no church and never spoke of religious matters"; he did not participate "in the pious joys of his Presbyterian family" or seem "to suffer from this deprivation."[11] After his father died when Sam was eleven, he promised his mother that he would "be a better boy," a pledge that he did not keep.[12] Sam admired his father in some ways and, as an adult, espoused some similar religious beliefs. However, he never forgave his father, who held numerous jobs including as a county judge, "for committing the cardinal sin of the Gilded Age . . . failing in business." Fathers in Twain stories are generally depicted as uncaring, ineffective, or tyrannical.[13]

His father's premature death significantly changed Sam's life, forcing him to leave school to help support his family financially. Clemens recalled that when a Presbyterian pastor asked his dying father, "Do you believe on the Lord Jesus Christ, and that through his blood only you can be saved?" his professedly skeptical father replied, "I do." After this, the minister prayed for him and "recommended him" to God.[14] Harold Bush argues that John Marshall's deathbed conversion, perhaps prompted by terror about his imminent demise rather than genuine faith, indicates that he was a hypocrite, a man who had no true convictions, or a profoundly confused individual.[15]

Sam's uncle, John Quarles, had eight children and owned about fifteen slaves. Clemens testified that he knew no better man than his uncle.[16] Quarles had strong religious convictions and an engaging personality, and Clemens undoubtedly admired his broadmindedness and tolerance about religious matters. During Sam's childhood, Jane Clemens repudiated Quarles's view that all people would eventually be saved.[17]

Train Up a Child in the Way He Should Go

Clemens's Sunday school experience significantly shaped his worldview as a youth, helped develop his "Presbyterian conscience," and contributed to his abhorrence of some aspects of Calvinism as he understood (and often misunderstood) this theology. Robert Raikes opened the first Sunday school in Gloucester, England, in 1780, and by the 1790s numerous congregations in the eastern United States, especially in urban areas, held Sunday school classes before or after their worship services. The American Sunday School Union (ASSU), created in 1824, helped establish many Sunday schools and produced literature for their pupils. Sunday schools instructed children on the Bible and basic Christian doctrines and strove to convert them. By the 1830s, Sunday schools had spread into Western frontier areas including Missouri. The ASSU, the Presbyterian Board of Publication, and other denominational publishers produced profiles of pious youth and stories designed to teach children about ethics and upright conduct and to guide their faith formation. Various Sunday school organizations also published magazines, such as *The Youth's Friend and Scholar's Magazine*, that contained biblical stories, engaging biographies, and didactic fiction.[18]

As a Sunday school pupil, Clemens memorized Bible verses to win prizes, although he claimed that only his mother seemed to notice when he repeatedly recited the same handful of verses. He also read the entire Bible as a child and was appalled by its violent and allegedly obscene aspects. Clemens claimed that he had to repeat the Westminster Shorter Catechism every Sunday and that he knew it well.[19]

In 1902, Clemens stated that he loved going to Sunday school and observed that often during his boyhood days, "I desired earnestly to stand in that Presbyterian pulpit and give instructions—but I was never asked until today." On the other hand, he told William Dean Howells that he learned "to fear God and dread the Sunday School." During the last decade of his life, Clemens wrote that in his youth Sundays were a "deadly bore" and that "the gladdest moment" of the church service was the benediction. Clemens's quip at a party celebrating his sixty-seventh birthday has the ring of truth: "We were good Presbyterian boys when the weather was doubtful; when it was fair, we did wander a little from the fold."[20]

What Clemens learned in Sunday school was reinforced by the elementary school he attended. During the 1830s and 1840s, in many American communities, public schools provided a nondenominational Protestant education. *McGuffey Readers*, which formed a central part of the curriculum, featured many biblical and moralistic stories. The school where Clemens learned the 3Rs met at First Presbyterian Church. His teacher Elizabeth Horr, he reported, always opened school by praying and reading a chapter from the New Testament, which she explained "with a brief talk."[21] Horr, a "devotedly pious" Calvinist and "a most disagreeable woman," was the prototype for Miss Watson in *Huckleberry Finn*.[22] Clemens contracted measles at age twelve when an epidemic afflicted Hannibal. He nearly died, and after he recovered, his mother, tired of his mischief and in need of more family income, removed him from school and apprenticed him to a printer.[23]

A Difficult Childhood

Clemens's childhood was a difficult one. In addition to losing his father and two older siblings, Clemens had many gruesome experiences. He saw drownings, a murder, corpses, and mayhem.[24]

Clemens had several encounters with death that deeply affected him. He witnessed his father's autopsy at age eleven, was frightened by seeing a corpse in the back room of his father's law office, and observed the murder of Sam Smarr, which served as the basis for the slaying of Boggs in *Huckleberry Finn*. In the novel, after Boggs was shot, some town folk placed a large Bible under his head and an open Bible on his chest. As Boggs gasped for breath, the Bible rose on his chest until he breathed for the final time—"and after that he laid still; he was dead."[25]

Clemens later explained that the shooting of Smarr was frequently replayed in his dreams. He always saw the same grotesque picture of "the great family Bible spread open upon the profane old man's breast . . . adding the torture of its leaden weight" to his dying struggle. Not one person in the "throng of gaping and sympathetic onlookers" had enough common sense to recognize that "an anvil would have been in better taste there than the Bible, less open to sarcastic criticism and swifter in its atrocious work. In my nightmares I gasped and struggled for breath under the crush of that vast book for many a night."[26] The weight of the Bible became for Clemens not a physical burden but a religious encumbrance as he strove to determine what was true.

Calvinism in Hannibal

Both scholars and Clemens have misrepresented the Calvinism that was preached and taught in antebellum Hannibal. No sermons and very few religious materials survive to help us interpret Presbyterians in Hannibal or northeastern Missouri during the 1840s, but evidence from nearby locales and antebellum Presbyterianism in general contradicts the way Twain biographers—and Twain himself in some of his novels, short stories, and recollections—present Calvinism. Their portrayal of God, election, human agency, and other matters depicts hyper-Calvinism rather than what the vast majority of Presbyterians and other Reformed Christians believed. With John Calvin, hyper-Calvinists (or hard-shell Calvinists) emphasized the sovereignty and glory of God, predestination, unconditional election, and irresistible grace. But unlike Calvin, they minimized humans' moral and spiritual responsibility, gave Christians a license to sin, and argued that evangelism was unnecessary.[27] Orthodox Calvinists, by contrast, insisted that God was sovereign in all matters including salvation, but they maintained that as free agents humans were responsible for their choices and that God used Christians as his instruments in the conversion process.

Twain, nineteenth-century opponents of Reformed theology, and many later scholars have all caricaturized antebellum American Calvinism as teaching that God was a monster who permitted the innocent to suffer, predestined most people to hell, and held people responsible for their actions even though they lacked the free will to choose their behavior.[28] Twain claimed that as a child, he heard pastors espousing these views, and as an adult, especially after 1880, he vehemently rejected them. Twain undoubtedly exaggerated Reformed tenets for humorous and dramatic effect in his published works, but his private diatribes about Calvinism indicate that he believed many false stereotypes to be true. Few printed sermons preached by Presbyterian clergy made any of these assertions. "Accusations of fatalism, infant damnation," and other "caricatures of Calvinism" were common, Presbyterian pastor George Duffield protested in 1854. Detractors, he complained, frequently misrepresented what Calvinists believed about human depravity, Christ's atonement, and regeneration by the Holy Spirit.[29]

All antebellum American Christians acknowledged the sovereignty of God over nations and history, but by the 1830s, however, Methodists, Disciples, many Baptists, and even some Congregationalists challenged traditional Calvinist soteriology by asserting that individuals played the principal role in their own salvation. As the title of Presbyterian turned Congregational evangelist Charles Finney's controversial 1836 sermon declared, "Sinners Bound to Change Their Own Hearts"—that it was sinners' responsibility to respond to God's gracious offer of salvation. Although the Holy Spirit was involved in the process of conversion, Finney argued, the Bible, reason, and experience all taught that the use of proper means—effective preaching, fervent prayer, inspiring revival services, and personal visitation—would produce a harvest of souls.[30]

An examination of Presbyterian sermons, Sunday school materials, and catechisms preached or used in various regions of the United States in the 1840s and 1850s raises questions about the sermons and the lessons Twain recalled from his childhood. In dozens of printed sermons, Presbyterian ministers stressed that, although God drew people to himself through the Holy Spirit, individuals were free moral agents who must accept God's gracious offer of salvation. Both Old School and New School (Presbyterians split into these two denominations in 1837) pastors in the North and South repeatedly insisted that redemption involved actions by both God and human beings.

As John Calvin and leading nineteenth-century Presbyterians argued, predestination was an antimony, a paradox; the Bible affirmed both God's sovereignty and human responsibility. The relationship between the two, Calvinists asserted, is a mystery. Albert Barnes, pastor of First Presbyterian Church in Philadelphia, contended in 1855 that the doctrines of divine sovereignty and election "are nowhere so steadily and so firmly maintained in preaching, and in the affections of the heart, as in the 'New School' churches." Its clergy sought to prove, however, that "these doctrines are not inconsistent with human freedom," the "unlimited offer of the gospel," the "willingness of God to save all," and the concept of moral accountability. In conversion, God did not compel people to believe, violate their freedom, or "interfere with the proper exercise" of their powers as moral agents.[31] "The doctrine of human depravity," Southern

Presbyterian Daniel Baker asserted similarly, did not destroy "all human responsibility." If people perished, it was their own fault.[32]

Presbyterian systematic theology texts made similar arguments. A. A. Hodge, the son of Charles Hodge and his successor as professor of theology at Princeton Theological Seminary, the flagship Presbyterian seminary in the nineteenth century, insisted in *Outlines of Theology* (1860) that the relationship between the doctrines of human freedom and the sovereignty of God is a "mystery." Reformed theologians emphasized that Scripture taught both that "human action is free" and that "God efficiently governs" people's actions. Therefore, these two facts must both be true "whether we can reconcile them or not." Hodge argued that God "continually controls and directs the actions of all his creatures" so that although he never violates the law of their natures, he "causes all actions and events" to occur according to his "eternal and immutable" plan. God did not force people to act in ways that robbed them of their free will.[33] While providing people with moral freedom and holding them accountable for their acts, God disposed all "actions and events according to his sovereign purpose." People were "perfectly free" in their willing, Hodge contended; they always acted according to their prevailing dispositions or desires. Individuals were responsible for their acts because they were free, rational, moral agents; their decisions were determined by their "own spontaneous affections and desires."[34] As free agents, Hodge added, people originated their actions and their reason and conscience enabled them to differentiate between right and wrong. People had the power to will as they pleased, to change their own subjective states, and to act based on the desires and preferences of their own hearts.[35]

In *The Adventures of Tom Sawyer*, the protagonist's pastor "thinned the predestined elect down to a company so small as to be hardly worth the saving." It seems unlikely that the Presbyterian ministers Clemens heard in Hannibal portrayed the elect as a tiny group. Speaking for many Presbyterians, *The Calvinistic Magazine* declared in 1830 that the Bible nowhere taught that only a small number of people would be saved; instead "more of the human family [would be] saved than lost."[36]

Undoubtedly, Clemens read some Sunday school literature that described God as greatly blessing Christians who obeyed biblical teaching and practiced piety. Like many scholars, however, Sherwood Cummings overgeneralizes when he claims that the religion in which

Clemens was raised taught that following religious rules brought not only heavenly bliss but material blessings, whereas disobeying them brought temporal punishments.[37] Few Presbyterian pastors preached such promises of earthly blessing from the pulpit; instead, they stressed that God's providence was inscrutable and that the righteous often suffered from afflictions that were designed to strengthen their faith. There was little correlation, Presbyterian ministers insisted, between being a devout Christian and having good health, material abundance, or a trial-free life. Moreover, they pointed out that non-Christians sometimes prospered and flourished. As prominent Presbyterian pastors such as Benjamin Morgan Palmer and George Duffield and Princeton Seminary professor Archibald Alexander all noted, believers and unbelievers alike had both positive and negative experiences. Presbyterian clergy acknowledged that those with whom "God is well pleased" were sometimes blessed with "fruitful seasons, health, success in their labours, and order and peace in their society." Those with whom "God is displeased," they added, did not, however, always suffer from famine, pestilence, the failure of their favorite enterprises, or the loss of their social status.[38] God used afflictions, Alexander maintained, to prevent believers from falling into sin, help them avoid great calamities, and prepare them for heaven.[39]

The sermons delivered at the First Presbyterian Church in Hannibal may have differed from those printed as pamphlets or in published collections. However, David Nelson, a former physician, Presbyterian minister, and abolitionist who organized this congregation in 1832 after conducting evangelistic meetings in the town, espoused the same positions held by most other antebellum Presbyterians. In *The Calvinistic Magazine,* Nelson and two co-editors included an essay on the doctrine of election asserting that God "predetermines whom he will convert," but that "wherever the gospel is preached every sinner who is willing to accept the offers of the gospel will be saved."[40] In addition, Nelson avowed that God worked "resistlessly in the hearts of men" without violating their free agency. The editors also affirmed that God's providential dealings with people "are mysterious." The wicked often experienced worldly success, prosperity, and longevity, whereas devout Christians suffered failure, poverty, adversity, and premature death. God's providence, they insisted, "is necessarily mysterious," because finite people could not comprehend the purposes of the infinite.[41]

Moreover, given the educational requirements for Presbyterian ministers by the 1840s—many of them had graduated from both college and seminary—and the careful scrutiny of ministerial candidates by presbyteries in a denomination whose pastors and laypeople were deeply concerned about theology, it is unlikely that the sermons Clemens heard differed substantially from those of other Presbyterian clergy.

On the other hand, Twain probably did hear sermons that accentuated the horrors of hell, which contributed to his personal fear of perdition and to the characterizations of hell in his novels. As he later quipped, "I don't believe in hell—but I'm afraid of it." In the 1830s and 1840s, many Presbyterian pastors stressed the terrors of hell to motivate sinners to repent and accept Jesus as their savior.[42] Presbyterian evangelists James McGready and Asahel Nettleton often depicted hell's revulsions in their revival messages.[43] Speaking for many Presbyterian ministers, Archibald Alexander declared that in hell lost sinners are "cast into the abyss of darkness and fire," where "their fire is not quenched" and where "there is weeping, wailing, and gnashing of teeth." "Who can conceive of the agonies of a soul tormented with remorse and despair, and the pressure of Almighty wrath?" he asked. "Who can dwell with everlasting burnings? One hour of this misery" would overbalance "all the pleasures of sin."[44] As late as the 1880s, numerous Presbyterians including T. DeWitt Talmage, pastor of the huge Central Presbyterian Church in Brooklyn, were still insisting that the fire of hell was literal and everlasting.[45]

Nevertheless, scholars often exaggerate the emphasis antebellum Presbyterians placed on God's wrath and hell. For example, in *Heretical Fictions: Religion in the Literature of Mark Twain*, Lawrence Berkove and Joseph Csicsila quote several portions of *A Short Catechism for Children* (1864) and argue that it was the kind of catechism Clemens would have learned as a child.

Q: Does your wicked heart make all your thoughts, words, and actions sinful? A: Yes; I do nothing but sin. Q: Is your life very short, frail, and uncertain? A: Yes; perhaps I may die at the next moment. Q: What would become of you if you die in your sins? A: I must go to hell with the wicked. Q: Cannot your good thoughts, words or actions recover you, by the covenant of works? A: No; everything I do is sinful. Q: What are you then by nature? A: I am an enemy of God, a child of Satan, and an heir of hell.[46]

Numerous scholars cite these excerpts in describing Clemens's religious socialization as a youth. Berkove and Csicsila, however, quote selectively from this catechism, omitting intervening and subsequent questions and answers that emphasize God's grace, the importance and nature of Christ's atonement that provides redemption for sinners, and the wonders of heaven as a counterpoise to the horrors of hell. *A Short Catechism* states, for example, that heaven is "a most glorious, holy, and happy place."[47]

Moreover, this catechism was written by Scottish Presbyterian minister John Brown in 1840, but it apparently was not published in the United States until 1859, when Clemens was twenty-four years old. He would much more likely have been instructed from *Catechism for Young Children: Being an Introduction to the Shorter Catechism* (1840) by Joseph Patterson Engles, a ruling elder at the Scots Presbyterian Church in Philadelphia and a Presbyterian Board of Publication agent. The tone of Engles's catechism is gentle, soothing, and positive. It accentuates God's love, grace, and mercy and declares that all who believe in Christ are pardoned and cleansed from sin. This catechism does not stress human depravity; it mentions hell only once and does not try to frighten children into accepting Christ as their savior.

Many parents used the Westminster Shorter Catechism to instruct their children in the faith, and, as noted, Clemens said he knew it well as a youth. It declares that because of their sin, all human beings "lost communion with God, are under his wrath and curse, and so made liable to all miseries in this life, to death itself, and to the pains of hell forever" (Answer 19). It then asserts, however, that God delivered the elect out of "the estate of sin and misery" and provided them with "salvation by a Redeemer" (Answer 20). Hell is mentioned only once in the catechism, and the concept of total depravity is not discussed. Like *Catechism for Young Children*, the Shorter Catechism focuses on the nature and benefits of the justification Christ supplies.[48]

The misrepresentation of the religion to which Clemens was exposed as a child and teenager leads to numerous false assertions. For example, Sherwood Cummings contrasts the sweet, devotional religion Olivia Langdon was taught, based on God's gracious promises in the New Testament, with the absolute, awesome religion in Hannibal that "depended for authority upon the threats of the Old Testament God."[49] Although major differences existed between the more liberal Congregationalism in which Olivia was raised and the theologically conservative Presbyterianism Clemens experienced as a child, they are not nearly as stark as Cummings and other scholars suggest.

Life Beyond Hannibal: Clemens, Age Seventeen to Twenty-Five

At age seventeen, when Clemens left Hannibal, which had become Missouri's second-largest city, he took with him many of its religious teachings, moral imperatives, and prejudices.[50] Before he left, his mother made him solemnly swear on a Bible not "to throw a card or drink a drop of liquor" while he was gone.[51] Clemens returned to Hannibal only six times for the rest of his life, but the town would play a prominent role in his stories. Although he was already questioning numerous Christian tenets he had been taught and had rejected some aspects of his Presbyterian socialization, his religious upbringing would permanently influence him.

For the next five years, Clemens worked as a printer in St. Louis, New York, Philadelphia, two Iowa cities, Warsaw (Illinois), and Cincinnati. During this period, he apparently attended church infrequently and he said little about his worldview. A letter he wrote to Orion in 1853 expresses his disgust with people's abuse of alcohol. "I always thought," he declared, that Easterners were models of uprightness, "but I never before saw so many whisky swilling, God-despising heathens" as he encountered in Philadelphia. "I believe I am the only person in the *Inquirer* office that does not drink."[52] Clemens's perspective on drinking would soon change, and thereafter he enjoyed consuming alcohol, usually (but not always) in moderation.

An episode that occurred in 1855 also illustrates his moral concerns during these years. While working in St. Louis, Clemens was appalled when parishioners in a Presbyterian church he attended collected a large sum of money to help the destitute "in some far off part of the world" while ignoring the desperate physical and material needs of a widow and her five children in their city. The family, Clemens noted, was destitute, half-starved, and almost naked, and "had suffered dreadfully from cold and fatigue." He observed that church members were not obeying the Bible's instruction to Christ's disciples "to carry their works into all the world *beginning with Jerusalem*." Despite occasionally expressing such concern for the plight of the poor, in 1876, Twain told a friend that at age 20, he had been "a callow fool, a self-sufficient ass" who had lifted "his bit of dung" while "imagining he is remodeling the world & is entirely capable of doing it right." He had been ignorant, intolerant, and egotistical and almost pathetically unaware of his personality flaws.[53] In 1855, Clemens started keeping a notebook to help improve his conduct, the first of fifty that still survive. For the next four decades, he filled them with observations about his experiences, opinions, and views on numerous philosophical and religious matters.

From 1857 to 1859, Clemens completed an apprenticeship and became a licensed river pilot. During these years, he voraciously read literary classics and philosophical works including Thomas Paine's strident attack on Christianity in *The Age of Reason* (1794). Clemens continued this work until the outbreak of the Civil War, which ended riverboat traffic on the Mississippi and prompted him to leave Missouri in July 1861 for the Nevada Territory with his older brother Orion.

Clemens experienced great traumatic and spiritual anguish when his younger brother Henry died at age twenty from injuries he sustained after a boiler on the *Pennsylvania* exploded in June 1858. Sam had encouraged his brother to take a job on a steamboat and had admonished him that if disaster occurred, he must rescue women and children. After the explosion hurled him into the Mississippi, the severely injured Henry swam back to the boat to assist the passengers. Henry died in a hospital a week after the explosion. Sam prodded a young doctor to give Henry a large amount of morphine, which Sam later concluded contributed to his death. Tormented by Henry's death and wracked with guilt, Sam wrote to his sister-in-law Mollie to inform her that Henry, "the light of my life," had "gone out in utter darkness. O, God!" Clemens cried, "this is hard to bear. Hardened, hopeless,—aye, lost—lost—lost and ruined sinner as I am—even I, have humbled myself to the ground and prayed as never a man

prayed before that the great God might let this cup pass from me—
that he would strike me to the earth, but spare my brother!" Clemens
protested that people called him "lucky" because he was not aboard
the steamboat when it exploded. Echoing Jesus' words on the cross,
Clemens proclaimed, "May God forgive them, for they know not
what they say." He beseeched his sister-in-law to "Pray for me, Mollie,
and pray for my poor sinless brother."[54] Deeply affected by Henry's
death, Clemens would resurrect his brother as a character in *Tom
Sawyer* and *Life on the Mississippi* and would also discuss Henry in his
autobiography. This soul-wrenching experience contributed to Clemens's doubts about Christianity and haunted him for the rest of his life,
as he often wrestled with his role in his brother's demise.[55]

The religious views Samuel Clemens was taught in Hannibal would
be challenged even more substantially in future decades as he lived in
the West and the East, worked as a journalist, became Mark Twain,
wrote best-selling books, riveting short stories, and provocative essays,
married, had children, traveled the world, and attained international
fame. After briefly (or almost) reaffirming the faith he was exposed to
as a youth while courting Livy, Clemens began to question and
criticize many aspects of Christianity.

Notes

1. AMT, August 15, 1906, 2:178.
2. Fragment #146, MTP, AMT, 2:545.
3. AMT, June 23, 1906, 2:178; Mark Twain, *The Adventures of Huckleberry Finn* (Hartford, CT: American Publishing, 1885), 11.
4. Thomas Cannon, "The Founders of Missouri Presbyterianism," *Journal of Presbyterian History* 46 (September 1968), 197–218. See also Timothy Flint, *Recollections of My Ten Years in the Mississippi Valley* (Boston: Cummings, Hilliard, 1826).
5. MTSC, 39–40; quotation from 39.
6. Curtis Dahl, "Mark Twain and Ben Ely," *Missouri Historical Review* 66 (July 1972), 552, 557, 559–60; session records, 1834–1859, First P.C. Hannibal. Missouri, 27, as cited in MTR, 14.
7. MTB 36; Wesley Britton, "Mark Twain: 'Cradle Skeptic,'" September 1997, http://www.twainweb.net/filelist/skeptic.html; Doris and Samuel Webster, "Whitewashing Jane Clemens," *Bookman* 61 (July 1925), 532 (second quotation).

8. Dixon Wecter, *Sam Clemens of Hannibal* (Boston: Houghton Mifflin, 1961), 86; Alexander Jones, "Heterodox Thought in Mark Twain's Hannibal," *Arkansas Historical Quarterly* 10 (Autumn 1951), 249.

9. Samuel Charles Webster, *Mark Twain. Business Man* (Boston: Little, Brown, 1946), 24. Also see Rachel Varble, *Jane Clemens: The Story of Mark Twain's Mother* (Garden City, NY: Doubleday, 1964).

10. TS, 42, 133; MTA, 1897–1898, I:115–16.

11. MTN, January 20, 1896, 271.

12. SMT, 32.

13. John Q. Hays, "Mark Twain's Rebellion Against God: Origins," *Southwestern American Literature* 3 (Spring/Fall 1973), 31 (quotation); Keith Coplin, *John and Sam Clemens: A Father's Influence* (Kirkwood, MO: Mark Twain Memorial Association, 1970), 3–5.

14. *Mark Twain's Hannibal, Huck, and Tom*, ed. Walter Blair (Berkeley: University of California Press, 1969), 40.

15. MTSC, 31.

16. "Random Abstracts," AMT, 1:210.

17. Jones, "Heterodox Thought," 251; MTR, 31; Minnie Brashear, *Mark Twain: Son of Missouri* (New York: Russell & Russell, 1964), 54.

18. Anne Boylan, *Sunday School: The Formation of an American Institution, 1790–1880* (New Haven, CT: Yale University Press, 1988); "Nineteenth Century Sunday School Books and Christian Literature for Children," https://library.upsem.edu/special-collections/nineteenth-century-sunday-school-books-christian-literature-children/.

19. CS, 73.

20. Mark Twain, "Remarks," May 30, 1902, MTS, 432; MMT, 125; Twain, "Letters from the Earth," WM, 407; Twain, "Dinner Speech," November 28, 1902, MTS, 458.

21. AMT, August 15, 1906, 2:178.

22. *Mark Twain's Satires and Burlesques*, ed. Franklin Rogers (Berkeley: University of California Press, 1967), 140.

23. Mark Twain, "The Turning Point in My Life," WM, 458.

24. Ron Powers, *Dangerous Waters: A Biography of the Boy Who Became Mark Twain* (New York: Basic Books, 1999), 274–89.

25. Twain, *Huckleberry Finn*, 112.

26. Written about 1898, MTA, 1:131.

27. Peter Toon, *The Emergence of Hyper-Calvinism in English Nonconformity 1689–1765* (London: Olive Tree, 1967); Michael Horton, "Reformed Theology vs. Hyper-Calvinism," https://www.ligonier.org/learn/articles/reformed-theology-vs-hyper-calvinism/.

28. See William Shurr, *Rappaccini's Children: American Writers in a Calvinist World* (Lexington: University Press of Kentucky, 1981), 30.

29. George Duffield, *American Presbyterianism* (Philadelphia: Isaac Ashmead, 1854), 21.

30. James Bratt, "The Reorientation of American Protestantism, 1835–1935," *Church History* 67 (March 1998), 58.

31. Albert Barnes, "The Agency of the Holy Spirit in Regeneration," in *The Way of Salvation* (Philadelphia: Parry and M'Millan, 1855), 263. Numerous other sermons make the same argument. E.g. David Merrill, "The Great Salvation," in *Sermons by the late Rev. David Merrill* (Windsor: Vermont Chronicle Press, 1855), 268; John Watson Adams, *Sermons on Various Subjects* (Syracuse, NY: Stodard and Babcock, 1851), 244, 253; Henry Bacon, *Sermons on the Lord's Prayer* (Auburn, IN: W. J. Moses, 1854), 82–4; Archibald Alexander, *Practical Sermons* (Philadelphia: Presbyterian Board of Publication, 1850), 34, 312.

32. Daniel Baker, "The Duty of Coming to Christ," in *A Series of Revival Sermons* (Pennfield, GA: J. S. Baker, 1847), 272–3.

33. A. A. Hodge, *Outlines of Theology* (Grand Rapids, MI: Zondervan, 1973), 272, 262, 267; first three quotations from 272, fourth from 262.

34. Hodge, *Outlines*, 68, 282, 285; quotations in that order.

35. Hodge, *Outlines*, 287, 289.

36. TS, 60; "A Familiar Dialogue, Between Calvinus and Arminius: Principally on the Doctrines of Election and Predestination," *The Calvinistic Magazine*, May 1830, 156–7; quotation from 157.

37. MTAS, 17.

38. J. W. Yeomans, "The Supremacy of the Moral Law," in *The Living Pulpit, or Eighteen Sermons by Eminent Living Divines of the Presbyterian Church*, ed. Elijah Wilson (Philadelphia: C. Sherman & Sons, 1859), 96.

39. Archibald Alexander, "The Benefits of Affliction," in *Practical Sermons*, 433.

40. "The Pastoral Letter of the Presbytery of Lexington, Virginia," October 27, 1827, *The Calvinistic Magazine*, February 1828, 38.

41. David Nelson, "What Is Free-Agency?" *The Calvinistic Magazine*, January 1830, 8; "Providence of God," *The Calvinistic Magazine*, May 1828, 144.

42. See, for example, Theodore Wright, *A Pastoral Letter, Addressed to the Colored Presbyterian Church in the City of New York* (New York: Sears and Martin, 1832), 7–8; Asahel Nettleton, "Great Sinners," in Bennet Tyler, comp., *Asahel Nettleton: Sermons from the Second Great Awakening* (Ames, IA: International Outreach, 1995), 130–1.

43. E.g., James McGready, "The New Birth," 2:92, 112; "The Doom of the Impenitent," 2: 178–80; "Nature and Tendency of Unbelief," 2:164–5 all

in James Smith, ed., *The Posthumous Works of the Reverend and Pious James M'Gready. Late Minister of the Gospel, in Henderson, Kentucky*, 2 vols. (Nashville, TN: Lowry and Smith, 1833); Asahel Nettleton, "Rejoice Young Man," http://www.sermonindex.net/modules/articles/index.php?view=article& aid=824.

44. Archibald Alexander, "The Misery of Impenitent Sinners," in *Practical Sermons*, 491–2. See also J. T. Smith, "The Worth of the Soul," in *The Living Pulpit*, ed. Wilson, 29, 32.

45. T. DeWitt Talmage, "Lazarus and Dives," in Talmage, *Sermons: First Series* (New York: Funk and Wagnalls, 1885), 330–1, 334. See Gary Scott Smith, "Changing Conceptions of Hell in Gilded Age America," *Fides et Historia* 47 (Winter/Spring 2015), 1–23.

46. Lawrence Berkove and Joseph Csicsila, *Heretical Fictions: Religion in the Literature of Mark Twain* (Iowa City: University of Iowa Press, 2010), 8–9. See also Mabel Donnelly, "Henry Ward Beecher and Infant Damnation," *The Harriett Beecher Stowe House and Library* (January/February 1992), 3.

47. "Westminster Shorter Catechism," https://www.opc.org/sc.html.

48. "Westminster Shorter Catechism."

49. MTAS, 24.

50. John Q. Hays, *Mark Twain and Religion: A Mirror of American Eclecticism* (New York: Peter Lang, 1989), 17.

51. MTB, 93.

52. SLC to Pamela Moffett, December 5, 1853, MTB, 101.

53. Samuel Clemens, to the editors of the Muscatine *Tri-Weekly Journal*, February 16, 1855, LTR, 1:47; SLC to J. H. Burroughs, November 1, 1876, MTL, 1:289.

54. SLC to Mollie Clemens, June 18, 1858, LTR, 1:80–1.

55. Ron Powers, *Mark Twain: A Life* (New York: Free Press, 2005), 89.

3

The 1860s

Journalism, a Pilgrimage, and Courtship

In May 1864 while working as the acting editor of the Virginia City *Enterprise*, Samuel Clemens traded insults in print with James Laird, the owner of the city's rival *Daily Union*. Egged on by friends, Clemens challenged Laird to a duel, even though dueling had been outlawed in the Nevada Territory. Much to Clemens's chagrin, Laird eventually accepted his challenge.

Dueling had a long and inglorious history in America. Most famously, as popularized by the 2015 Broadway musical *Hamilton*, Aaron Burr, the nation's vice president, killed founding father Alexander Hamilton in a duel in 1804. Andrew Jackson participated in several duels before becoming president in 1829. Hamilton, a Revolutionary War soldier, and Jackson, a War of 1812 commander, were both crack marksmen. Clemens was not. He claimed that he tried for an hour before the duel to hit a barn door and failed. He feared that Laird would figure out what a terrible shot he was. At that moment of dread, however, a small bird flew by, and Steve Gillis, Clemens's second for the duel and an excellent marksman, shot its head off. Just then Laird and his friends came over a ridge to the spot designated for the duel. When Laird asked who had shot the dead bird, Gillis told him that Clemens had killed it from thirty yards away. Laird's second, who had assumed Clemens could not hit a church, declared, "That is astonishing shooting. How often can he do that?" Gillis replied, "About four times out of five." Alarmed by this lie, Laird decided not to fight a duel with Clemens "on any terms whatever." Clemens later credited Gillis's deadeye shooting with saving his life. "I don't know what the bird thought about that interposition of Providence," Twain wrote, "but I felt very, very comfortable over it—satisfied and content."[1]

Scholars have called Clemens's account of the duping of Laird apocryphal, but it is significant that he attributed his safety to God's intervention. During the 1860s and throughout the rest of his life, Clemens would express ambivalent views about God's Providence. Sometimes, especially during his courtship of Olivia Langdon, he affirmed belief in God's direction of the universe and his own life; at other times, however, he criticized and even rejected the doctrine of divine Providence and espoused a bleak determinism.

The 1860s took Twain from Hannibal to Virginia City, Nevada; San Francisco; Europe; the Holy Land; Elmira, New York, to court Olivia (Livy) Langdon; and finally Buffalo. In 1869, the publication of *The Innocents Abroad* brought Twain fame and fortune and helped cement his reputation as a professional writer.

Clemens worked as a riverboat pilot until the Civil War broke out in April 1861, curtailing traffic on the Mississippi River. Following a two-week stint with the Missouri State Guard in June, he traveled to Virginia City, Nevada, near Carson City, the capital of the territory. After failing as a silver miner, Clemens took a job as a journalist with the *Territorial Enterprise* in Virginia City. Violating Nevada's law against dueling forced him to leave the territory in mid-1864. After briefly prospecting for gold in Calaveras County, near Sacramento, Twain settled in San Francisco and wrote articles for newspapers and magazines. The publication of "The Celebrated Jumping Frog of Calaveras County," a critique of the dangers of gambling, in the *New York Saturday Press* in November 1865 brought him national publicity, prompting the *Sacramento Union* to commission him to travel to Hawaii for four months in 1866 to write articles about his experiences. The next year, Twain journeyed to Europe and the Middle East under the auspices of the San Francisco-based newspaper, *Alta California*. This five-month trip enabled Twain to write his very popular *The Innocents Abroad*. On this excursion, he learned about Livy from her brother Charles, a fellow traveler. Twain spent the next two years wooing and winning her while primarily lecturing about his book throughout the United States. After they wed in February 1870, the Clemenses spent a year in Buffalo, where Twain was a co-owner and co-editor of the *Express*.

During this decade, Twain developed friendships with several ministers in San Francisco, battled depression, struggled to determine his vocation, and carefully examined Christianity while striving to win Livy's heart and hand. He also strove to abandon his boorish, rough-neck Western behavior, adopt Eastern mores and ethical practices, and reinvent himself as a Christian husband who could provide financial security and emotional and spiritual guidance for his future family.

God's Providence

During the late 1860s and early 1870s, especially in his courtship letters to Livy, Twain often argued that God directed events and praised God's good, wise, and kind providence. "Let us believe," Twain wrote Livy, "that God has destined us for each other." "Let us hope," he proclaimed, "that we shall walk hand in hand in love and worship of Him . . . and stand redeemed and saved, beyond the thresh-old and within the light of that land whose Prince is the Lord of rest eternal." Twain was "unspeakably grateful to God" for bringing them together. "If ever a man had reason to be grateful to divine Provi-dence," he avowed, "it is I." Five years into their marriage, on Livy's thirtieth birthday, he told her that Providence had prepared for his happiness "by sending you into the world."[2]

Providence made many more appearances in Twain's letters around this time. In February 1869 Twain informed Mary Fairbanks, a devout Presbyterian and wife of the publisher of the Cleveland *Herald*, whom he had met on the *Quaker City* excursion, that "the hand of Providence" had rearranged his lecture schedule. In August, he wrote to her that his decision not to go to Cleveland to become a politician had occurred "as Providence intended." Referring to a scheduling mix-up in November, Twain declared to Livy, "let us find no fault with circumstances that may have been ordered by Providence." In April 1870, he urged his older brother Orion to accept a generous offer to purchase their family property in Tennessee because God would not deliver another buyer if they rejected God's "beneficent care for us." He advised William Dean Howells in 1874 that if he left a scheduling issue "to Providence for 24 hours" it would "come out all right." He told other friends that year that events had been "designed by Providence" and that God's Providence often frustrated the best laid plans "of mice & men."[3]

Twain's references to God's Providence diminished after the mid-1870s, as his religious skepticism increased, but he still made occasional statements on the topic. "I'm glad Providence knew better what to do," he told Twichell in 1879, "than I did." When Twain suffered a serious illness the next year, he wrote to a pastor, "thanks to a kind Providence [I] am wholly out of danger this morning, & recovering quite fast." He claimed in 1888 that God had brought a blizzard to prevent Livy from joining him in Washington, DC on one of his speaking tours. "If I had known it was going to make all this trouble and cost all these millions," Twain quipped to Livy, "I would never had said anything about your going to Washington."[4] When discussing God's Providence, Twain often insisted that it included suffering, even for the world's most righteous people. Twain portrayed Joan of Arc, his most revered reformer, as an agent of Providence but emphasized that she died as a martyr. God chose Abraham Lincoln to "bind up the nation's wounds," but he was assassinated. An unfinished story Twain penned in 1898, posthumously titled "The Great Dark," describes a captain who loses his bearings during a storm on the ocean. When his crew threatens to mutiny, the captain exhorts them to do what God "commands and die when He calls.... I don't know where this ship is, but she's in the hands of God.... If it is God's will that we pull through, we pull through—otherwise not." Twain declared again in 1906 that "the hand of Providence" had enabled him to win his beloved Livy.[5]

On the other hand, Twain sometimes professed that he believed in luck. Throughout his life, Twain was fascinated with "instances of luck, coincidence, accident, and turning-points" in people's lives, and the topics of chance and destiny permeate his writings. Reflecting on a business crash in the mid-1890s, Twain wrote, "The proverb says, 'Born lucky, always lucky,' and I am very superstitious." As a youth, he had been at risk of drowning and pulled out of water nine times, leading to his being called a "cat in disguise." Twain agreed with his uncle that he had been "born lucky" because he was not on the *Pennsylvania* when it blew up, even though he had helped pilot it during the previous eighteen months. "I am so superstitious," Twain confessed, "that I have always been afraid to have business dealings with certain relatives and friends" who "were unlucky people. All my life I have stumbled upon lucky chances of large size, and whenever they were wasted it was because of my own stupidity and carelessness."[6]

Many of the stories Twain wrote during the 1860s parody the Westminster Confession of Faith's definition of Providence as God upholding, directing, disposing, and governing "all creatures, actions, and things, from the greatest even to the least."[7] Twain attacked the idea taught in some Sunday school literature, Christian periodicals, and religious books such as *Willy Graham: or The Disobedient Boy* (1844) that God intervenes to protect devout Christians and bless them with good health and material prosperity and to punish wicked individuals for their sins. These "special providence" stories misled readers by asserting that the good were always rewarded and protected while the evil were either redeemed or punished.[8] Such stories, Twain protested, were contrary to human experience and contradicted the Bible's teaching that God's Providence is mysterious. Twain also criticized these Sunday school books for emphasizing fear and guilt.

In Twain's "The Christmas Fireside" (1864), the characters who skip church to hunt or fish on Sunday are not injured. In "Christian Spectator" (1865), Twain mocks "one of those entertaining novelettes, so popular among credulous Sabbath-school children, about a lone woman silently praying a desperate and blood-thirsty robber out of his boots."[9] In "The Story of the Bad Little Boy" (1865), the protagonist pilfers apples, slips a penknife he stole into the cap of an upright boy who is thrashed as a result, and goes boating on Sundays without drowning. As an adult, the protagonist kills all the members of his large family one night with an ax, becomes wealthy by "cheating and rascality," and, despite being "the infernalest wickedest scoundrel" in his community, "is universally respected" and elected to the legislature. By contrast, "nothing ever went right" for Jacob Blivens, the principal character in "The Story of the Good Little Boy Who Did Not Prosper" (1870), even though he always obeyed his parents and faithfully attended Sunday school.[10] In "The Story of Mamie Grant, the Child Missionary" (1868), the nine-year-old heroine's evangelistic efforts destroy her family because instead of doing her assigned task of paying their bills, she gives religious tracts to bill collectors and her family is evicted.

In *Roughing It* (1872), based on Twain's experiences in the West in the 1860s, Jim Blaine appeals to special Providence to explain why bad things happen to upright people like his uncle Lem. God, according to Jim's account, placed Lem in a particular place to break an Irishman's fall, but in the process Lem's back was fractured in several places. Twain continued to parody tales of providential protection in *Tom Sawyer* (1876), "About Magnanimous-Incident Literature" (1878), and "Edward Mills and George Benton: A Tale" (1880), depicting various incidents where "a bountiful Providence" does not produce beneficent outcomes. Such stories were similar to Twain's personal experiences. In his *Notebook*, for example, he contrasted the lives of two men he knew—a rich, "unspeakable villain" who never broke a bone, "led a joyous life till 80, [and] then died a painless death" and another man who became partially paralyzed while rescuing a drowning priest and had to beg for thirty-eight years to survive.[11]

While criticizing standard Christian Providence tales, Twain, like many Calvinists, saw the workings of God's Providence as mysterious. Providence stories tried to make manifest what John Calvin called God's secret counsel. "Calvin defines a 'special providence' as simply the belief that 'particular events' are designed by God for a specific end," such as the whirlwind that threw Jonah overboard.[12] Twain asserts that in a fallen world, tragic events happen; people break their backs or die in industrial accidents; for him, as Joe Fulton contends, "providence explains the everyday 'roughing it'" people experience. Twain exhorted Christians to acknowledge both Providence's baleful and beneficial aspects. Like God in the book of Job, Twain censures people for presuming they can understand and explain God's purposes.[13]

In "The Second Advent" (1881), Twain depicts the disasters that would occur if God answered everyone's intercessory prayers. Burlesquing the biblical account of God dividing the Jordan River so the Israelites led by Joshua could more easily cross it, Twain portrays the damming of a river to enable a group to traverse it, which causes massive flooding that kills untold people and animals and destroys numerous farms. Every time an answered prayer brings blessings to some individuals, it produces calamity for others. This realization prompts residents of the Arkansas town where the story is set to adopt two resolutions. The first one states, "Whoever shall utter his belief in special providences in answer to prayer, shall be adjudged insane" and incarcerated. "Since no one can improve the Creator's plans by procuring their alteration," the only prayer allowed hereafter, according to the second resolution, is "'*Lord, Thy will, not mine, be done*'; and whosoever shall add to or take from this prayer, shall perish at the stake."[14]

Twain reprimanded people for praising God for his blessings and ignoring the suffering he believed God caused. Many Americans credited Providence with making possible their "fine and showy new civilization" but overlooked the poverty of previous ages that made their improved social conditions so conspicuous. Twain described such an attitude as analogous to a sailor being thrown overboard during a tempest and starving and freezing for days before being washed ashore on a deserted island, where he lived on fish and grasshoppers for months until he was rescued by an infidel ship captain. The sailor quickly forgot that Providence had hurled him overboard "and only remembers that Providence rescued him."[15]

Twain also occasionally complained about the impact of Providence on his own life. "When Providence sets out to deliver retribution upon a certain man, the plans of a lot of 'instruments' are knocked galley-west," he protested. "I have lost just about half my time, since I was born, acting as an instrument." He tried not to feel resentful, he told Howells in 1875, but "the partialities of Providence" seemed to be "slathered around" without the "gravity & attention to details" that important matters required.[16] "Providence always makes it a point to find out what you are after," he griped to Mary Fairbanks in 1877, to ensure "that you don't get it." "My experience with Providence," Twain wrote in 1895, has not given "me great confidence" in God's judgment; "my wife," whom Twain adored, must have "crept in while his attention was occupied elsewhere."[17]

Twain sometimes also denounced the concept of "special providence," especially in his twilight years. In his version of the Apostles' Creed, penned sometime in the 1880s, he declared, "I do not believe in special providences."[18] The phrase "Special Providence," Twain thundered in 1885, "nauseates me—with its implied importance of mankind and triviality of God." God does not even "know we are there and would not care if He did." Twain insisted in 1906 that God had never shown any interest "in any human squabble, nor whether the good cause won out."

That same year Twain used the San Francisco earthquake, which demolished the building that housed the newspaper where he had worked, to "ridicule the selfishness implicit in some applications of the doctrine of special Providence." While living in San Francisco in

1866, he had watched "some hoodlums" chase and stone a Chinese man. A policeman saw the attack but did not stop it. Twain penned an article filled with "holy indignation" about the incident for the San Francisco *Morning Call*, but the editor refused to print it because the newspaper depended financially on its Irish subscribers, who despised the Chinese. In addition, the *Morning Call* fired Twain. His "Presbyterian Training" taught Twain that the newspaper had thereby "brought disaster upon itself. I knew the ways of Providence" and that the newspaper would have to answer for this offense. The editor who had sacked Twain was the guilty party, but he was certain that the newspaper itself would suffer some day for the editor's crime. In 1906 the punishment finally came, in the form of an earthquake. Although some would think it strange that God destroyed an entire city to settle a forty-year-old account between a discharged reporter and a newspaper, Twain, as a Presbyterian, "knew that in Biblical times, if a man committed a sin," a whole nation was likely to be exterminated.[19]

As another example of a misguided statement about "special providence," Twain cited Edgar Cope, rector of St. Simeon's Episcopal Church in Philadelphia. Cope thanked God for saving the lives of more than 100 people when a train ran off its rails near Johnstown, Pennsylvania, in 1907. Cope, Twain protested, had wrongly praised God for providing an "inexpensive kindness to one little handful of His earthly children" while allowing many others to experience "misery and death"; in 1906 alone, 10,000 people had been killed and 60,000 injured on American railroads, all of whom God could have saved. Twain ridiculed Cope for believing that God "is so all-comprehensively powerful that He can rescue from death and mutilation any of His children that are in peril by the simple exercise of His will, and at no inconvenience to Himself" and that God's extension of his grace to the passengers on this one train "was a most praiseworthy act."[20]

Twain and Religion, 1861–1867

The years from 1861 to 1867 are often referred to as Twain's bohemian ones, and he admitted that he sowed some wild oats during this period. While working as a reporter for the *Territorial Enterprise* in Virginia City, Nevada—a city known for its theaters, houses of prostitution, gambling palaces, bars, riots, and murders—Clemens was labeled a "Profaner of Divinity." He often drank heavily and narrowly avoided fighting several duels because of the provocative and insulting language he employed in articles and letters. Clemens confessed to his mother that he did not attend church regularly.[21] Nevertheless, he did go periodically to the newly established First Presbyterian Church in Carson City (where Twain was living), to which Orion also belonged. In March 1862, he described listening to one of the depressing sermons of A. F. White, a "whining, nasal, Whangdoodle preacher," at that church. In January 1864, Twain parodied White's series of prosperity-gospel sermons in "Doings in Nevada," published in the New York *Sunday Mercury*.[22] This congregation met in a courtroom above the city jail, leading Twain to quip that "they save men eternally in the second story of the new court house, and damn them for life in the first."[23]

When he agreed to give lectures to raise funds for this church, where Orion was an elder and the treasurer, Twain declared lightheartedly, "Although I am not a very dusty Christian myself, I take an absorbing interest in religious affairs, and would willingly inflict my annual message upon the church itself if it might derive benefit thereby." In a letter to the *Territorial Enterprise* in December 1863, Twain asked, perhaps thinking of his father, "Why will a man" take "chances on fire and brimstone, instead of joining the church and endeavoring with humble spirit and contrite heart, to ring in at the eleventh hour, like the thief on the cross?"[24]

While working in Virginia City, Twain developed a friendship with Franklin Rising, an Episcopal rector and a recent graduate of General Theological Seminary in New York City. Twain claimed that Rising and he "were fast friends" for two of the years he spent in Nevada. Twain occasionally attended Rising's church and tried to teach him how to construct his sermons to appeal to "the better natures of the rough population around him." Rising served as the model for the young minister who conducts Buck Fanshawe's funeral in *Roughing It*, as Twain parodies the pastor's inability to speak effectively to miners in Virginia City. Twain wrote, however, that Rising "has done as much as any man among us to redeem this community from its pristine state of semibarbarism."[25]

Twain and Rising rekindled their relationship when they journeyed together to Hawaii in 1866. Rising led the services during the five

Sundays on the return voyage to San Francisco, and Twain directed the choir. "I hope they will have a better opinion of the music in Heaven than I have down here," Twain joked. "If they don't a thunderbolt" would "knock the vessel endways." They were together day and night during the cruise, Twain reported, and Rising "tried earnestly to bring me to a knowledge of the true God." The journalist kept in touch with Rising after the minister became financial secretary of the (Episcopal) American Church Missionary Society and moved to New York City. Twain mourned when he learned of Rising's death at age thirty-five in December 1868 when two steamboats collided on the Ohio River.[26]

When Twain moved to San Francisco in June 1864 and began working as a reporter for the San Francisco *Morning Call*, he wrote in an article that for "a Christian" who for months had toiled and lived in primitive conditions amidst the barren landscape of Washoe County, Nevada, residing in the city's Occidental Hotel was "Heaven on the half shell. He may even secretly consider it to be Heaven on the entire shell, but his religion teaches a sound Washoe Christian that it would be sacrilege to say it."[27] In San Francisco, Twain attended church more regularly than in Nevada and cultivated friendships with some of the city's leading ministers.

Nevertheless, Twain lived a morally and socially unconventional life and suffered from financial problems, loneliness, and depression. Like Rising, Twain's older sister Pamela strove to win him to Christ. She noted that he wrote to her about pursuing but never achieving happiness. Those whose hopes of happiness are based on worldly matters, she warned him, never find it. Genuine Christians, by contrast, saw the hand of God in every trial, bereavement, and apparent misfortune. She implored her brother to "Let the Spirit of God, which has been knocking at the door of your heart for years, now come in, and make you a new man in Christ Jesus." Everyone in the family except him had displayed "an interest in religion." "Will you stand alone," she asked, "and be separated from the rest, not only in this world, but in the world to come?" Pamela exhorted him to seriously reflect on at least one biblical chapter every day and promised to send him religious papers to read.[28]

Whether Twain responded to Pamela's letter is not known, but he assured Orion and his wife Mollie in September 1864 that "I do go to church." On the other hand, Twain was clearly perplexed about religious matters, as a letter to them a year later reveals: "I have a religion—but you will call it blasphemy. It is that there is a God for the rich man but none for the poor." He added, "I am utterly miserable—so are you. Perhaps your religion will sustain you, feed you—I place no dependence in mine. Our religions are alike, though, in one respect—neither can make a man happy when he is out of luck. If I do not get out of debt in 3 months—pistols or poison for one—exit *me*." Twain was probably referring to this period in his life when he despondently wrote in 1909, "I put the pistol to my head but wasn't man enough to pull the trigger. Many times I have been sorry I did not succeed, but I was never ashamed of having tried. Suicide is the only really sane thing the young or old ever do in this life."[29]

During his sojourn in San Francisco, Twain developed friendships with clergymen Charles Wadsworth, Henry Martyn Scudder, Andrew Leete Stone, Horatio Stebbins, and Henry Bellows. Wadsworth pastored Calvary Presbyterian Church, which Twain sometimes attended. Scudder was a minister at Howard Presbyterian Church, and Stone served First Congregational Church. Bellows and Stebbins successively pastored First Unitarian Church. Prior to coming to San Francisco, Bellows had edited *The Christian Inquirer* and founded and served as president of the United States Sanitary Commission, the principal soldiers' aid society during the Civil War. Twain called him "a man of imperial intellect and matchless power" and "a Christian in the truest sense of the term."[30] Twain claimed that Stebbins, a Harvard graduate who helped found Stanford and the University of California, and he were "thick as thieves."[31]

Twain was attracted to ministers because they were among the nation's most educated citizens, and because many of them excelled at oratory and worked diligently to create a more just society. "There are none I like better to converse with" than ministers, Twain told his mother; "if they're not narrow minded and bigoted they make good companions." "Small-fry ministers" attacked him, Twain wrote to Mary Fairbanks, but "all those of high rank and real influence I visit, dine and swap lies with." Preachers, he insisted, are always pleasant company when off duty. Albert Bigelow Paine argued that ministers "did not always approve" of Twain because he "was hopelessly unorthodox" and "rankly rebellious" about creeds, "but they adored him." Twain's relationships with San Francisco clergymen, Harold Bush, Jr. argues, led him to realize his lifestyle was unfulfilling, and to crave greater meaning and self-identify as a Christian. Moreover, these ministers helped transform "the wild humorist of the West into the more mature and steady New Englander" who could court Olivia Langdon and be accepted into Hartford's highest social circles.[32]

While enjoying cordial relationships with several San Francisco pastors, Twain ridiculed the hypocrisy and greed of American clergy in a fictitious exchange of letters with three leading eastern ministers: Bishop Francis Hawks of New York, Episcopal rector Phillips Brooks of Philadelphia, and Cummings of Chicago. He invited them to accept a call to pastor Grace Cathedral, a prominent Episcopal congregation on Nob Hill.[33] To entice them, he pointed out that San Francisco was a great mission field. Its "sinners are so thick that you can't throw out your line without hooking several of them." Twain humorously claimed to have written a sermon that an Episcopal, Methodist, Presbyterian, and Unitarian pastor had successively used (with adaptations to suit their doctrinal differences), resulting in the conversion of 118 of "the most abject reprobates that ever traveled on the broad road to destruction." He also promised them that preaching would be easy in San Francisco: "Bring along a barrel of your old obsolete sermons; the people here will never know the difference."[34] In his parody, all three ministers decline the offer, however, because they are earning considerably more money in their current pastorates and "because their respective investments in the cotton, petroleum, and grain markets required their constant close attention."[35] His essay satirized clergy who claimed to promote the gospel but instead focused on enlarging their personal wealth.

Another essay describing Twain's humorous depiction of his battle to pay attention in church may well have portrayed his own experience. He began the service devoutly, listening "attentively and expectantly for awhile." Then, however, he fidgeted, grew absent-minded, looked furtively at the minister and members of the congregation, and began counting lace bonnets, bald heads, and drowsy parishioners. He conjectured whether a buzzing fly could escape through an open window and then relapsed "into a dreary reverie." About this time, the minister again captured his attention by saying "a kind word for the poor 'sinners at large'" like him.[36]

Twain's critique of wildcat religion and the treatment of Chinese immigrants in San Francisco also reveal his religious mindset during the mid-1860s. In "The New Wildcat Religion" (1866), Twain censured the frenzied atmosphere and activities of revivals and camp meetings and expressed his preference for "regular stock religions." "You never heard of a Presbyterian going crazy on religion"; people "never see us ranting and shouting and tearing up the ground," Twain declared. "Let us all be content with the tried and safe regular religions, and take no chances on wildcat."[37] Twain considered the followers of William Miller (later called Seventh-Day Adventists) an example of wildcat religion. On October 22, 1844, which Miller forecast to be the end of the world, his disciples had assembled at Lover's Leap near Hannibal and in many other locales around the country to wait for Christ to return. "A multitude of lunatics in America," Twain later explained, "put on their ascension sheets, took a tearful leave of their friends, and got ready to fly up to heaven at the first toot of the trumpet."[38]

Although he preferred the more orderly, sedate worship of Presbyterians, Episcopalians, and Unitarians, Twain sometimes satirized it as bland, boring, unemotional, and uninspiring. These groups donned their best clothes, stood solemnly, bowed their heads, sang hymns (ensuring that people did not "shirk any of the stanzas"), listened quietly while their ministers prayed, sat silently and gravely while their pastor preached, furtively noticed what others were wearing and who caught flies, and grabbed their hats and bonnets when the minister began the benediction. "Like horses, Presbyterians know what they are supposed to do, for it is routine." There was no frenzy, fanaticism, or skirmishing; their worship was safe, tried and true, and "perfectly serene."[39]

As a reporter, Twain attended court hearings, visited jails, and witnessed the extensive, often brutal discrimination against the Chinese living in San Francisco. In various articles written for local and national newspapers, he deplored the inhumane treatment of the Chinese in both the judicial system and employment. As noted above, Twain was infuriated by the *Morning Call*'s refusal to print his story about the beating of a Chinese laundry worker. He wrote a short story about a boy who, on his way to Sunday school, stoned a Chinese man because he believed God would not love him unless he did. On the other hand, Twain penned several parodies of Asian religions.

In various essays, especially three about a Chinese temple constructed by the Ning-Yong Company, he portrays Buddhism as an alien, inferior religion, lampoons the "fat and happy" Chinese god who looks as if "he had eaten too much rice and rats for dinner," pokes fun at "the infernal odors of opium and edibles cooked in an unchristian way," and mocks Chinese Americans' "unchristian devotions."[40]

A Pilgrimage

An 8,000-mile pilgrimage to Europe and the Middle East in 1867 dramatically changed Twain's life. His description of the trip, *The Innocents Abroad* (1869), which became one of the most popular travel books of all time, brought him fame and significant income. Most significantly, it led to his meeting and marrying Olivia Langdon.

Recognizing Twain's writing ability and wit, the editors of the *Alta California* reasoned that its readers would find his account of a trip to the Holy Land entertaining and offered to finance his travel. The voyage of the *Quaker City*, a refitted Civil War battleship, "the first prepackaged luxury cruise in American history, promised to be a star-studded affair." Its prospective passengers included Henry Ward Beecher (America's most famous preacher), former Union general William Tecumseh Sherman, and Broadway actress Maggie Mitchell. The trip's promoters emphasized the excursion's educational and religious benefits and its exclusivity—its $2,000 price tag at a time when a first-class round trip to Paris cost just one-tenth as much limited its sixty-five passengers to the very affluent. Bidding his family goodbye, Twain wrote that he expected the tour to be tranquil and satisfying. "God bless you all," he declared.[41]

The excursion, which lasted from June 10 to November 19, 1867, stopped at numerous European ports and included visits to other European cities, Turkey, Syria, and Palestine. In writing his travel account, Twain rejected the approach of other American guidebooks of his day, which told readers "what to admire and how to behave" and insisted that "European culture was superior to American culture."[42] Twain, by contrast, harshly criticized many aspects of Europe's religious and social life.

Beecher, Sherman, and Mitchell did not make the trip; most of the "pilgrims" who accompanied Twain came from small towns and had never been abroad before, and he viewed many of them as narrow-minded hypocrites. They met every night on the *Quaker City* to pray, sing, and listen to Scripture readings and homilies by fellow travelers, but they largely ignored the plight of the millions of destitute people they encountered during the excursion. In the Holy Land, they "cried crocodile tears" at the alleged site of Christ's crucifixion, chiseled off souvenirs from temple walls, and haggled with impoverished locals over the price of a boat ride on the Sea of Galilee.[43]

Probably speaking for numerous passengers, Colonel William Denny of Winchester, Virginia, called Twain "a wicked fellow" who took the Lord's name in vain. Twain was "liberal, kind and obliging" and "if he were only a Christian would make his mark." Most of the travelers were devout Christians, but Twain described Dan Slote, who owned a stationery manufacturing business in New York, as "a splendid, immoral, tobacco-smoking, wine-drinking, godless roommate who is as good & true & rightminded a man as ever lived."[44] Twain's future in-laws, the Langdons hoped that their seventeen-year-old son Charles who was making the trip without them would become more spiritually-minded and mature by socializing with the pious pilgrims, but he instead preferred to spend time with Twain, Slote, and a few other cigar-smoking, gambling, irreverent passengers.

Innocents Abroad does not parody Christianity itself but rather people's misrepresentation and improper application of Christ's teachings and their egotism, pretension, and foolishness. As Fred Kaplan argues, Twain avoided "offending reasonable and temperate Christians. His satire was directed not at Christianity but at human folly, hypocrisy, and selfishness." Twain criticized the hollow spirituality, gullibility, and misplaced priorities of his fellow Protestant travelers as well as the traits and actions of European Catholics, the Eastern Orthodox, and various Christian groups in Jerusalem who despised each other. He was appalled by the crass commodification, greed, and gaudiness connected with many sacred places, icons, and relics the pilgrims viewed in Europe and the Holy Land; these places and items, he protested, were shams that promoted religious superstition, political despotism, and human exploitation. Twain also censured many of the beliefs, practices, and actions of Muslims whom the pilgrims encountered. *Innocents Abroad* expresses many conventional Christian beliefs: Twain refers to Jesus fifty-two times as "the

Saviour," twice as "our Saviour," and seven times as the Lord and professes to be profoundly moved by "standing on ground that was once actually pressed by the feet of the Saviour."[45]

Innocents Abroad frequently parodies *Tent Life in the Holy Land* (1857) by William Cowper Prime, an American attorney, art historian, and travel writer. Twain uses the fictitious character William Grimes to lampoon Prime's sentimental prose and his depiction of numerous violent clashes with local residents. His fellow pilgrims had read *Tent Life*, Twain joked, and kept themselves ready for battle. If violence did occur, Prime should be prosecuted as an "accessory before the fact." Prime, Twain later complained, frequently damned "to the nethermost hell three or four men whom he hated with his whole heart."[46]

When Twain embarked on the *Quaker City* excursion, he accepted many of the fundamental tenets of Protestantism, but he questioned some doctrines, denounced religious emotionalism and false piety, and abhorred religious deception and manipulation. Although he sometimes attended church and had befriended numerous ministers, Twain viewed himself as a sinner; he had strong opinions about some religious matters and occasionally felt and expressed intense spiritual feelings. During the trip, he regularly (although often not enjoyably) participated in the pilgrims' devotions, attended church services much more frequently than he had in a long time, and engaged in considerable introspection and soul-searching. *Innocents Abroad* provides glimpses into the spiritual struggle that preoccupied Twain for the next several years as he sought to determine what he believed and to win Livy's heart, as they began their marriage and started a family, and as he pursued various writing projects.[47]

Twain decried the widespread European use of religious relics to subsidize churches and enrich individuals as a horrible sacrilege and ridiculed people for accepting relics as genuine. Almost every old church they visited in Europe, he protested, had a piece of Christ's cross "and some of the nails that held it together." The cathedral in Milan alone contained two of St. Paul's fingers and one of St. Peter's, bones of all the other disciples, part of Christ's crown of thorns (even though Notre Dame in Paris had the entire crown), a fragment of the robe Jesus wore at his crucifixion, and a picture of Mary and the baby Jesus painted by St. Luke. Expressing a combination of piety, frustration, and humor, Twain declared, "I trust I am a humble and a consistent Christian. I try to do what is right. I know it is my duty to 'pray for them that despitefully use me'; and therefore, hard as it is, I shall still try to pray for these fumigating, maccaroni-stuffing [sic] organ-grinders" that they encountered in Bellagio, Italy.

Twain admitted that he had been taught to view the Catholic Church with hostility and therefore found it much easier to "discover Catholic faults than Catholic merits." When they visited Italy, he declared, "we were in the heart and home of priestcraft—of a happy, cheerful, contented ignorance, superstition, degradation, poverty, indolence, and everlasting unaspiring worthlessness." The Catholic Church in Italy had abundant resources, including large estates, the most fertile land, great forests, mills, and factories, but, he protested, it had not paid a cent in taxes and did almost nothing to alleviate the country's immense poverty and wretchedness. For 1,500 years Italy had starved half its citizens while devoting its energy and resources to building magnificent cathedrals. All the churches combined in an average American city could not buy the ostentatious jewelry housed in one of Italy's hundred cathedrals, but Italy had a hundred beggars for every one in the United States.

On the other hand, Twain praised the virtue, charity, and unselfishness that motivated the Dominican friars to care for thousands of cholera victims in Naples even though it cost many of them their lives. "They must unquestionably love their religion, to suffer so much for it," Twain reasoned. Their commitment to their faith and good deeds "would save their souls though they were bankrupt in the true religion—which is ours [Protestantism]." He also lauded the Convent Fathers in Palestine whose doors were always open as a "priceless blessing to the poor."

When visiting Greece, Twain was struck by the fleeting character of fame. During antiquity, many Greek orators, generals, and authors had toiled arduously to leave an enduring legacy, but all that remained twenty centuries later was small inscriptions on blocks of stone. Moreover, he declared, despite Greece's many impressive achievements in the centuries before Christ's birth, poverty, misery, and mendacity abounded in the 1860s.

Twain expressed animosity toward Muslims several times in *Innocents Abroad*. Muslims' "natural instincts," he wrote while touring Turkey, "do not permit them to be moral." The sultan had eight hundred wives, which, he quipped, "almost amounts to bigamy." Americans, he joked, thought this was shameful in the Middle East, but they tolerated it in Salt Lake City. Twain expressed his contempt for Muslims who had slaughtered five thousand Christians in Damascus in 1861. "I never disliked a Chinaman as I do these degraded Turks and Arabs," Twain thundered, "and when Russia is ready to war with them again, I hope England and France will not" interfere. Twain also blamed Muslim rulers for the deplorable conditions in Jerusalem where wretchedness, poverty, dirt, lepers, cripples, and the blind abounded.[48] When they visited Egypt, Twain declared that unless the Muslim guides who were helping them climb the Pyramids repented, someday "they would go straight to perdition." They would, however, never repent; they would "never forsake their paganism. This thought calmed me, cheered me." Standing before "the overshadowing majesty" of the Sphinx "with its accusing memory of the deeds of all ages," Twain added, provided a foretaste of what people would feel when they stood "in the awful presence of God."

Visiting Turkey also prompted Twain to lambast Orthodox Christians for attending church regularly on Sundays but constantly breaking the Ten Commandments throughout the week. Missionaries told him that many Orthodox Christians complimented fellow believers for being "charming swindler[s]" and "most exquisite liar[s]!"

Twain denounced contemporary Christians several times in *Innocents Abroad* for misinterpreting prophecy. When the pilgrims visited Smyrna, he noted that it had "the only church against which no threats were implied" among the seven addressed by John in Revelation 2–3, and that it was the only city to have survived. The light of Ephesus, by contrast, "had been put out." Christians, who often found prophecies in the Bible where none existed, Twain argued, spoke "cheerfully and complacently of poor, ruined Ephesus as the victim of prophecy." Revelation, however, did not promise, its destruction "without due qualification." Rather, Jesus warned that it would be destroyed only if its Christians did not repent. Twain also accused modern interpreters of "arbitrarily fitting" prophesies to serve their purposes. Their erroneous interpretations, he contended, caused worldly men to speak disparagingly about "sacred subjects."

Twain made a similar complaint when the tourists visited Capernaum in Palestine. Some of his fellow travelers were very gratified that the town lay in ruins, because Christ had allegedly prophesied that it would be demolished if its residents did not repent after witnessing the great works he had done there. "As usual," these pilgrims "fit the eternal words of gods to the evanescent things of this earth," Twain wrote. In Twain's view, Christ was referring to the punishment the inhabitants of Capernaum who rejected his miracles would receive at the final judgment, not to the destruction of the city.

Twain censured some his fellow pilgrims for their unwillingness to travel on Sunday, which necessitated compressing a three-day journey to Damascus into two days. He and others argued that their tired horses deserved to be treated kindly for "their faithful service" and that this grueling pace might injure some travelers. Jesus had insisted that oxen be rescued from the mire on the Sabbath, he added, but the self-righteous travelers refused to show their horses any pity. Men and horses might die, but they must enter the Holy Land next week "with no Sabbath-breaking stain upon them." Making an argument he would repeat many times in his subsequent writings, Twain complained that these pilgrims "were willing to commit a sin against the spirit of religious law" to preserve its letter. He was happy "to keep the Sabbath day," but sometimes obeying the letter of the law was sinful. Many *Quaker City* travelers were likable, "honorable, upright, [and] conscientious," Twain avowed, but their understanding of "the Saviour's religion" was distorted. They lectured other pilgrims about their "shortcomings unsparingly" and read chapters of the Bible at their evening devotions that accentuated gentleness, charity, and mercy but failed to live by these virtues. Their actions led people to view Christianity unfavorably.

In Damascus, the travelers visited the reputed home of Ananias, whom God had used in Paul's conversion to Christianity. Seeming to accept the Bible's divine authorship, Twain wrote that a "fierce supernatural light" had blinded Paul who thereafter acted "under Divine inspiration."

Not surprisingly, the Holy Land was the high point of the trip for Twain and his fellow travelers. They galloped through the Louvre and numerous other galleries, the Vatican, and the frescoed cathedrals of France, Italy, and Spain, "but the Holy Land brought out all our enthusiasm. We fell into raptures by the barren shores of Galilee" and at numerous other biblical sites. The Holy Land was an appropriate place "for the birth of a religion able to save the world" and "for the stately Figure appointed to stand upon its stage and proclaim its high decrees." Their tour of many Old Testament sites prompted Twain to complain that human nature had not improved over the centuries. He especially faulted the Israelites for not "withstanding the seductions of a golden calf" and for frequently exterminating their enemies.

The pilgrims visited the Western Wall and the Temple Mount, the Mount of Olives, the Garden of Gethsemane, Calvary, the traditional houses of the rich man and Lazarus in Christ's parable, the Tombs of the Kings, the place where Stephen was stoned, the room where the Last Supper was held, and the fig tree that Jesus cursed. Twain walked the Via Dolorosa, a route one-third of a mile long in the Old City of Jerusalem that Jesus had taken to his crucifixion, and bought a Bible for his mother. Twain spent several hours contemplating that he was actually in the illustrious city where Solomon resided, Abraham conversed with God, and walls still stood "that witnessed the spectacle of the Crucifixion."

Christ's actual burial place was greatly disputed, Twain noted, but no doubt existed about where he was crucified—at Golgotha, the Mount of Calvary. When Christ was executed, many in Jerusalem "believed that he was the true Son of God." This, coupled with "the storm, the darkness, the earthquake, the rending of the veil of the Temple, and the untimely waking of the dead," would have indelibly impressed the place where Jesus died on people's minds.

On the other hand, Twain was disappointed and disgusted because he believed that no significant events had occurred at many of the other sites they visited in Palestine; rather, the monks had created "imaginary holy places." He had hoped to enjoy a genuine religious experience by encountering "sites so rich in religious significance and biblical history," but the deceptive nature and commercial exploitation of many of the locations rendered this impossible. Bethlehem, filled with countless beggars and relic peddlers, was particularly disgusting. Twain was especially skeptical about the Holy Sepulchre, a fourth-century site that was the alleged burial place of Adam and Jesus.

Visiting the place where Jesus declared, "Thou art Peter; and upon this rock will I build my church, and the gates of hell shall not prevail against it," prompted Twain to complain that Peter's confession had led to the creation of "the mighty edifice of the Church of Rome," the supremacy of popes over emperors, and popes' "godlike power to curse a soul or wash it white from sin." For many centuries, Twain asserted, Rome had fought to sustain its position as "the only true Church," which popes claimed Christ "conferred upon her," and would continue to do so until the end of time.

Twain lamented that the various sects of Christians, including Syrians, Copts, and Greeks, that had chapels under the roof of the Church of the Holy Sepulchre could not "worship together around the grave of the Saviour of the World in peace." The priests of all these chapels were permitted to visit an altar, built over the place where soldiers reputedly cast lots for the Savior's raiment, to "pray and worship the gentle Redeemer." They were not allowed to do so "at the same time, however, because they always fight." Ironically, Twain observed, much blood had been shed throughout history because of people's veneration of "the last resting-place of the meek and lowly, the mild and gentle, Prince of Peace!"

Twain's reaction to other aspects of the Holy Land was mixed. It was astonishing, he argued, that "the now flourishing plant of Christianity" had sprung from such an "exceedingly small portion of the earth." Most of Christ's ministry occurred within an area about the size of a typical county in the United States. The Jordan River and the Sea of Galilee were much smaller than the impression of them he had received in his Sunday school classes. Twain was also surprised that the grapes they saw were not nearly as large as the ones that (according to the pictures in his Sunday school books) Joshua and Caleb brought back to the Israelites when they spied on Canaan. On the other hand, after visiting Noah's tomb, Twain declared that henceforth, his "memorable voyage will always possess a living interest for me."

Twain described the topography of the Holy Land as "monotonous and uninviting" and bemoaned its widespread destitution. Its scenery was the most dismal on earth. The present poverty of Bethlehem and Bethany clashed with their earlier "high honor" of having "the Saviour's presence" and being "the hallowed spot where the shepherds watched their flocks by night, and where the angels sang Peace on earth, good will to men." Jerusalem was impoverished, Capernaum was in ruins, and Bethsaida and Chorazin had vanished. Poking fun at the premillennialists of his era, Twain wrote that if Jesus did come to earth again, it would not be to Jerusalem. No sensible person who had been there would want to return.

Twain professed great admiration for Christ and belief in his miracles, including his healings of the afflicted and multiplying the loaves and fishes to feed a huge crowd. Jesus, Twain declared, "knew how to preach" to Palestine's "simple, superstitious, disease-tortured creatures." His ability to cure the sick led multitudes to follow him and made him "the talk of the nation." Christ was a "majestic Personage" and "the Messiah of the Christians" who walked on water, released people from demon possession, and raised Jairus's daughter from the dead. Twain referred to "the Lord's Transfiguration," called Christ's crucifixion a "tremendous event," and seemed to affirm Christ's bodily resurrection. Twain also noted that many viewed Jesus as "a mysterious stranger who was a god" and who "had stood face to face with God above the clouds."

Twain was very moved by standing on the same ground where the Savior had once walked. This experience clashed with the mystery and vagueness normally associated with "the character of a god"; in his previous experience, the gods had always been "hidden in the clouds and very far away." It was difficult to realize that he was sitting where "a god has stood" and looking at the same brook and mountains Jesus saw, surrounded by the ancestors of individuals who had talked with Christ face to face.

Twain's reaction to the Holy Land was reverent, agonizingly honest, and pensive, and he regretted that he could not respond more deeply on a spiritual level. He recognized, however, after greater contemplation that his experiences had given him "profound and genuine spiritual nourishment."[49] On the second Christmas eve after the trip, Twain wrote to a fellow traveler, that 1,869 years earlier "Shepherds watched their flocks—& the hovering angels were singing Peace on earth, good-will to men" because "the Saviour" had come. "[D]on't you realize . . . that Jesus *was* born there, & that the angels *did* sing in the still air above . . . ? *I* do." Twain effused, "It is more real than ever. And I am glad, a hundred times glad, that I saw Bethlehem."[50]

In light of Twain's struggle to embrace Christianity, as revealed in his courtship letters to Livy soon after this excursion, it is difficult to determine whether he truly believed Christ was indeed the Savior who performed many miracles and rose from the dead or was simply saying what he knew his many pious readers wanted to hear. In *Innocents Abroad*, he does distinguish biblical stories and statements about Christ performing miracles from other accounts that he calls traditions or legends. In addition to the other instances where Twain seemed to affirm God's intervention in history, he appeared to believe that Mary had received a message from an angel telling her that she would give birth to the savior, and that the apostle John saw a vision of "the New Jerusalem glimmering above the clouds of Heaven."

The Elmira *Saturday Evening Review* predicted incorrectly that *Innocents Abroad*'s "apparent irreverence" and "playful allusions to matters that a large portion of mankind have been taught to regard as sacred" might limit its sales. Although Twain undoubtedly meant no harm, the reviewer presumed, his satire of the place where "all Christian hearts" turned with awe and devotion might disturb many potential readers. *Packard's Monthly* warned similarly that some might "see in the descriptions of the Holy Land a conspicuous lack of reverence" for sacred matters. The *New York Herald*, by contrast, faulted "over-pious and fastidious critics" for condemning the book because of "its levity." Some of Twain's accounts did not express "austere piety," but they were not sacrilegious. The *National Standard* praised *Innocents Abroad* as "satirical, comical, and funny" and insisted that "its morals are of a high tone." The *New York Tribune* criticized Twain's horrid disrespect "for tradition and authority" for sometimes degenerating into "an offensive irreverence for things which other men hold sacred." Most of his book, however, "is pure fun." *Zion's Herald*, a Methodist periodical, faulted Twain for using *Pilgrim's Progress*, "a sacred name" to which "every Christian's heart clings," as the book's subtitle. It also protested that amid its rollicking, *Innocents Abroad* featured "too much wine, whist [an English card game], theatres, and swearing." Nevertheless, the editor praised the travelogue's "many excellent descriptions" and declared reading to it be a joy. *Innocents Abroad* contained no homilies, political essays, or philosophical discussions, the *Liberal Christian* asserted, but it "preaches nevertheless, and is full of health and aglow" with a "cheerful, hopeful, wholesome religion" that "does not fear to crack a joke."[51]

Courtship and Faith

After returning from his pilgrimage, Twain worked very briefly as personal secretary to William M. Stewart, the first US Senator from Nevada, and then as a correspondent in Washington, DC, from late November 1867 until March 1868. While there, he partnered with another journalist, William Swinton, to create a newspaper syndicate consisting of twelve weekly journals that published some of the same articles. Twain called Swinton a Presbyterian "of the old and genuine school" who loved his religion and found serenity in it. They needed more money for this enterprise to succeed; Swinton's strong faith gave him confidence they would obtain the capital they required, but Twain did not share his certainty. Twain concluded that Swinton "was ashamed of me, privately, because of my weak faith." Swinton declared in a "confident and unquestioning way, 'The Lord will provide.'" Influenced by Swinton, Twain was "almost convinced that the Lord really would provide."[52] The syndicate was short-lived, however.

During his excursion, Twain had learned about twenty-two-year-old Oliva Iona Louise Langdon when her younger brother Charles showed him an ivory replica of her. Twain was immediately captivated and arranged to meet Livy soon after the pilgrims returned to the United States. They met in New York City during the 1867 Christmas season. Instantly smitten, Twain resolved to win Livy's love and wed her. He confronted a major obstacle, however. Livy and her parents—Jervis and Olivia Lewis Langdon—were devout Christians, and the author was known for neither his uprightness nor his Christian commitment. Evaluating what Mark Twain believed about religious matters is immensely complicated by statements he made while courting Livy.

Jervis Langdon, a prosperous merchant, settled in Elmira, New York, in 1845. The next year he helped founded Park (Congregational) Church. The Langdons played a very active role in this church, which was pastored from 1854 to 1900 by Thomas Beecher, the son of prominent theologian and educator Lyman Beecher and the brother of America's most renowned preacher, Henry Ward Beecher. Langdon was an ardent abolitionist who served as a conductor in the Underground Railroad. He also strongly supported prison reform, women's rights, and the temperance movement. When Langdon died of stomach cancer in 1870, Twain called him a "good, & noble Christian" who aided the church, Elmira, and the needy through his service, advice, and money. "All the impulses of Mr. Langdon's heart," Twain declared, "were good & generous." Langdon strove to abolish slavery even though it brought him "disgrace, insult, hatred & bodily peril."[53]

Although Twain signed a November 1867 letter to John Russell Young, an editor of the *New York Tribune*, as "Your obliged fellow-servant in Christ" and denounced "the stupid gang of scholastic asses who go browsing through the Holy Land reducing miracles to purely natural occurrences," at this point in his life he did not profess to be a Christian. Moreover, Twain appeared to want a faith to give meaning and direction to his life. While in Palestine, he wrote, "Oh for [the ability] to kneel at the Sepulchre & look at the rift in the rock & the socket of the cross & the tomb of Adam & feel & know & never question that they were genuine."[54] The thirty-three-year-old bachelor admitted that he had engaged in actions the Langdons considered immoral admitted that he had.[55] To win Livy's hand and her parents' consent, Twain realized that he needed to become a Christian, reform his behavior, and convince them that his character was sound and that he could provide financially for Livy and their future family.

Biographers disagree about whether Twain's efforts to overcome his religious doubts and embrace Christianity while wooing Livy were genuine, but the preponderance of the evidence indicates that his attempt was both strenuous and heartfelt. Twain's love letters to Livy reveal "convincingly the depth and sincerity of his quest for religious faith."[56] Several factors suggest that Twain's effort to embrace Christianity while courting Livy was authentic. He showed a strong sense of integrity at other times; he hated hypocrisy; he frankly admitted that he struggled to accept basic Christian doctrines and experience closeness with God; and throughout life he wrestled with guilt about other acts he had committed; dishonesty about his search for faith would have exacerbated the guilt he wished to avoid. Some scholars, however, depict Twain as a charlatan, a master manipulator who allegedly stopped practicing Christianity soon after his wedding.[57] Others argue that Twain's quest to accept Christianity was genuine but deluded. Twain certainly had powerful reasons to declare himself a Christian—Livy was very unlikely to agree to marry him unless he did, and her parents were equally unlikely to give their permission. Nevertheless, his courtship letters demonstrate that his endeavor to espouse Christianity on intellectual, emotional, and moral grounds was valiant and valid.

As noted, Twain frequently admitted to Livy his doubts about Christianity and his struggle to believe. His love letters reveal his battle to accept fundamental Christian doctrines and to overcome his cynicism about some Christian practices produced by his child-hood and young adult religious experiences, personal tragedy, and reading the works of religious skeptics. Livy's letters have not been preserved, so we know about her views only through Twain's responses.

That Twain won the confidence of Livy's parents is remarkable. Twain was ten years older than her, and her parents' vetting of him undoubtedly revealed that he drank excessively, swore habitually, and was poorly educated and financially unstable. In his attempt to gain the approval of Livy's parents, Twain furnished the names of six respected San Francisco residents including two pastors—Charles Wadsworth and Horatio Stebbins—several of whom provided lukewarm assessments. Stebbins, for example, said, "Mark is rather erratic, but I consider him harmless." Another reference, James Roberts, the superintendent of the Calvary Presbyterian Church's Sunday school, called Twain a drunkard and declared, "I would rather bury a daughter of mine than have her marry such a fellow."[58]

To win the Langdons' approbation, Twain enlisted the aid of Mary Fairbanks. She became his mentor on morals and manners, his spiritual guide, and a close confidante on religious matters. Like the Langdons, she was a highly respected member of America's upper crust because of her wealth, status, and religious involvement.[59] Shortly after the excursion, Fairbanks stated that Mark Twain "may have ridiculed our prayer-meetings and our psalm-singing" because "his newspapers expected it of him," but Samuel Clemens, "the better man," revered "the sacred mission of prayer" and often happily recalled the evening services on the ship when "his voice blended with others" in singing hymns.[60]

As the Langdons came to know Twain, they were impressed by his character, personality, integrity, and future promise and eventually gave him their blessing to marry Livy.

Her parents' acceptance of Twain was facilitated by Livy's confidence that he could become a Christian and an upright man. Livy believed that she could help him accept Christ as his savior and reform his life. She willingly accepted the responsibility from Mary Fairbanks of helping tame "the wild humorist of the Pacific slope."[61]

Throughout a courtship that lasted more than two years, Twain described his painstaking battle to become a Christian. He also frequently quoted Scripture, professed to be faithfully reading the Bible and praying, mentioned church services he attended and prayer sessions with his friend Joseph Twichell, described sermons he heard, referred to hymns, discussed theological issues, affirmed his belief in God's Providence and the afterlife, and peppered his letters with "God bless you" and other religious rhetoric. Twain spent much of the period when he was courting Livy traveling throughout the country to give speeches. From November 1868 through March 1869, for example, Twain gave forty-three lectures in nine states from New York to Iowa on "The American Vandal Abroad."

Twain was painfully honest about his spiritual struggle. He candidly admitted he was trying to avoid improper motives for embracing a religious faith, especially his desire to please Livy. "I have been praying that I might seek the Savior for his own sake," he declared in December 1867, rather than for a "selfish motive"—securing "your loving approbation" or removing "Mrs. Fairbanks' uneasiness concerning my eternal future." And he prayed, Twain added, that nothing he said or did might deceive Livy "even in the faintest degree." He did not want her to conclude that he was "already a Christian" when "the Father knows I am only trying to be—only groping in the dark." Twain reported a year later that after three months of praying earnestly, he had begun "to comprehend that one must seek Jesus for himself alone," not influenced "by selfish motives." However, whenever he sought "the Savior," he "was confronted" by a selfish impulse—his "measureless love" for Livy and the impossibility of being content while causing her pain "by my separation from the Christian fold if you were my wife." His conversion would also cheer his "aged mother's closing days," "descend like a benediction" upon his sister Pamela, and thrill his "faithful pilgrim mother," Mary Fairbanks. [62]

Despite his struggles, Twain was optimistic that he would soon become a Christian. Twain reported to Livy regarding Twichell's confidence that after he espoused Christianity, he would become a very "useful man." "Part of my mission on earth," Twain insisted, was "to be a benefactor to the clergy" through his humor. Twain promised Fairbanks that "I shall do no act which you or Livy might be pained to hear of" and "I shall be a Christian." "If I am not to be a Christian," he declared, "it will take many & many a month of discouragement to *prove* it to me."[63]

A year after Livy and Twain met, she asked Fairbanks what kind of man the author had been and was likely to become. Livy noted that he appeared to have adopted "a new manner of life, with higher & better purposes actuating his conduct," but she especially wanted to know if Fairbanks thought Twain "resolutely" aimed to act more virtuously because he had accepted "a Christian life."[64] Meanwhile, Twain shared with Livy that Twichell was trying to help him become a Christian. He quoted Twichell's statement that he hoped Twain would experience "the dear life eternal which our Savior gives for repentance & faith." Twichell urged Twain to pray diligently to receive the peace that "believing in Jesus Christ & knowing Him" provided and to give his "heart to God." Twain added that Twichell had gently and tenderly "taught the religion that is all in all to him. And shall be to me, likewise, I hope & pray."[65] Twichell prayed fervently for Twain's conversion and that Twain and Livy's love "might grow until it was made *perfect* love by the approving spirit [of] God."[66] Nevertheless, Twain lamented in December 1868 that Livy was troubled because she had "small faith" that his "efforts to become a Christian will succeed" or because she believed he still leaned on her spiritually. Twain insisted that when he became a Christian his "life will have an object! What an amazing value the thought gives to this life of mine, which was so perfectly valueless before!"[67]

Twain's examination of his conscience and his search for religious meaning were especially intense in late 1868 and early 1869. Emulating Augustine and the Puritans, Twain scrutinized his life for signs of genuine conviction. He sought to follow Fairbanks's advice to put himself "out of sight" when considering an action and "do it for the comfort & benefit of others," thereby adopting "a Christ-like spirit."

He told Livy that he had become a moral man—one who did not swear, steal, or drink. He was not yet, however, a Christian, "a fruit-bearer." He performed his duties well, but he lacked the "chief ingredient of piety"—the "inner sense which tells me what I do I am doing for love of the Savior." "You know," Twain added, that "the child must crawl before it walks—& I must do right for love of you while I am in the infancy of Christianity; & then I can do right for love of the Savior when I shall have gotten my growth." Three days later, he bemoaned that he had gone through a period when faith seemed "far away and well-nigh unattainable" and he felt like "giving up in despair." He lamented that godliness escaped him, prayer seemed "unavailing," and his strenuous searching appeared to be "a mockery." Twain claimed that he read the Bible every night, along with all the religious literature he could obtain. He avoided all wrongdoing, but he nevertheless sometimes experienced "a chilly apathy" toward God. At the same time, he confessed to Livy's father, "I am upon the right path—I shall succeed, I hope. Men as lost as I, have found a Savior, & why not I?"[68] He promised that "I won't be satisfied with anything short of the highest Christian attainment."[69]

Livy strongly encouraged Twain's quest to become a Christian, and he redoubled his efforts to experience the elusive "religious emotion." He was living morally, but this feeling had not come despite his fervent prayers. Twain confessed, "I know not how to compel an emotion." He prayed every day that Livy would "not be impatient or lose confidence" in his "final conversion" and that his "poisonous & besetting apathy" would depart.[70] Twain's letters to Livy during this period disclose his vacillation as he examined his conscience. His "thirty-three years of ill-doing & wrongful speech" had shackled him with "a deadly weight of sin." "I see the Savior dimly at times," he declared, but at other intervals Christ was "very near." Sometimes praying was pleasurable, and he did so "night and morning, in cars and everywhere, twenty times a day." On other days, however, the "spirit of religion" was "motionless within me from the rising . . . to the setting of the sun." Nevertheless, he "would distrust a religious faith that came upon me suddenly." Only a faith that developed deliberately, step by step, could be trusted.[71]

In late January 1869, Twain asked God to guard him "from even unconsciously or unwittingly saying anything" to Livy that she "might misconstrue & be thereby *deceived*." He did not want to "be guilty of any taint or shadow of *hypocrisy*" in his dealings with her. Instead, he strove to "be *wholly* true & frank & open" even if "it cost me your priceless love." Twain repudiated some of his previous behaviors and pledged to attain "the highest Christian excellence." He promised that he would not conceal any of his earlier misdeeds from her parents, and he assured her that after they wed, he "would never desire to roam again." "Once a Christian" who was equipped with God's strength, Twain avowed, "what should I fear?"

Six weeks later, Twain explained to Livy that he had believed sowing wild oats in his earlier years was "the surest way to make" him "a steady, reliable, wise man, thoroughly fitted for his life, equal to its emergencies, & triple-armed against its wiles & frauds & follies." But, he reasoned, "here is a deeper question": is it "justifiable to trample the laws of God under foot at any time in our lives?" Livy's deep spirituality had enabled him to "catch glimpses of my own shallowness." Twain asked God to keep Livy "free from the taint of my misshapen, narrow, worldly fancies" until her sweet influence helped him see the light.[72]

Following the custom of the Victorian era, Livy refused Twain's first marriage proposal, but his charm, wit, persistence, sincerity, and apparent acceptance of Christianity convinced her that they could enjoy life together, and the fragile damsel—who would suffer many health problems during their marriage—consented when the ambitious author asked her a second time in November 1868, contingent upon her parents' approval. Overjoyed, Twain wrote to Twichell, citing 2 Timothy 4:7: "Sound the timbrel!" for "I have fought the good fight & lo! I have won." The next day the author told his sister, "When I am permanently *settled*—& when I am a Christian—& when I have demonstrated that I have a good, steady, reliable character, her parents will withdraw their objections, & she *may* marry me—I say she *will*."[73]

When their engagement was announced on February 4, 1869, Twain informed Livy that "I devour religious literature, now, with a genuine interest & pleasure" that is "growing—& I hope it may always grow." Nine days later, judging himself more by his conduct than his beliefs, Twain professed that he was a Christian. His friends had previously known him as "a profane swearer" who drank socially, "a man without a religion; in a word, as a 'wild' young man." Now, however, "my conduct is above reproach" and "I now claim that I am a Christian"; he hoped that "my bearing shall show that I am justly entitled to so name myself." Twain thanked Livy for reclaiming his life from waste and worthlessness. She had taken his previously aimless "worldly ambitions" and given him "a direction, a goal to be attained." Twain wrote to his family that Livy "said she never could or would love me—but she set herself the task of making a Christian of me. I said she would succeed, but that in the meantime she would unwittingly dig a matrimonial pit & end by tumbling into it—& lo! the prophecy is fulfilled." Twain told Twichell that "in the presence of God only," Livy and he had devoted their "lives to each other & to the service of God." Twain added that "my future wife wants me to be surrounded by a good moral & religious atmosphere" and he would "unite with the church as soon as I am located." Echoing this commitment, Twain promised Livy, "we shall spend our joined lives in the sincere & earnest service of God."[74] "Praise & thanks unto God, whose servant I am," he declared. Marriage would give them a new reason "to love, a new depth to sorrow, [and] a new impulse to worship."[75]

In their love letters, Twain and Livy also discussed biblical passages, prayer, providence, and the afterlife. "You are worth a dozen preachers to me," Twain told Livy in January 1869, "& I love to follow your teachings. Every day in my little Testament I track you by your pencil through your patient search for . . . wisdom." Every verse she marked reminded him of one of her remarks and "shows me how deeply the beautiful precept had sunk into your heart & brain." Twain reported to Livy in August 1869 that each night he would go to bed only after reading the Bible and praying for them "as usual."[76]

As their relationship began, Twain was deeply moved by Livy's promise to pray for him daily, and he beseeched her to continue. Twain promised that he would "so mend my conduct that I shall grow *worthier* of your prayers" and that "I *will* 'pray with you'" as she asked with as much vigor as his feeble faith permitted. When Twain told Twichell that Livy was praying for him, the pastor responded, "Clemens, you don't know what limitless power there is in a woman's prayers!—the prayers of a hundred men cannot lift me up like one prayer from a woman!"[77] Twain admitted that Christ sometimes seemed far from him and noted that he prayed sometimes hopefully but other times despairingly because he felt overwhelmed by "a firm-set mountain of sin."

As their courtship progressed, Twain continued to discuss both his prayers and his efforts to improve his conduct. In December 1868, he told Livy, "I prayed that at last you might come to love me freely & fully, & that He would prepare me to be worthy of it."[78] Twain urged Livy to "pray unceasingly" and promised that although he was a sinner and "unworthy to approach the Throne," he too would pray continuously. "It is easy to pray for you," he added, "but it seems dreadful *presumption* to ask favors for myself. You have earned them—but I do not deserve them." Perhaps recalling his own father, Twain told Livy he felt like a son who had dishonored "a generous earthly father all his life" and then at the last hour asked "for food & shelter under his roof."[79] "I do not & shall not neglect my prayers, Livy, but somehow they do not seem as full of life as when you or Twichell are [near]by," he wrote. Every beat of his heart, Twain declared, "is a prayer for you" that "all your days may be filled with the ineffable peace of God." He promised her that "I will pray, as customary, for light & guidance, for faith & love, for patience & strength—praying also, that the peace of God may rest in your heart" and the Holy Spirit may shield "you from all harm." Every time Twain prayed that God would give him "His strength to do the task that is set before me," he told Livy, his lecture had been "infallibly a success." Twain described the prayers he participated in with the family of Azel Stevens Roe, a Hartford friend, in May 1869 as "beautiful & earnest & touching." "I pray for you" every night, Twain declared in January 1870, "ever since you moved my spirit to prayer seventeen months ago."[80]

As we have seen, Twain later frequently questioned the doctrine of Providence, but in his courtship letters to Livy, he consistently affirmed it. "I believe in the Savior in whose hands our destinies are," he asserted. "With the favor & the blessing of Him who rules our destinies, I *shall* succeed" in becoming a Christian. "Don't grieve, Livy," Twain counseled, "that you cannot" fight wrong "with strong fierce words & dazzling actions." God appointed "His instruments" and equipped them to do his work, Twain argued, and Livy was admirably performing the work God created her to do. "Therefore, be content. Do that which God has given you to do, & do not seek to improve upon His judgment. . . . You might as well reproach yourself for not being able to win bloody victories in battle, like Joan of Arc. In your sphere you are as great, & as noble, & as efficient as any Joan of Arc that ever lived."[81]

In several letters, Twain affirmed belief in an afterlife. After they were married, Twain effused, they would labor together until the "journey of life is done & the great peace of eternity descends upon us . . . . We shall never be separated on earth, Livy; & let us pray that we may not [be] in Heaven." Twain reminded Livy that after ten million years, their time on earth would seem "trifling & insignificant." They would chuckle when they remembered that they sometimes failed to fulfill "duties to God & man because the world might jeer at us." The world's petty opinions would be only a fleeting memory in "that distant day." "We sow for time," Twain declared, "seldom comprehending that we are to reap in Eternity."[82]

How should we interpret Twain's keen interest in religious matters and his professed desire to become a Christian while courting Livy? As noted, some biographers view it as a ruse, a deliberate deception designed to gain the hand of the woman with whom he was infatuated. Other scholars argue that Twain's close examination of and deep involvement in Christianity during this period was genuine but deluded. He carefully read the Bible and sermons, attended church, prayed, sought to understand Christianity, and strove to reform his behavior to win Livy's heart, but given his life experience and religious skepticism, these interpreters contend he was never able to truly overcome his doubts. Harriet Smith and Richard Bucci contend, for example, that Twain may have been deceived "about his own character and beliefs," but it is impossible to read his letters from 1869 to 1871 "without realizing that if he was, he was not aware of it at the time."[83] Still others, including myself, maintain that Twain's participation in Christian activities and Christian commitment was authentic but short-lived. Harold K. Bush, Jr. maintains, for example, that Twain, like Augustine, engaged in an often emotionally painful quest to "discover true faith in God."[84] For the rest of his life, Twain would struggle to reconcile his head and heart, his intellect and his emotions.

Speaking for those who see his conversion as disingenuous, Jeffrey Holland declares that falling in love with Livy "was the closest thing to an orthodox religious conversion Sam Clemens ever experienced."

She became his goddess, "the only one in which he ever fully believed." Clearly, Twain highly esteemed Livy. His romantic rhetoric was effusive even by the standards of Victorian love letters. He extolled her as "my matchless, my beautiful Livy—my best friend, my wise helpmeet, my teacher of the Better Way." Using language that probably made her cringe, Twain called her "my sacred idol." She was "a living breathing sermon; a blessing delivered straight from the hand of God," a messenger who carried "refreshment to the weary" and "hope to the despondent" whom he compared with the saint he revered—Joan of Arc.[85]

Conclusion

The frequent argument that Twain abandoned religion soon after his wedding is based on a very narrow definition of religion. As Bush demonstrates, Twain expressed religious yearnings for the rest of his life.[86] As the 1860s ended, Twain seemed to be rediscovering and reaffirming aspects of his childhood religious socialization and to be developing a more mature understanding of Christian orthodoxy. However, after he and Livy married, moved to Hartford, Connecticut, settled in an exemplary Christian community, and had children, his questions and doubts about Christianity reemerged. His close friendship with Twichell continued, and he participated in the worship and ministry of Asylum Hill (Congregational) Church, supported a mission to aid the city's poor, conversed about religious matters with numerous individuals, and wrote about many religious topics. His faith, however, began to waver and his critique of Christianity steadily increased; it is very unlikely that he ever again discussed religious issues as intensely and extensively with any individual as he had with Livy during their courtship.

Notes

1. AMT, January 19, 1906, 1:297–8. See also Paul Fatout, *Mark Twain in Virginia City* (Bloomington: Indiana University Press, 1964), 196–213; and Leland Krauth, "Mark Twain Fights Sam Clemens' Duel," *Mississippi Quarterly* 33 (Spring 1980), 141–53.

2. SLC to OL, January 7, 1869, LTR, 3:11 (first two quotations); SLC to OL, January 22, 1869, LTR, 3:64 (third quotation); SLC to OL, March 2, 1869, LTR, 3:131 (fourth quotation); SLC to OLC, November 27, 1875, LTR, 6:597 (fifth quotation).

3. SLC to MMF, February 27 and 28, 1869, LTR 3:123; SLC to MMF, August 14, 1869, MTMF, 104; SLC to OL, November 25, 1869, LTR, 3:409; SLC to Orion Clemens, April 21, 1870, LTR, 4:114; SLC to WDH, February 27, 1874, LTR, 6:52; SLC to Francis Finlay, April 23, 1874, LTR, 6:114; SLC to Thomas Bailey Aldrich, March 24, 1874, LTR: 6:90.

4. SLC to JHT, January 26, 1879, MTL, 1:349; SLC to Edwin Pond Parker, May 15, 1880, *Mark Twain's Letters, 1876–80*, ed. Michael Frank and Harriet Elinor Smith (Berkeley: University of California Press, 2007), 104; SLC to OLC, March 1888, MF, 54; quotations in that order.

5. "A Lincoln Memorial: A Plea by Mark Twain for the Setting Apart of His Birthplace," *New York Times*, January 13, 1907, 8; CT, 2:343; AMT, February 14, 1906, 1:357.

6. MTC, 151; SLC to Henry Rogers, January 3, 1895, MTB, 995.

7. https://www.apuritansmind.com/westminster-standards/chapter-5/; RMT, 43.

8. RMT, 44.

9. Edgar Marquess Branch, Robert Hirst, and Harriet Elinor Smith, eds., *Early Tales & Sketches, Volume 2: 1864–1869* (Berkeley: University of California Press, 1981), 395.

10. Mark Twain, "The Story of the Bad Little Boy," CSS, 7–8; quotations from 8; Twain, "The Story of the Good Little Boy," CSS, 67–70; quotation from 68.

11. Mark Twain, "Edward Mills and George Benton: A Tale," CSS, 145; MTN, May 27, 1898, 363.

12. RMT, 54. See *Calvin's Institutes*, 3.22.4.

13. RMT, 54 (quotation), 56.

14. Mark Twain, "The Second Advent," MTFM, 66–8; quotations from 68.

15. AMT, January 1904, 1:236.

16. SLC to Louise Chandler Moulton, January 8, 1875, LTR, 6:344; SLC to WDH, January 26, 1875, LTR, 6:357. Nevertheless, Twain added, he hoped Providence would take an interest in a trip they had planned, and if it did, the trip would "clip right along to the entire satisfaction of all parties concerned."

17. SLC to MMF, October 31, 1877, MTMB, 211–12; Twain, as quoted in *Melbourne Age*, October 28, 1895, http://www.twainquotes.com/Clemens_Olivia.html.

18. Mark Twain, "Three Statements of the Eighties," WM, 56. His rejection of special providence is also evident in "Letter from a Recording Angel" (1887), *Pudd'nhead Wilson* (1894), "As Concerns Interpreting the Deity" (1905), *The Refuge of the Derelicts* (1905–1906), and the "Little Bessie" dialogues (1908–1909).

19. MTN, December 11, 1885, 190; AMT, June 23, 1906, 2:138; AMT, June 13, 1906, 2:115 (first quotation), 117 (remainder of the quotations).

20. AMT, February 25, 1907, 2:440–1; quotations from 441.

21. *Territorial Enterprise*, May 3, 1863, LTR, 1:253; SLC to Jane Clemens, October 20, 1861, LTR, 1:138.

22. SLC to William Clagett, March 8 and 9, 1862, LTR, 1:171. See Henry Nash Smith, ed., *Mark Twain of the Enterprise* (Berkeley: University of California Press, 1957), 121–6.

23. Branch and Hirst, eds., *Early Tales & Sketches*, 1:222.

24. SLC to Seymour Pixley and G. A. Sears, January 23, 1864, LTR, 1:272; SLC to *Territorial Enterprise*, December 5, 1863 in *Mark Twain of the Enterprise*, ed. Smith, 93.

25. SLC to OL, December 19 and 20, 1868, LTR 2:333 (first two quotations); Mark Twain, *The Washoe Giant in San Francisco*, ed. Franklin Walker (San Francisco: Fields, 1938), 63 (third quotation).

26. SLC to Jane Lampton Clemens and Pamela Moffett, August 6, 1866, LTR, 1:352 (first two quotations); SLC to OL, December 19 and 20, 1868, LTR, 2:333 (third quotation). See also Andrew Forest Muir, "Franklin Samuel Rising, Radical Evangelical," *Historical Magazine of the Protestant Episcopal Church* 24 (January 1, 1955), 366–99.

27. Mark Twain, "In the Metropolis," June 26, 1864, *Golden Era*, in *Washoe Giant*, ed. Walker, 74–6.

28. Pamela Moffett to SLC, March 6, 1864, LTR, 1:147–8.

29. SLC to Orion and Mollie Clemens, September 28, 1864, LTR, 1:315; SLC to Orion and Mollie Clemens, October 19 and 20, 1865, LTR, 1:324; Twain wrote this on April 21, 1909 in the margin of the *Letters of James Russell Lowell*, ed. Charles Eliot Norton, 2 vols. (New York: Harper and Brothers), responding to a comment Lowell made about suicide. See Alan Gribben, *Mark Twain's Library: A Reconstruction* (Boston: G. K. Hall, 1980), 1:425–6. Cf. MTN, September 17, 1898, 368: "The suicide seems to me the only sane person."

30. SLC to Jane Clemens and family, December 4, 1866, LTR, 1:368.

31. SLC to Jane Clemens, n.d., MTB, 372.

32. SLC to Jane Clemens and family, June 1, 1867, MTL, 1:126; SLC to MMF, June 17, 1868, LTR, 2:221; ("off duty") Mark Twain, letter to San Francisco *Alta California*, June 10, 1867; MTB, 371; MTSC, 44, 53–4.

While in Hawaii, Twain became friends with Samuel Damon, the pastor of the Oahu Bethel Church in Honolulu; he admired Damon for "always collecting and caring for the poor" (quoted in SMT, 144).

33. "Important Correspondence between Mr. Mark Twain of San Francisco, and Rev. Bishop Hawks, D.D., of New York, Rev. Phillips Brooks of Philadelphia, and Rev. Dr. Cummings of Chicago, Concerning the Occupancy of Grace Cathedral," *The Californian*, May 6, 1865 in CT, 1:113. Brooks served as the rector of Trinity (Episcopal) Church in Boston from 1868 to 1891 and was one of America's most renowned preachers.

34. Mark Twain, "Letter from Myself to Bishop Hawks," May 6, 1865, CT, 1:114 (first two quotations), 115 (third quotation).

35. John Howell, *Sketches of the Sixties* (New York: Putnam & Sons, 1899), 176–7.

36. Twain, "Important Correspondence," 119–20; all quotations from 120.

37. Mark Twain, "The New Wildcat Religion," *Golden Era*, March 4, 1866, in *Gold Miners and Guttersnipes: Tales of California by Mark Twain*, ed. Ken Chowder (San Francisco: Chronicle Books, 1991), 173–4.

38. *Alta California*, September 6, 1867, quoted in MTR, 34.

39. "Wildcat Religion," 174.

40. Mark Twain, "Disgraceful Persecution of a Boy," May 1870, CT, 1:381; Twain, "The New Chinese Temple," August 19, 1864, in Edgar Marquess Branch and Robert Hirst, eds., *Early Tales and Sketches*, vol. 2: *1864–1865* (Berkeley: University of California Press, 1981), 41–3 (first and third quotation, 41); Twain, "The Chinese Temple," in ibid., 44; "The New Chinese Temple," in ibid., 45–6 (second quotation, 45).

41. Roy Morris, Jr., American Vandal: Mark Twain Abroad (Cambridge, MA: Harvard University Press, 2015), 11; SLC to Jane Clemens and family, June 7, 1867, MTP, https://www.marktwainproject.org/xtf/view?docId=letters/UCCL00134.xml;query=%E2%80%9CGod%20bless%20you%20all,%E2%80%9D%20;searchAll=;sectionType1=;sectionType2=;sectionType3=;sectionType4=;sectionType5=;style=letter;brand=mtp#1.

42. Jerome Loving, *Mark Twain: The Adventures of Samuel L. Clemens* (Berkeley: University of California Press, 2011), 141.

43. Morris, *American Vandal*, 25; Kimberly Winston, "New Film on Mark Twain Highlights His Religious Doubts," https://religionnews.com/2017/10/16/new-film-on-mark-twain-highlights-his-religious-doubts/ (quotation).

44. William Denny's journal, MTP, as quoted in Loving, *Adventures*, 139; MTL, 1:126.

45. SMT, 207; IA, 504.

46. IA, 540; AMT, October 31, 1908, 3:270.

47. REV, 156.

48. Twain was referring to England and France's "interference" in the Crimean War (1853–1856).

49. REV, 164.

50. SLC to MMF, December 24, 1868, MTMF, 59.

51. Ausburn Towner, Elmira *Saturday Evening Review*, August 21, 1869, as cited in Explanatory Note accompanying To Elisha Bliss, Jr., August 15, 1869, LTR, 3:301; *Packard's Monthly*, October 1869, https://twain.lib. virginia.edu/innocent/packard.html; "Literature," *New York Herald*, August 31, 1869, 8; *National Standard* as published by Twain in Buffalo *Express* (October 9, 1869), https://twain.lib.virginia.edu/innocent/ blurbs.html; "Mark Twain Book," *New York Tribune*, August 27, 1869, 6, as quoted in LTR, 3:343; *Zion's Herald*, December 30, 1869, https:// twain.lib.virginia.edu/innocent/zionherald.html; New York *Liberal Christian*, August 21, 1869, 3.

52. Mark Twain, "Miscellany," October 3, 1907, MTE, 353–5. It is not clear whether this incident actually happened.

53. SLC to Josephus Larned, August 7, 1870, LTR, 4:181–2.

54. SLC to John Russell Young, November 24, 1867, LTR, 2:113. Late September 1867, N&J, 1:368.

55. SLC to OL, January 24, 1869, LR 3:74–5.

56. REV, 167.

57. Susan K. Harris, *The Courtship of Olivia Langdon and Mark Twain* (Cambridge: Cambridge University Press, 1996), 79; MTATB, 39.

58. Stebbins and Robbins, as quoted in Explanatory Note to Olivia L. Langdon, January 20 and 21, 1869, LTR, 3:57.

59. After her death, Twain told Fairbanks' daughter Mollie and her husband that Mary "was a beautiful spirit, & her approval & her love were an enrichment to any who were privileged to win them." He confessed, "I was never what she thought me, but was glad to seem to her to be it. She was always good to me, & I always loved her" (SLC to Charley and Mollie, July 31, 1899, MTMF, 279).

60. Mary Fairbanks, (Cleveland) *Herald*, December 14, 1867, LTR, 2:107.

61. Resa Willis, *Mark and Livy: The Love Story of Mark Twain and the Woman Who Almost Tamed Him* (New York: Athenaeum, 1992), 43; OLC to MMF, January 15, 1869, LTR 3:42 (quotation).

62. SLC to OL, December 5 and 7, 1867, LTR, 2:312; SLC to OL, with a note to Charles Langdon, December 9 and 10, 1868, LTR, 2:319.

63. SLC to OL, October 30, 1868, LTR, 2:217 (first two quotations); SLC to MMF, November 26, 1868, MTMF, 50 (third quotation); SLC to MMF, December 12, 1868, MTMF, 55 (fourth quotation).

64. OL to MMF, December 1, 1868, LTR, 2:286.

65. SLC to OL, December 4, 1868, LTR, 2:306.

66. SLC to OL, December 9 and 10, 1868, LTR, 2:319.

67. SLC to OL, December 4, 1868, LTR, 2:308; SLC to OL, December 12, 1868, LTR, 2:329; quotations in that order.

68. SLC to MMF, MTMF, xxix; SLC to OL, December 27, 1868, LTR, 2:353–4; SLC to OL, December 30, 1868, LTR, 2:363–4; SLC to Jervis Langdon, December 29, 1868, LTR, 2:359.

69. SLC to MMF, January 7, 1869, MTMF, 65.

70. SLC to OL, January 2, 1869, LTR, 3:5.

71. SLC to OL, January 6, 1869, LTR, 3:12–13.

72. SLC to OL, January 24, 1869, LTR, 3:74 (all quotations except the last one which is from 3:75); SLC to OL, March 8, 1869, LTR, 3:153.

73. SLC to JHT, November 28, 1868, LTR, 2:293; SLC to Pamela Moffett, November 29(?), 1868, LTR, 2:295.

74. SLC to OL, February 4, 1869, LTR, 3:82; SLC to OL, February 13, 1869, LTR, 3:90 (first two quotations), 95–6 (third quotation); SLC to Jane Clemens and family, February 5, 1869, LTR, 3:85; SLC to JHT, February 14, 1869, LTR 3:101; SLC to OL, February 17, 1869, LTR, 3:104.

75. SLC to OL, March 5, 1869, LTR, 3:137 (first quotation); SLC to OL, December 5, 1869, LTR, 3:348 (second quotation).

76. SLC to OL, January 12, 1869, LTR, 3:26; SLC to OL, August 21, 1869, LTR, 3:317.

77. SLC to OL, September 21, 1868, LTR, 2:250; Twichell, as quoted in SLC to OL, October 18, 1868, LTR, 2:268.

78. SLC to OL, October 30, 1868, LTR, 2:217; SLC to OL, December 4, 1868, LTR, 2:301; quotations in that order.

79. SLC to OL, December 12, 1868, LTR, 2:330.

80. SLC to OL, December 19 and 20, 1868, LTR, 2:336; SLC to OL, January 20 and 21, 1869, LTR, 3:55; SLC to OL, January 21, 1869, LTR, 3:60; SLC to OL, January 26 and 27, 1869, LTR, 3:79; SLC to OL, May 24, 1869, LTR, 3:250; SLC to OL, January 14, 1870, LTR, 4:25; SLC to OL, January 20, 1870, LTR, 4:32; quotations in that order.

81. SLC to OL, November 28, 1868, LTR, 2:289 (first quotation); SLC to OL, December 4, 1868, LTR, 2:308 (second quotation); SLC to OL, January 22, 1869, LTR, 3:63 (remainder of the quotations).

82. SLC to OL, September 8 and 9, 1869, LTR, 3:348 (first quotation); SLC to OL, January 14, 1869, LTR, 3:40 (remainder of the quotations).

83. "Introduction," MTL, 2:xxiv.

84. MTSC, 62.

85. Jeffrey Holland, "Soul-Butter and Hogwash: Mark Twain and Frontier Religion," March 8, 1977, https://speeches.byu.edu/talks/jeffrey-r-holland/soul-butter-hogwash-mark-twain-frontier-religion/; SLC to OL, March 12, 1869, LTR, 3:163; SLC to OL, June 8, 1869, LTR, 3:264; SLC to OL, January 22, 1869, LTR, 3:63; quotations in that order.

86. MTSC, 62.

4

The 1870s

Hartford as a Religious Haven

Although the Clemenses suffered one major tragedy—the death of their nineteen-month-old son Langdon in 1872—the 1870s were generally happy and successful years for them as they became part of a congenial community in Hartford and writings flowed from Twain's pen. During this decade, Twain wrote *Roughing It* (1872), *The Gilded Age* (1873), and *The Adventures of Tom Sawyer* (1876). He lampooned greed and political corruption in *The Gilded Age* and "Revised Catechism" (1871) and in numerous other essays. *Tom Sawyer* contains several stories about Sunday school escapades and revival meetings based on Twain's childhood.

A series of "catastrophes and near-catastrophes" that occurred within the first six months of their marriage on February 2, 1870 made the Clemenses' stay in Buffalo, where Twain was the co-owner and co-editor of the *Express*, short. For six weeks, they watched the suffering and decline of Livy's father Jervis, their benefactor, who died of stomach cancer on August 6. A month and a half later, Livy's close friend Emma Nye became ill during a visit and died of typhus in their home. After nearly having a miscarriage in October, Livy gave birth to their son Langdon on November 7. His premature birth and numerous illnesses led to constant visits by physicians and nurses. Exhausted from caring for Langdon on top of her other household management responsibilities, Livy contracted typhoid fever in February 1871, remaining near death for five weeks. Under these circumstances, Twain made little progress on his writing.[1] The "infernal damnable chaos" of their lives led Twain to loathe Buffalo and caused the Clemenses to leave the city.[2]

In September 1871, they moved to Hartford, Connecticut, a town of 38,000 where three daughters would be born: Susy in 1872, Clara in 1874, and Jean in 1880. Hartford was the home of numerous small, skilled-based enterprises (most notably Colt's Fire Arms Company), the center of America's expanding insurance industry, and the location of the nation's leading subscription publishing company. The Clemenses craved a community where they could enjoy respectability, stability, security, and warm friendships.

The Clemenses also moved to Hartford to participate in the life of Asylum Hill (Congregational) Church, pastored by Twain's good friend Joseph Twichell, who had co-officiated at their wedding. They soon built a nineteen-room house that included a solarium, a billiards room, and five bathrooms in Nook Farm, a pleasant, intellectually stimulating Hartford community where the church was located. This mansion was their home until 1891. Many of their neighbors were devout Christians, including Harriet Beecher Stowe, author of *Uncle Tom's Cabin* (1852); her husband, religion professor Calvin Stowe; her sister, social activist Isabella Beecher Hooker; publisher Elisha Bliss; editor Dudley Warner; and Congregational ministers Horace Bushnell, Nathaniel Burton, and Edwin Parker. Most Nook Farm residents attended either Twichell's newly constructed Asylum Hill Church, Burton's Fourth Congregational Church, or Parker's South Congregational Church. The close-knit Nook Farm community functioned as a religious support group that helped residents raise their children and nurtured its members in the Christian faith. Moreover, Asylum Hill's theology and the faithful practice of Christian morality by Nook Farm residents set standards that contributed to Twain's critique of Christians in other locales. After their wedding, Twain and Livy attended church fairly often, said grace before meals, and read the Bible daily with their children, but Twain soon discontinued having devotions and praying with his wife.

Twain and Twichell

Twain told Twichell in 1869 that he and Livy wanted "to live a useful, unostentatious & earnest religious life" and planned to "unite with the church" as soon as they settled in Hartford. They looked forward to being "surrounded by a good moral & religious atmosphere." While visiting Hartford before moving there, Twain helped lead the singing for a service at an almshouse where Twichell preached, which Twain described as very touching. Although the Clemenses never joined Asylum Hill Church, Twichell's journals and numerous newspaper articles indicate that Twain frequently attended church services in the 1870s (usually at Asylum Hill but occasionally at South Congregational Church because he liked its choir and Parker's preaching), participated in Asylum Hill's ministry and social activities, and contributed to the church financially. Because its male members were wealthy businessmen, Twain dubbed it "the Church of the Holy Speculators."[3] The Clemenses rented a pew at Asylum Hill until 1891, and Twain sometimes raised funds for the church by giving lectures.[4] Leah Strong argues that Twain accepted Twichell's taking "the attitude of pastor toward parishioner" in their relationship.[5] Examining their friendship shines a light on Twain's religious views, especially during the 1870s.

Members of the Nook Farm community gathered two or three times a week to engage in religious or social activities, and when the Clemenses were in Hartford they usually attended the Sunday worship service.[6] Peter Messent contends that Twain attended Asylum Hill Church and took part in its ministry more out of a sense of social obligation and desire to support his close friend than because of a genuine Christian commitment. After one sermon, Twain jokingly complained to Twichell that "I go to church to pursue my own train of thought. But to-day I couldn't do it" because of Twichell's sermon. "You have forced me to attend to you—and I have lost me a whole half hour. I beg that it might not occur again." Like Tom Sawyer, Twain struggled to worship attentively, reverently, and wholeheartedly. In a letter to Livy, Twain praised a child's joyful worship, describing it as the homage "of overflowing life & youth, health, ignorance of care," the "tribute of free, unscarred, unsmitten nature to the good God that gave it!" He, by contrast, "had been decorous & reverent" but had "picked flaws in the minister's logic and damned his grammar."[7] By the mid-1870s, Twain rejected some fundamental Christian doctrines, but he viewed Christianity as the best foundation for a just and equitable society and supported Nook Farm's strong emphasis on personal and public morality.[8]

Twichell was Twain's closest male friend for more than forty years. He was Twain's hiking partner, travel companion, intellectual peer, spiritual confidant, mentor, moral guide, and sounding board. The author admired the pastor's character, appreciated his friendship, and, despite jibes like the one quoted in the previous paragraph, valued his sermons. Twichell, Twain declared, was "my oldest friend—and dearest enemy on occasion" and "my pastor."[9] Twain also called the minister "a good man, one of the best of men, although a clergyman."[10] During the course of their long friendship, they often discussed theological issues and prayed together. Twichell viewed Twain's theological ruminations as sincere attempts to discover the truth and strove to provide reasoned, compassionate responses to his questions and comments.

Twichell's father was an affluent tanner and carriage hardware maker who lived in Southington, Connecticut. After graduating from Yale in 1859, Twichell attended Union Theological Seminary in New York City for two years. He then served for two years as a Union chaplain in the Civil War, leading religious services and providing spiritual counseling for soldiers from Manhattan, predominantly Irish Catholic laborers, who formed a regiment led by General Dan Sickles. Twichell witnessed some of the war's most brutal battles at Fredericksburg, Chancellorsville, Gettysburg, the Wilderness, and Spotsylvania. In 1865, he completed his divinity degree at Andover Seminary in Boston and became the first pastor of the newly established Asylum Hill Church. Athletic, extraverted, articulate, and sensitive, Twichell was a proponent of muscular, socially active, liberal evangelical Christianity. A disciple of prominent Congregational pastor and theologian Horace Bushnell, Twichell stressed the value of prayer and the advancement of God's kingdom on earth.

As previously mentioned, Twichell strove diligently to convert his friend to Christianity during his courtship of Livy, and he frequently prayed for and with the author. On their many hikes, they discussed numerous theological topics. In addition, Twichell and Twain both supported an educational ministry to the Chinese in Hartford as well as Father David Hawley's Hartford City Mission. Twain gave lectures in 1873 and 1875 to raise money for the mission's work to provide sustenance, clothing, and spiritual aid to the city's poor, many of whom were immigrants. In advertising his first lecture in the Hartford *Evening Post*, Twain praised Hawley's work during harsh winter weather to help "women broken down by illness & lack of food, & children who are too young to help themselves."[11] Twain lauded Hawley, who directed the mission for almost a quarter-century, for his "generous selflessness" and "tireless zeal." Hawley, a social worker, was greatly loved by members of all social classes in Hartford, who called him "Father" to express their affection and esteem. At Hawley's memorial service in 1876, Twichell declared that he had done "a great service for the cause of Christ in this city."[12]

Twichell accompanied Twain to Bermuda in 1877 and to Switzerland in 1878; the latter trip led Twain to write *A Tramp Abroad*. While there, Twain confessed to Twichell, "I don't believe in your religion at all. I've been living a lie right straight along whenever I pretended to. I have been almost a believer, but it immediately drifts away from me again. I don't believe one word of your Bible was inspired by God any more than any other book." This statement prompted Twain's first biographer, Albert Bigelow Paine, to claim that after Twain's admission the two men stopped discussing "the personal aspects of religion."[13] A review of the two men's paper trail, however, proves that Paine was mistaken. Until the end of Twain's life, they dialogued and debated about religious issues, with Twichell providing rebuttals to Twain's attacks on Christianity.[14] Responding to one of Twain's many diatribes, Twichell wrote in 1904 that he hoped they could pray together "as we have done in times past." This, Twichell argued, is what people should do in the face of the "unfathomable realities" Twain had described as he put forth his solipsistic views.[15] Despite Twain's growing skepticism, which resulted in an increasing divergence between their worldviews, the two men clearly loved and respected each other and tolerated each other's theological differences. Paine himself wrote in 1902 that the author and the pastor had "one of their regular arguments on theology and the moral accountability of the human race, arguments that had been going on between them for more than thirty years."[16]

Twichell reported to his wife, Harmony, that on this trip to Switzerland he had an opportunity "to declare the gospel truth" to Twain. This conversation was initiated by Twain's admission that nothing "makes me hate myself so . . . as to have Livy praise me and express a good opinion of me, when I know . . . I am a humbug and no such good person as she takes me to be." As Twichell explained it, this comment led to a discussion of "character and the state of the heart, and the application of Christ's gospel to the wants of a sinful man." The pastor hoped that God's "grace might touch him with power and lead into larger views of things spiritual than he has ever yet seen!!" Twain was "exceedingly considerate" whenever they discussed religious matters. "And when we kneel down together at night to pray," Twichell declared, "it always seems to bring the spirit of gentleness upon him." He added that Mark was coarse at times, but "he is a genuinely loveable fellow." While they were in Switzerland, Twichell recounted, they prayed together many evenings.[17] After Twain's death, Twichell declared that whenever they stayed together, Mark "knelt with me in the evening when I prayed" for church members "and in the morning repeated the Lord's prayer with me. When it was time for our prayers he would say, 'come on, Joe.'"[18]

Twichell was originally attracted to Twain "by the brightness of his mind, the incomparable charm of his talk, and his rare companionableness," but he soon discovered "that he had a big, warm and tender heart." When their twenty-four-year-old daughter Susy was gravely ill in Hartford in 1896 and neither Twain nor Livy, who were abroad at the time, was able to return home before she died, Twichell stayed with her for hours, bringing her "peace and comfort." Twain was deeply grateful to Twichell for this kindness. When Livy was dying in Italy in 1903 and 1904, Twain poured out his heart to Twichell in numerous letters. At his sixty-seventh birthday celebration, Twain declared that his wife and Twichell had reared him "and what I am I owe to them."[19] Over the years, Twain frequently vented his frustration, despair, and anger toward God to his friend, who listened patiently and sympathetically and provided comfort, consolation, and hope.

Life in Hartford

Throughout the 1860s and 1870s, Twain was drawn to ministers who were perceptive, compassionate, and sensitive and who, like him, cared about justice, efficient and honest government, moral business practices, and the plight of the indigent. Pastors like the ones he befriended in San Francisco and Hartford as well as Thomas Beecher in Elmira had a strong, sincere, intellectually vibrant faith that inspired their social activism—a combination that Twain admired.[20] The Congregational churches of Twichell, Burton, and Parker in Hartford were centers for community good works, spiritual enrichment, socialization, and recreation.[21]

Horace Bushnell, a leading proponent of American theological liberalism, whom Twain labeled in 1902 the "greatest clergyman that the last century produced," significantly influenced the religious beliefs of many members of the Nook Farm community.[22] Bushnell died in 1876, limiting Twain's friendship with him. The humorist read Mary Cheney's 1880 biography of Bushnell and identified with the influence his mother had on his theology, his skepticism as a youth, the premature death of his children, and his battles to defend himself against heresy.[23] Like most other theological liberals, Bushnell rejected the conventional view of Christ's atonement as substitutionary—i.e., that Christ died in place of sinners—and instead espoused a moral influence theory, which treated Christ's death as an example of God's righteous, suffering love.

In raising their children, many Nook Farm residents were guided by Bushnell's *Christian Nurture* (1847), which argued that parents should help their children gradually accept the Christian faith rather than encouraging them to have a definitive conversion experience. When Livy became pregnant with their first child, the Clemenses purchased a copy of the book to instruct them in how to create a Christian family environment; they agreed with Bushnell that teaching children about God's love was a primary parental responsibility.[24] When their first-born son, Langdon, died in 1872 at nineteen months, Twain blamed himself (because he had taken Langdon for a carriage ride on a chilly spring day) rather than diphtheria, the direct culprit, for his son's death.

Although safely cocooned in Nook Farm, surrounded by like-minded neighbors, and enjoying friendships with numerous literary colleagues, Twain continued to seek social respectability and to battle with guilt, which plagued him his entire life. In December 1877, he spoke at a celebration for poet John Greenleaf Whittier's seventieth birthday in Boston. Twain regaled the nearly sixty distinguished authors in attendance with a burlesque about three rogues he had supposedly met in a mining town in California. In his sketch, these three scoundrels called themselves "Ralph Waldo Emerson," "Oliver Wendell Holmes," and "Henry Wadsworth Longfellow." All three authors were present at the party, and none of them displayed any amusement at Twain's tale about the three scalawags imbibing whiskey, cheating at cards, and misquoting the famous writers they claimed to be. Reflecting on this painful experience, Twain told Howells, "My sense of disgrace ... grows." It added to "a list of humiliations that extend back to when I was seven years old, & which keep on persecuting me regardless of my repentancies [sic]." Because his action had injured his reputation throughout the country, he thought it would "be best that I retire before the public at present." Twain confessed, "I must have been insane when I wrote that speech & saw no harm in it, no disrespect toward those men whom I reverenced so much."[25]

The Adventures of Tom Sawyer

As the United States celebrated its centennial, Twain published *The Adventures of Tom Sawyer*. This renowned book is replete with stories based on his religious experiences as a child, including Tom's battles with his conscience and discussions of sin, repentance, religious awakenings, sermons, prayers, and Sunday school shenanigans. Twain later called this book "a sermon ... a hymn put into prose form to give it a worldly air." *Tom Sawyer*, like many other Twain works, exposes the pretense, cant, and deception he saw prevalent throughout the world. He pokes fun at the town of St. Petersburg's "hypocrisies, vanities, prejudices, customs, values, and dreams."[26] Tom's hometown "is a complex fabric of lies: of half-truths, of simulation, dissimulation, broken promises, exaggerations, and outright falsehoods." Its residents fail to recognize their duplicity. Churchgoers turn religious rituals intended to express devotion and provide edification into opportunities to show off and receive acclaim.[27]

Aunt Polly, Tom's caregiver, frequently quotes Scripture, regularly leads family worship, and seeks to rear the incorrigible trickster lovingly. Family worship features Polly's prayers, filled with biblical quotations and her authoritative discourses on scriptural themes, law, and morality. Twain also uses Polly, who subscribes to "all the

'Health' periodicals and phrenological frauds" and their "quack medi-
cines," to lampoon the scams perpetuated by fake healers, a theme he
develops in other works, especially *Christian Science* (1907).

Motivated by tangible rewards, Tom memorizes five verses from
the Sermon on the Mount, the shortest verses he could find, to win a
prize at Sunday school. Mocking the emphasis many Christians
placed on rote memorization of biblical passages without understanding their meaning, Twain depicts one boy who "recited three thousand verses without stopping; but the strain upon his mental faculties
was too great," making him thereafter "an idiot." Tom supposedly
memorizes two thousand verses (he had actually traded material items
given to him for the "privilege" of whitewashing his aunt's fence to
gain tickets indicating that he had memorized this number of verses),
which qualified him to receive a Bible. However, when he is asked to
name the first two disciples Jesus chose, Tom replies, "David and
Goliath," demonstrating his biblical ignorance.

As in several Twain short stories, *Tom Sawyer* features a "model
boy" whose conduct is exemplary. Willie Mufferson tenderly cares for
his mother and brings her to church every Sunday. He is "the pride of
all the matrons," but all the other boys in St. Petersburg hate him
because he is so good. Huckleberry Finn is the foil to the model boy;
the town's mothers dread this "juvenile pariah" because he is lazy,
immoral, and vulgar and because their children admire him and
want to be like him. "Every harassed, hampered, respectable boy in
St. Petersburg" envies Huck's independent, carefree lifestyle.

Based on his personal experiences, Twain spoofs a Presbyterian
church service, which includes hymns, a lengthy prayer, and a boring
sermon. In his "good, generous prayer," the pastor entreats God to
watch over the town's children, his congregation, all the nation's
churches, the town, county, state, United States, all government
officials, sailors, "the oppressed millions groaning under the heel of
European monarchies and Oriental despotisms," and "the heathen in
the far islands of the sea." The minister hopes that his words will "find
grace and favor" and "be as seed sown in fertile ground, yielding in
time a grateful harvest of good." The restless Tom endures the prayer
and considers the addition of any new petitions unfair and "scoun-
drelly." During the pastor's prayer, a fly lands on the pew in front of
Tom and appears to mock him, convinced that "it was perfectly safe."

And it was, because Tom "believed his soul would be instantly destroyed" if he grabbed the fly during the prayer. As soon as the prayer ends, however, the fly becomes "a prisoner of war."

Tom is bored by the pastor's monotonous sermon, which emphasizes hell's "limitless fire and brimstone" and the small number of God's elect. Tom's ears perk up, however, when the minister paints "a grand and moving picture" of the millennium, in which the lion and lamb lie down together and a little child leads the assembled host. Tom would have been glad to be that child if the lion were tame. *Tom Sawyer*, Joe Fulton argues, contrasts dead, formalized, traditional worship in churches with the free, spontaneous, unfettered worship that occurs in fields and forests as people play.[28]

Throughout the book, Tom, mirroring Twain's own life, suffers from a guilty conscience and self-recrimination. He periodically experiences remorse about his misdeeds and the pain they cause his Aunt Polly. He cries, pleads for her forgiveness, and repeatedly promises to reform.

When Tom and Huck see Injun Joe murder Doctor Robinson using Muff Potter's knife in the town graveyard, they fear that if they disclose the truth, Injun Joe will kill them. Tom's "gnawing conscience" about not revealing the murderer's name disturbs his sleep. He promises to change his ways and faithfully attend Sunday school if God would get him out of this jam. Tom and Huck try to appease their troubled consciences by giving the falsely accused Muff tobacco and matches, and they feel even more guilty when he tells them they have treated him better than anyone else in town. Tom's "harassed conscience" eventually prompts him to go a lawyer's house to confess that he and Huck had witnessed the murder, and then to testify in court to exonerate Muff. Tom's conscience also convicts him for running away from his aunt and causes him to regret that he, Huck, and Joe Harper violated a biblical commandment by stealing bacon and ham. Convinced that the mischievous, good-hearted Tom has drowned, Polly declares, "The Lord giveth and the Lord hath taken away—Blessed be the name of the Lord! But it's so hard." She prays for Tom, who is hiding within earshot, so movingly and with such "measureless love," that he is again conscience-stricken. Tom also blames himself for getting his classmate Becky Thatcher into a "miserable situation" when they are lost in a cave.

Tom Sawyer deals with people's eternal destiny and its protagonists' belief that salvation depends on good behavior and that God punishes evil deeds. Tom half-envies a boy who had recently died. "If he only had a clean Sunday-school record," Tom meditates, he would be willing to die "and be done with it all." When Tom and Huck fear that Injun Joe may kill them, Huck declares, "Oh, Tom, I reckon we're goners. I reckon there ain't no mistake 'bout where I'll go to. I been so wicked." Huck and Tom expect God to strike Injun Joe with lightning for killing a man and then allowing Muff Potter to be arrested for the crime. When Injun Joe claims under oath that he is innocent and is not struck dead, the boys conclude that he "had sold himself to the devil."

When Tom, Huck, and Joe Harper are presumed to have drowned, a St. Petersburg church holds a funeral service. After congregants sing a moving hymn, the pastor reads John 11:25: "I am the resurrection and the life." He brings the large audience to tears by describing the boys' positive traits, "winning ways," and rare promise and laments that he had previously seen only their faults and flaws. He recounts many touching incidents to illustrate the boys' "sweet, generous natures"; unfortunately, these incidents had previously been viewed wrongly as "rank rascalities, well deserving of the cowhide." The boys, who have been hiding in the gallery and watching their own funeral, then run down the aisle of the church, to the amazement and delight of their families and friends. The minister exhorts congregants to sing the doxology—"Praise God from whom all blessings flow"—and their heartfelt gratitude to God shakes the rafters. Polly thanks "the good God and Father of us all" that the boys are alive. God, she declares, is "long-suffering and merciful to them that believe on Him and keep His word." She professes that she is unworthy of God's beneficence but insists that if only the worthy received God's blessings, few people would enjoy life on earth or "enter into His rest" when they died.

Later, at a local revival service, everyone except Tom "got religion." Tom tries in vain to find at least one unrepentant sinner. Joe Harper is studying the Bible, another boy is handing out tracts, and even Huck is quoting Scripture. Brokenhearted, Tom concludes that he is the only person in St. Petersburg who is "lost, forever and forever." That night a terrible storm hits the town, and Tom is convinced that God sent it to exterminate a bug like him who "had taxed the forbearance of the powers above to the extremity of endurance." God does not take Tom's life after all, and Joe and Huck soon suffer "a relapse" and steal a melon.

Some town residents, inspired by their faith, do act lovingly. When Huck is delirious with a fever, the Widow Douglas promises to "do her best" to care for him, "because, whether he was good, bad, or indifferent, he was the Lord's." The town's residents offer public and wholehearted private prayers for Tom and Becky while they are lost in a cave.

After Tom and Huck take possession of a treasure of gold previously discovered by Injun Joe, Huck struggles greatly with the restrictions civilized life imposed on him. Huck dreaded Sundays with its expectation of attending church and limitations on activity, one of the numerous constraints he experienced in antebellum Southern society. When he is forced to go to church, Huck sweats profusely and hates the "ornry sermons." He is not allowed to catch a fly or chew tobacco. On Sundays he is required to wear shoes all day and cannot smoke, yell, stretch, or scratch. Being forced to live an urbane life is almost more than the newly wealthy Huck can bear. Wherever "he turned, the bars and shackles of civilization shut him in and bound him hand and foot." After bravely bearing his miseries for three weeks, he reverts to his earlier life. Tom finds him "unkempt, uncombed, and clad" in his ragged clothing but free and happy. Being affluent, Huck laments, did not live up to its advertisements; instead, it caused him to worry and desire to die. As in many other Twain tales, people's quest for money has a deleterious effect. Many townfolk gloat over and glorify Tom and Huck's bonanza, causing them to experience "the strain of the unhealthy excitement" and become obsessed with finding similar windfalls. Men ransack every "haunted" house in St. Petersburg and the neighboring villages in search of hidden treasure.

Many mid-1870s reviews of *Tom Sawyer* refer to passages dealing with its religious themes or stories. A San Francisco newspaper noted that "the old Adam possesses" Tom Sawyer "from the very cradle, making him the plague of the household, the terror of goody-goody folks, [and] the persecutor of those colorless little seraphs known as 'good boys.'" The *Alta California*, for which Twain had worked, declared that Tom Sawyer "had special aversions for church, Sunday school, pious people, [and] devout conversation." The *Hartford*

Christian Secretary regretted that "Tom lies and smokes," but recognized that Twain's "intention was not to describe a model boy." Some reviewers advised young readers to avoid *Tom Sawyer*. The *British Quarterly Review*, for example, warned that the book would make "boys think that an unscrupulous scapegrace is sure" to become a "noble man." Tom Sawyer, the *Hartford Daily Times* emphasized, "isn't one of the orthodox boys who love their Sunday schools" and "read about the good little boys who die early and go to heaven. He evidently preferred the other place where they don't have any Sunday schools, and the boys don't have to keep quiet every seventh day in the week." Writing in the London *Examiner*, Twain's friend, Unitarian pastor Moncure Conway, by contrast, praised the novel's description of "the salient, picturesque, droll, and at the same time most signifi-cant features of human life."[29]

Christ "Made Trouble Enough" the First Time

During much of his life, Twain referred reverently to Jesus, typically calling him "the Saviour," "the Lord," or "Christ" or using titles such as "Prince of Peace"; he "was never flippant or mocking" when discussing Jesus.[30] In his courtship letters to Livy and his exchanges with Mary Fairbanks, Twain frequently expressed admiration and appreciation for Jesus and called him an exemplary role model. In *Innocents Abroad*, he professed amazement to "be standing on ground" where the Savior had walked, and sitting "where a god has stood." He credited Jesus with performing numerous miracles and described the place where Christ was crucified as "the most sacred locality on earth." In an 1868 essay, Twain described Calvary as "the theatre of the noblest self-sacrifice man has yet conceived." "The Teacher of Nazareth," he added, would say to those who mourned the world's desolation, "Peace! *I* am the Resurrection and the Life!"[31] Twain was fascinated by Gustave Doré's 1872 painting "Christ Leaving the Praetorium," which he viewed at the British Museum in London. The only other painting Twain had seen that made Jesus appear divine was Leonardo DaVinci's "The Last Supper." To truly portray God, Twain asserted, an artist must depict divine forgiveness as Doré's painting did. "Pictured Christs," Twain complained, were almost always exasperating, but Doré's Jesus "is not a man"; he is instead an unforgettable "stately figure."[32]

To Twain, it was "stupefying" that Jesus, who except for several short trips, "preached his gospel, and performed his miracles within a compass no larger than an ordinary county in the United States," could have had such a huge influence.[33] "All that is great and good in our particular civilization," Twain proclaimed in an 1871 essay, "came straight from the hand of Jesus Christ."[34] He valued many of Christ's teachings, especially the Golden Rule (although he contended that Jesus had borrowed the principle from Confucius) and "Love thy neighbor as thyself."[35] Jesus' statement, "Come unto me all ye that labor and are heavy laden, and I will give you rest," Twain declared, "is the most beautiful sentence that graces any page—the tenderest, the softest to the ear."[36] He hoped that people would act "for the comfort and benefit of others" and thereby exhibit "a Christ-like spirit."[37]

Moreover, Twain frequently portrayed Christ as the supreme exemplar of empathy. He wished that "the Lord would disguise Himself" and personally examine the suffering of the poor in London: "He would be moved, and would do something for them Himself."[38] In many of his stories, a character emulates Christ by at least temporarily sacrificing his life for another's. Examples include Prince Edward for Tom Canty in *The Prince and the Pauper*, Huck for Jim in *Huckleberry Finn*, and Lord Berkeley for One-Armed Pete in *The American Claimant*.[39] Most significantly, he viewed the sacrificial death of Saint Joan as resembling that of Jesus. In "A Dog's Tale," *Joan of Arc*, and other works, Twain used the symbol of Christ's incarnation to prod readers to "empathize with people of other races and classes."[40]

By the late 1870s, however, Twain rejected the orthodox Christian doctrine that Jesus was God's unique son and the second person of the Trinity, although he did not publicly state this. He told his brother Orion in 1878 that "neither [William Dean] Howells nor I believe in . . . the divinity of the Savior." Christ was nevertheless "a sacred Personage" who should never be referred to "lightly, profanely, or otherwise than with the profoundest reverence."[41] Although Twain seemed to affirm belief in Christ's bodily resurrection in *Innocents*

Abroad, by the late 1870s, he privately disavowed Christianity's most cherished tenet, but avoided acknowledging it publicly.

Twain also repudiated the doctrines of Christ's virgin birth and substitutionary atonement. He called the virgin birth, which he often incorrectly referred to as the Immaculate Conception, a very "puerile invention," one of "the impossibilities recorded in the Bible."[42] In his autobiography, Twain maintained that Mary invented the story of the virgin birth to conceal her indiscretions from Joseph.[43] Twain parodied the concept of the virgin birth in "The Second Advent" (1881). In this story, set in Black Jack, Arkansas, Nancy Hopkins is expecting a child before her wedding and insists that the baby in her womb has been miraculously conceived. The town's residents, however, "do not believe a word of this flimsy nonsense." They think instead that Hopkins had sex with her fiancé and concocted the story of a virgin birth to cover her misdeed.[44] Twain asked British novelist Elinor Glyn in 1908 if she had ever met "an intelligent person who privately believed" in the virgin birth; Glyn replied that "of course, she hadn't." Nor had she ever met a person who was "daring enough to publicly deny his belief in that fable" in print.[45]

Twain was amazed that Charles Briggs, a Presbyterian professor at Union Theological Seminary in New York City and perhaps the nation's "most daringly broad-minded" religious leader, defended the virgin birth. The efforts of Briggs and others to prove this "impossible fact" were amusing. Briggs argued that the angels who announced Christ's birth were "reliable witnesses" and that giving false testimony was inconsistent with the character of Joseph and Mary. Moreover, James and Jude, Jesus' half-brothers, sanctioned the story, and it was "too near the birth of Jesus, in temporal, geographical and personal relations, to go astray in so important a matter." Mary's reason for believing that the Holy Spirit conceived the child she carried, Twain protested, was the report she received from a total stranger, "an alleged angel" who could also "have been a tax collector." She probably had never encountered an angel before; she would not have known an angel's trademarks, and "he brought no credentials." The virgin birth rested entirely on the "testimony of a single witness"—a young peasant woman "whose husband needed to be pacified." If Briggs was asked to believe that Krishna, Osiris, and Buddha were the products of a virgin birth as other religions claimed, he would "probably be offended."[46] If the virgin birth could be duplicated in New York City today, Twain maintained, almost none of its four million residents would believe it. "It would produce laughter, not reverence and adoration." Jesus was the product of a promiscuous relationship, Twain asserted, and the foundation of "the Christian religion, which required everybody to be moral and to obey the laws," is based on a lie.[47]

While the virgin birth was a fabrication, the doctrine that Christ died on the cross to atone for humanity's sin, Twain avowed, was absurd; the concept of the atonement was neither rational nor unique in human history. Rejecting the biblical assertion that Christ was both God and man, Twain could not understand why God would condemn himself to die to wipe humanity's slate clean. God's wrath toward people's sin was so great that he illogically committed suicide to appease it and settle his score with humanity. Many people, Twain argued, had freely sacrificed their lives for the sake of others who were in danger, even risking "eternal damnation" because they did not have an opportunity to settle "their sin account with God" before rushing to the rescue. Every soldier offered his life to defend his country, recognizing that his death "may land him in hell, not on the great white throne, which was Christ's sure destination." Moreover, "For God to take three days on a Cross out of a life of eternal happiness and mastership of the universe is a service which the least among us would be glad to do upon the like terms"; it was not impressive or praiseworthy.[48] And Jesus did not "save many, anyway; but if he had been damned for the race that would have been an act of a size proper to a god." Ignoring the Bible's contention that Christ suffered intense spiritual anguish as he bore the sins of human beings and was temporarily forsaken by his father, Twain insisted that Christ's suffering on the cross was no greater than that of women in childbirth.[49]

Twain censured Jesus for inventing the fiendish concept of hell, an act that made him "a thousand billion times crueler" than God ever was in the Old Testament.[50] "Nothing in all history," Twain protested, "remotely approaches in atrocity the invention of Hell." Christ, "the earthly half" of God, required people to be merciful, but he invented "a lake of fire and brimstone" where all "who fail to recognize and worship Him as God are to be burned" throughout eternity.

Worse yet, billions of people who never heard of Christ would also "suffer this awful fate."[51] How could someone who had devised a place of eternal punishment, Twain asked, be considered sweet, gentle, merciful, and forgiving? He had known only three or four people during his entire life whom he would want to suffer agony in hell for a year, much less forever. And Twain doubted that he would even let them burn for a year: "I am soft and gentle in my nature, and I should have forgiven them seventy-and-seven times, long ago."[52]

During the final decade of his life, Twain questioned other biblical assertions about Christ. He argued that the story of Christ's temptation by Satan in the wilderness made no sense, because Jesus already owned the whole world.[53] Twain did not think that Jesus had done any miracles, but if he had, they were another example of Christ's cruelty because they were so selective; if he had the power to perform miracles, he should have restored sight to all the blind, cured all the crippled, fed all the hungry, and raised all the dead.[54] Moreover, "if Christ had really been God, He could have proved it," Twain insisted, "since nothing is impossible with God. He could have proved" his divinity to everyone in his time, the current time and "all future time."[55] Twain even argued that "a Christ with the character and mission related by the Gospels" had never existed. He told Albert Bigelow Paine, "It is all a myth. . . . There have been Saviors in every age of the world. It is all just a fairy tale, like the idea of Santa Claus." On the other hand, Twain hoped that Christ would not come again because "he made trouble enough" the first time.[56]

"Man Is Prone to Evil as the Sparks Fly Upward"

Twain sometimes highlighted the positive aspects of people being created in God's image, but much more often he faulted God for creating people so shabbily. He theorized that human beings had emerged "from the primeval slime, through some unhappy accident, much to the surprise and grief of the Creator."[57] The humorist occasionally affirmed the biblical concept that people shared God's nature as spiritual beings and therefore could enjoy companionship with others and should care for one another. "We are fearfully and wonderfully made," Twain avowed, and "occasionally astonish the God that created us." Being the recipients of a divine spark, an "all-pervading effulgence," lifted humans "far above other creatures & confer[red] upon us kinship with God," which was "a noble possession." "God puts something good and lovable in every man His hands create," Twain declared.[58]

In his eulogy in 1910, Joseph Twichell declared that Twain clearly recognized "the ignoble side of human nature," but "his predominant mood toward humanity was that of sympathy."[59] Twain, he added, had a "penetrating insight" into the "weaknesses of humanity" and "an equally keen appreciation" of people's "nobler aspects and capabilities." People possess "*far* more goodness than ungoodness," Twain told Livy.[60] Many individuals, he insisted, engaged in frequent acts of benevolence, sympathy, and self-sacrifice. Twain often exuded these qualities in his own life, and compassion and tenderheartedness characterized his relationships with family and friends. Twain's numerous charitable deeds were inspired in part by his belief that people were valuable because they were created in God's image.

Influenced by his Calvinist heritage, Twain strongly emphasized human degeneracy, which he struggled to reconcile with the optimism of the Social Gospelers whom he admired and worked with to remedy various social ills. Twain, Harold Bush, Jr. argues, was obsessed "with the darkness and sinfulness of humanity" and participated in the century-long debate between American Calvinists, Arminians, and Pelagians about the nature of human beings and the means of salvation.[61] Twichell jokingly reprimanded Twain for being "too orthodox on the Doctrine of Total Human Depravity." Citing Job 5:7, Twain asserted that "*man is prone to evil as the sparks fly upward.*" The Calvinist perspective that human beings are fallen, sinful, and worthy of damnation, Lawrence Berkove contends, underlies *Roughing It*, *Huckleberry Finn*, and *A Connecticut Yankee* and significantly impacts many of Twain's other books and short stories.[62]

Twain's assessment of what he termed "the damned human race" (for him this phrase referred to humanity's estrangement from and judgment by God) was often brutal.[63] Livy, when confined to her room by illness, found one benefit: she could not hear Twain's diatribes about the "damned human race." Twain called human beings the "grotesquest of all the inventions of the Creator." "Our Heavenly Father invented man because he was disappointed in the monkey," Twain quipped, but the human being "is no considerable improvement."[64] Humans are "far and away the worst animal that exists."[65] "Man is a museum of disgusting disease, a home of impurities," Twain avowed; "he begins as dirt and departs as stench."[66] Humanity was a "shabby poor, ridiculous thing." Twain was amazed that more books did not scoff at "the vile & contemptible human race."[67] "Pretty poor materials went into the making of man," he jested; "God must have made him at the end of the week when he was tired."[68] Several essays from the last two decades of Twain's life—some of which were not published until the 1960s—including "Man's Place in the Animal World" (1896), "Was the World Made for Man?" (1903), and "The Ten Commandments" (1905 or 1906), display his greatest pessimism about human nature.[69]

Humanity, Twain told Twichell, was "a *ridiculous invention*." "Let us hope," he added, that "there is no hereafter; I don't want to train with any angels made out of human material." "Isn't human nature the most consummate sham & lie that was ever invented?" Twain asked Howells. "Isn't man a creature to be ashamed of?"[70] "I have been reading the morning paper," Twain told Howells in 1899, "knowing that I shall find in it the usual depravities and basenesses & hypocrisies & cruelties." As a result, he would spend "the rest of the day pleading" with God to damn "the nasty stinking little human race."[71] Twain disputed the claim of biologist Alfred Russel Wallace that human beings were "the chief love and delight of God." Given the size of the universe and age of the earth, this seemed very unlikely.[72] People had advanced in material prosperity and knew more than their predecessors, but their character had not improved. "Good and evil impulses" were the same as they had always been. Humanity was clearly progressing, Twain sarcastically stated, evident in the Inquisition, witch burning, imperialism, and America's militarism, racism toward blacks and the Chinese, mistreatment of immigrants, political corruption, and many other unsavory practices.[73]

In numerous stories and essays, Twain highlighted human incompetence, limitations, and wickedness. He especially castigated human selfishness. From the cradle to the grave, Twain complained, people's primary objective was to obtain personal peace of mind and comfort. If an individual can achieve this "by *helping* his neighbor, he will do it"; if he can do so more easily "by *swindling* his neighbor, he will do that." Most individuals acted lovingly toward their families and friends but not toward any other people. People sought to please God, Twain contended, only after pleasing themselves.[74]

Twain frequently excoriated his own degeneracy. "What a man sees in the human race is merely himself in the deep and honest privacy of his own heart. [Lord] Byron despised the race because he despised himself. I feel as Byron did, and for the same reason." Twain's "trained Presbyterian conscience" had "but one duty—to hunt and harry its slave upon all pretexts and on all occasions."[75] This conscience, which Twain called the Moral Sense, continually tormented him. He often reproached himself for his contemptible behavior and then scolded himself for being so guilt-ridden.[76] Why cannot his conscience, Twain asks in one story, "haul a man over the coals once, for an offense, and then let him alone?" His conscience retorts, "It is my business—and my joy—to make you repent [repeatedly] of everything you do." Responding to a flattering introduction at a banquet, Twain declared, "Everyone believes I am a monument of all the virtues," but "I've got a wicked side." Twain confessed, "I have led a life full of interior sin." Someday a Chairman (presumably God) would reveal "the true side of my character." In his life, Twain quipped in 1898, "I have committed millions of sins. Many of them I probably repented of—I do not remember now." In seventy years, "I have done eleven good deeds." Humanity "is a race of cowards," Twain declared, "and I am not only marching in that procession but carrying a banner."[77]

Twain did revel in one "detestable" behavior: swearing, usually using "hell" and "damn," but sometimes taking God's name in vain. Some people, especially Livy, were irritated by his frequent cursing. Out of respect for his wife, Twain did not swear in her presence. "Profanity is more necessary to me than is immunity from colds," Twain told his brother Orion, because it "furnishes a relief denied even to prayer." A person "can swear and still be a gentleman if he does it in a nice and benevolent and affectionate way," Twain jested. "If I cannot swear in heaven," he quipped, "I shall not stay there."[78]

Twain sometimes stressed the insignificance of humanity; he called people microbes, and many of his stories challenge people's sense of importance. Rejecting Charles Darwin's argument, Twain asserted that people were descending rather than ascending the evolutionary ladder. In his essay "The Descent of Man from the Higher Animals,"

Twain contended that human beings were morally lower than other species because they alone acted with willful perversity.[79] People were vitiated by their lies, self-deception, and various forms of pretense. "All men are liars, partial or hiders of facts, half tellers of truths, shirks, moral sneaks," Twain pontificated. "When a merely *honest* man appears he is a comet—his fame is eternal—Luther, Christ, and maybe God made two others—or one—besides me," he joked. People are also easily self-duped. In one of his stories, young Satan, presumably speaking for Twain, declares that people practice "continuous and uninterrupted self-deception."[80]

Twain repeatedly berated God for creating humanity. He wondered why God even made the human race, or why he did not create something credible in its place. God committed a "grotesque folly," which he must have regretted when he observed human actions. In "The Czar's Soliloquy" (1905), Nicholas II asks, "Is the human race a joke?" and whether God devised humanity during "a dull time when there was nothing important to do."[81] Although placed in the mouth of a despicable tyrant, these words seem to express Twain's actual perspective. If human beings "are the noblest works of God," Twain inquired, "where is the ignoblest?" Was there any "plausible excuse" for the horrific "crime of creating the human race?"[82] "If I had invented" humans, Twain maintained, "I would go hide my head in a bag."[83]

Twain also railed against the doctrine of original sin. Adam and Eve's trial in the garden was unfair. Adam was told that if he ate from a particular tree, he would die. But Adam had no "idea what the word death meant. He had never . . . heard of a dead thing before." All Adam's descendants, Twain protested, had unfairly been "unceasingly hunted and harried with afflictions" as a punishment for "the juvenile misdemeanor which is grandiloquently called Adam's sin."[84]

Faith versus Works

Like his views of other Christian doctrines, Twain's perspective on salvation is complicated and inconsistent. He appeared to struggle for most of his life with a strong sense of sin and guilt and to believe that he must act righteously to be acceptable to God. On the other hand, several characters in Twain's stories express the orthodox Christian view that salvation is based on God's grace rather than people's good works. In *Pudd'nhead Wilson*, for example, Roxy declares, "dey ain't nobody kin save his own self—can't do it by faith, can't do it by works, can't do it no way at all. Free grace is de on'y way, en dat don't come from nobody but jis' de Lord; en he kin give it to anybody he please, saint or sinner." Or as Twain put it humorously, "Heaven goes by [God's] favor. If it went by merit you would stay out and the dog would go in."[85]

Despite making such statements and sometimes referring to himself as a prodigal son, Twain seemed unable to believe the Christian concept that God's love and grace are unconditional and that salvation depends on individuals' acceptance of Christ as their savior rather than on their good deeds. Influenced by Horace Bushnell, Twain reasoned that it was much better for children to gradually embrace the Christian faith through nurture by Christian parents and their church, or by deliberate, thoughtful reflection as adults, than to have a sudden religious conversion at a revival. This perspective was probably reinforced by his own lack of a definitive salvation experience as well as by his temperament and epistemology. "I would distrust a religious faith," he declared, that was not deliberately adopted and proven "step by step." In numerous Twain tales such as "The Recent Carnival of Crime in Connecticut" (1876), characters have dramatic conversion experiences that have only a temporary impact. Worse yet, such conversions could be bogus, like that of Tom Sawyer who duplicitously claimed, "I am one of the gang [of cutthroats], but have got religgion [sic] and wish to quit it [the gang] and lead a honest life again."[86]

Reflecting on his childhood, Twain wrote, he realized that tragedies "ought to bring me to repentance." At night he had often been frightened by his failure to truly repent, but broad daylight always banished his fears of God's judgment. He experienced many "nights of despair" and expressed remorse "after each tragedy," but only because doing so was in his own interest. He admitted, however, that "in all my boyhood life I am not sure that I ever tried to lead a better life in the daytime—or wanted to." As an adult, Twain strove to act uprightly, but he seemed to have little desire to confess his sins to God or to commit his life to Christ.[87] He also complained that God "made it hard to get into heaven and easy to get into hell."[88]

Christianity and the Church

In the mid-1870s, Twain read W. E. H. Lecky's *History of European Morals from Augustus to Charlemagne* (1869). In its margin he wrote, "If I have understood this book aright, it proves two things beyond shadow or question: 1. That Christianity is the very invention of Hell itself; 2. & that Christianity is the most precious and elevating and ennobling boon that ever was vouchsafed to the world."[89] As Harold Bush, Jr. observes, scholars analyzing Twain's religion have focused primarily on the first of these two points, emphasizing his ridiculing of religion as a source of much of the world's problems and pain. They have paid much less attention to Twain's positive appraisals of Christianity.[90] As discussed earlier, Twain was strongly influenced by his religious socialization, his quest to understand Christianity in his mid-thirties, his support of the Social Gospel, and his many friendships with ministers. Nevertheless, Twain's analysis of religion in general and Christianity in particular was more negative than positive. Much of his critique can be seen, however, as a jeremiad that contrasts what he considered the dismal state of Christian practice with the ideal Christian ethics as embodied in the Nook Farm community.[91]

Twain occasionally mentioned the contributions of Christianity and the church to the world, but he more often criticized Christians and their congregations. "Nine-tenths of all the kindness and forbearance and Christian charity and generosity in the hearts of the American people today," he proclaimed in 1871, was "filtered down from their fountainhead, the gospel of Christ," but this came through plays and "the despised novel" rather than through "the drowsy pulpit!" In a 1906 speech to raise money for Booker T. Washington's Tuskegee Institute, Twain praised the school for thoroughly grounding students in the Christian code of morals. Tuskegee instilled into them "the indisputable truth" that Christianity "is the highest and best of all systems of morals, that the Nation's greatness, its strength, and its repute among other nations is the product of that system." Its faculty insisted that all Americans are under Christianity's "character-building powerful influence and dominion from cradle to grave." By accentuating "the humaner passages of the Bible," Protestantism,

Twain added, had produced the world's "highest and purest and best individuals."[92]

Twain admired those who faithfully emulated Jesus and practiced the Golden Rule. For example, he praised Christian social workers serving in New York City's dangerous inner-city neighborhoods as "sincere and zealous religious men" who were trying to convince "the prostitutes who infest the alleys and byways" of the city to change their profession. Twain also valued thoughtful, ethically centered sermons designed to motivate parishioners to live righteously and remedy social ills. He complained, however, that many sermons were boring, trite, and filled with platitudes and "uninflammable truism about doing good."[93]

Twain, however, more often deplored the flaws, foibles, and failures of Christianity and the church. No Christian communion escaped his critique; he lampooned Catholics, mainstream Protestants, Mormons, and Christian Science alike. William Dean Howells reported that Twain told him that "Christianity had done nothing to improve [human] morals and [social] conditions." When Howells provided "abundant proof" that Twain was wrong by citing evidence from Charles Loring Brace's *Gesta Christi, or History of Humane Progress* (1882), Twain quickly recanted and thereafter, Howells claimed, "was more tolerant" in his criticism of Christianity.[94]

From the 1860s until his death, Twain, like Jesus, attacked hypocrisy, protesting that what people said they believed and what they did often differed substantially.[95] The "hound of Hannibal," writes Daniel Pawley, "had a blood-hound's instinct for sniffing the trails of hypocrites" and modern-day Pharisees. "There are two separate and distinct kinds of Christian morals," Twain complained, that were "no more kin to each other than are archangels and politicians." On one hand, many Americans were "clean and upright" in their "private commercial life." For 363 days a year, they practiced Christian private morals and kept "the nation's character at its best and highest." The other two days, however, they abandoned their Christian private morals and instead abided by "Christian public morals" as they did their best to undo their "whole year's faithful and righteous work." Those two days were election day and tax day, as most Christians voted for corrupt candidates and underreported their income. Twain exhorted them instead to help make holding public office "a high and honorable distinction."[96]

Twain despised the smug religiosity, false spirituality, self-righteousness, and pious judgmentalism of many Christians, traits that Jesus condemned in the Pharisees. In many Twain stories, the openly profane like Huck Finn and Jim obey the Bible's commands more faithfully than professed Christians such as Miss Watson, Uncle Silas, Aunt Sally Phelps, and the Grangerfords and Shepherdsons. "The liberating and genuine spirituality of Huck and Jim" as they float on a raft sharply contrasts with "the oppressive and hypocritical religious orthodoxies of the society onshore."[97]

Twain was especially upset when people cited Christianity to justify their use of violence. In 1906, Twain commented sarcastically that during the last generation every Christian nation had sought to find newer and more effective ways to kill Christians and a few pagans; therefore, "the surest way to get rich quickly, in Christ's earthly kingdom, is to invent a gun" that could more effectively kill more people. Twain also objected that the spirit of patriotism clashed with the Christian emphasis on forgiveness and love. Christ commanded his followers to pardon people for all the insults they uttered and all the crimes they committed, whereas patriotism (or nationalism) prompted citizens to contest boundaries, refuse to forgive affronts, and demand their rights.[98]

Twain also denounced the failure of Christians to practice compassion and mercy. He deplored the church's callous treatment of the destitute and vulnerable, caused in part, he contended, by its emphasis on individual salvation. Christian charity was often sentimental and impersonal and did little to help the marginalized and outcasts. Responding to Presbyterians' decision to repudiate the doctrine of infant damnation, Twain wrote sarcastically in 1907 that "everything is going to ruin"; soon "we shall have nothing left but the love of God."[99]

Twain complained further that churches often resisted constructive change. "The church is always trying to get other people to reform," he declared; "it might not be a bad idea to reform itself" to set a good example. The church, he lamented, was frequently "an obstructor and fighter of progress," but when "progress arrives, then she takes the credit." The church had often strongly opposed advancements in philosophy and science and had long supported slavery and persecuted alleged witches. For nine centuries, Twain complained, the church "had imprisoned, tortured, hanged, and burned whole hordes and armies of witches" until it was finally discovered that witches did not exist. "The so-called Christian nations are the most enlightened and progressive," Twain opined, "but in spite of their religion, not because of it. The Church has opposed every innovation and discovery from the day of Galileo down to our own time," including the use of anesthetics in childbirth, which, he incorrectly claimed, it regarded "as a sin because it avoided the biblical curse pronounced against Eve."[100]

Twain deplored both the anti-intellectualism of numerous Christians, especially their antagonism to scientific knowledge, on one hand and their tendency toward theological abstraction on the other. His reading of Andrew Dickson White's *A History of the Warfare of Science with Theology in Christendom* (1896) prompted him to ask, "What is the order of theological evolution: does a person first become an idiot & then a theologian, or is it the other way about?" "Theology & dysentery," he added, "are two of the most enervating diseases a person can have." Twain complained in an 1870 letter to Livy that Christians argued about "vexed questions in theology" instead of surveying "the grand universe" and saying, "Great is God, who created all things for Us."[101]

Twain was especially upset when Christians supported oppressive social structures rather than working to abolish them. He told a Russian revolutionary in 1906 that "Christianity of which we have always been so proud" had become "nothing but a shell, a sham, a hypocrisy" and that Christians had "lost our ancient sympathy with oppressed peoples struggling for life and liberty." "For two years," Twain lamented, Russian Christians had been repeating "the massacre and mutilation" their forebears had engaged in for nineteen hundred years, while ironically commending Christianity as "the one and only true religion of peace and love." They had committed untold atrocities to try to convince nonbelievers "to come into the fold of the meek and gentle Savior."[102]

In a 1905 letter, Twain repudiated Twichell's claim that the kingdom of God was making "steady progress from age to age." The world, Twain insisted, was advancing in material goods but not in morality. Moreover, if humanity had made "any progress toward righteousness," it had occurred only among ten percent of the population of Christendom, which, excluding Russia, Spain, and South America, he estimated to be 320 million. Therefore, he concluded, 32 million people had helped to promote the Kingdom of God while 1.2 billion had not.[103]

At times, Twain even predicted the demise of Christianity or called for a better religion to supplant it. "If Christ were here now," Twain reasoned, "there is one thing he would not be—a Christian." The authority of the Bible, he warned, "had been used to commit the religious atrocities of the Middle Ages," and someday it might "again become as heavy a curse to the world." "Christianity will doubtless still survive" ten centuries from now, he declared—"stuffed and in a museum." He called for replacing Christianity with a "New Religion" based on "God and Man as they are, and not as the elaborately masked and disguised artificialities they are represented to be in most philosophies and all religions."[104]

Conclusion

Though he enjoyed a safe haven in a caring religious community during the 1870s, Twain continued to struggle with guilt and his relationship with God. This struggle was exacerbated by his focus on most Christians' failure to live by biblical teachings and his largely negative appraisal of church history. Although he would actively participate with Christians in the 1880s to alleviate social problems, his antipathy toward aspects of Christianity would intensify and his personal quest to find a worldview that supplied purpose and personal peace would persist.

Notes

1. "Introduction," LTR 4:xxviii.
2. SLC to Elisha Bliss, March 17, 1871, LTR 4:365–6.
3. MTB, 370.

4. SLC to OL, February 15, 1869, LTR, 3:101 (quotations); SLC to OL, October 18, 1868, LTR, 2:268; Peter Messent, *Mark Twain and Male Friendships: The Twichell, Howells, and Rogers Friendships* (New York: Oxford University Press, 2009), 70–3; entries in Twichell's journals at the Beinecke Rare Book and Manuscript Library of Yale University also confirm Twain's regular church attendance in the 1870s. See also MTSC, chapters 3 and 4.

5. MTFP, 92.

6. NF, 50.

7. Messent, *Male Friendships*, 74; *Human Life: A Magazine of Today*, May 1906, Twichell Family Scrapbooks, Beinecke; SLC to OL, LTR, 4:529–30.

8. NF, 70.

9. AMT, July 25, 2007, 3:79.

10. Mark Twain, "Some Rambling Notes of an Idle Excursion," I, *Atlantic Monthly* 40 (October 1877), 443.

11. Hartford *Evening Post,* January 28, 1873.

12. Twain, as quoted in Robert Owen Decker, *Hartford's Immigrants: A History of the Christian Activities Council* (New York: United Church Press, 1987), 48–9; AMT, November 21, 1906, 2:281; quotations in that order; Twichell, as quoted in N. Maria Landfear, *Reminiscences of Father Hawley* (Hartford, CT: Case, Lockwood & Brainard, 1877), 85.

13. MTB, 631–2; quotations in that order. See also MTFP, 105–6.

14. Messent, *Male Friendships*, 75–8.

15. JHT to SLC, August 17, 1904, MTP. See also SLC to JHT, December 6, 1899, MTL, 2:683; SLC to JHT, July 28, 1904, MTP; JHT to SLC, September 5, 1901, MTP; and JHT to SLC, September 28, 1902, MTP.

16. MTL, 2:719.

17. JHT to Harmony Twichell, August 11, 1878, *The Letters of Mark Twain and Joseph Hopkins Twichell*, ed. Harold K. Bush, Steve Courtney, and Peter Messent (Athens: University of Georgia Press, 2017), 33–4.

18. David Twichell, "Memoranda on His Mother's Death," in Joseph Twichell Papers, Beinecke, 3.

19. *Hartford Courant*, April 22, 1910; quoted in NF, 2; SLC to JHT, September 27, 1896, MTL, 2:635; Twain, "Dinner Speech," 458.

20. REV, 156–7.

21. NF, 69. Andrews argues that Twain did not conceal his religious views from Asylum Church members or from members of the Hartford Monday Evening Club, a lecture and discussion group in which he regularly participated (70).

22. Mark Twain, "Speech on Art," June 7, 1902, MTS, 444.

23. MTR, 121.

24. Albert Stone, *The Innocent Eve: Childhood in Mark Twain's Imagination* (Hamden, CT: Archon, 1970), 11; MTR, 125.

25. SLC to WDH, December 23, 1877, MTHL, 212.

26. SLC to W. R. Ward, September 8, 1887, MTL 1:261; Wesley Britton, "Mark Twain: 'Cradle Skeptic,'" September 1997, http://www.twainweb.net/filelist/skeptic.html.

27. Forrest Robinson, *In Bad Faith: The Dynamics of Deception in Mark Twain's America* (Cambridge, MA: Harvard University Press, 1986), 26 (first quotation), 27–9, 20–1 (second quotation).

28. RMT, 84–6.

29. San Francisco *Daily Evening Bulletin*, January 20, 1877, https://twain.lib.virginia.edu/tomsawye/sfbulletin.html; San Francisco *Daily Alta California*, January 15, 1877, https://twain.lib.virginia.edu/tomsawye/altacal.html; Hartford *Christian Secretary*, May 17, 1877, https://twain.lib.virginia.edu/tomsawye/xiansect.html; *British Quarterly Review* 64 (October 1876), 547; *Hartford Daily Times*, December 20, 1876, https://twain.lib.virginia.edu/tomsawye/harttime.html; Moncure D. Conway, London *Examiner*, June 17, 1876, https://twain.lib.virginia.edu/tomsawye/londonex.html.

30. MTATB, 23.

31. IA, 504, 601; quotations in that order; Mark Twain, "I Rise to a Question of Privilege," May 1868, in *Who Is Mark Twain?*, ed. Robert Hirst (New York: HarperStudio, 2009), 181.

32. Mark Twain's 1872 *English Journals*, 68–70, LTR, 5:616.

33. IA, 502.

34. Mark Twain, "The Indignity Put Upon the Remains of George Holland by the Rev. Mr. Sabine," WM, 53.

35. Mark Twain, "Concerning the Jews," in *The Man That Corrupted Hadleyburg and Other Essays and Stories* (New York: Collier, 1917), 152; AMT, June 20, 1906, 2:130.

36. SLC to Mrs. Solon Severance, December 24, 1867, MTMF, 11.

37. SLC to OL, December 30, 1868, LTR, 2:364.

38. MTN, early January 1897, 324.

39. RMT, 88.

40. Joe Fulton, "Jesus Christ and Vivisection: Mark Twain's Radical Empathy in 'A Dog's Tale,'" *CCTE Studies* 71 (2006), 186.

41. SLC to Orion Clemens, March 23, 1878, LTR, 1:323.

42. AMT, June 20, 1906, 2:132. See also Twain, "Last Visit to England," July 1, 1907, MTE, 341.

43. AMT, June 20, 1906, 2:131.

44. Mark Twain, "The Second Advent," MTFM, 57.

45. Mark Twain, "Elinor Glyn," MTE, January 13, 1908, 317.

46. AMT, June 10, 1906, 2:131. See Charles Briggs, "Criticism and Dogma," *North American Review* (June 1906), 865–6.

47. AMT, June 20, 1906, 2:132.

48. MTN, March 28, 1896, August 7, 1898, MTN, 289 (first quotation), 290 (second and third quotations), 364 (fourth quotation).

49. Unpublished Notebook #42, transcription number 51, December 27, 1896, https://daybyday.marktwainstudies.com/page/24/; unpublished Notebook #29, transcription number 45, MTP.

50. Mark Twain, "Letters from the Earth," WM, 443.

51. June 19, 1906, AMT, 2:130 (first quotation), 129 (second and third quotations).

52. Twain, "Letters from the Earth," 443; AMT, January 9, 1907, 2:368 (quotation).

53. MTB, 1469.

54. October 13, 1904, MTN, 393; AMT, June 19, 1906, 2:129.

55. AMT, June 25, 1906, 2:140–1.

56. MTB, 1482; SLC to WDH, January 25, 1900, MTHL, 2:716.

57. MTMW, 117. See also Tom Quirk, *Mark Twain and Human Nature* (Columbia: University of Missouri Press, 2007).

58. Mark Twain, "The Bolters in Convention," *Territorial Enterprise*, December 30, 1863; Mark Twain, "The Divine Spark," unpublished essay, MTP; SLC to MMF, October 12, 1868, LTR, 2:265, explanatory note; quotations in that order.

59. Unidentified news clipping, book 5 of Twichell family scrapbooks.

60. Twichell, as quoted in MTFP, 90; SLC to OLC, July 17, 1899, LLMT, 253–4.

61. MTSC, 209. See also William Shurr, *Rappaccini's Children: American Writers in a Calvinist World* (Lexington: University Press of Kentucky, 1981), 29.

62. JHT to SLC, September 5, 1901, MTP (first quotation); Mark Twain, "Schoolhouse Hill," in *The Bible according to Mark Twain*, ed. Howard Baetzhold and Joseph McCullough (New York: Touchstone, 1995), 310 (second quotation); Lawrence Berkove, "Mark Twain's Vision of Truth," *Journal of American Studies* (English Edition) 26 (December 1994), 204–22.

63. MTUF, 149; BA, 168.

64. MTB, 1153; SLC to WDH, November 21, 1901, MTHL, 2:733 (first quotation); AMT, November 24, 1906, 2:288 (second quotation).

65. Quoted in MF, 264.

66. MTMS, 55.

67. SLC to WDH, May 12–13, 1899, MTHL, 2:698–9 (first quotation); MTN, November 6, 1895, 256 (second quotation).

68. As quoted in LMT, 213. Cf. MTN, March 19, 1903, 381.

69. John Bird, "Swinging the Pendulum: Mark Twain and Religion," *Papers on Language & Literature* 46 (Summer 2010), 345.

70. SLC to JHT, July 16, 1900, MTP; SLC to WDH, August 31, 1884, Writings, 35:443.

71. SLC to WDH, April 2, 1899, MTL, 1:376.

72. MTB, 1358.

73. AMT, January 15, 1907, 2:371; SLC to JHT, March 14, 1905, Writings 35:769 (quotation); Twain, "Miscellany," September 7, 1906, MTE, 383–4.

74. WM, 140 (quotation); MTN, August 7, 1898, 365.

75. MTB, 1539; Twain, "Chapters from My Autobiography," *North American Review*, May 3, 1907, 5; quotations in that order.

76. MTC, 152.

77. Mark Twain, "The Recent Carnival of Crime in Connecticut"; Twain, "Speech," November 15, 1900, MTS, 357; Twain "Something about Repentance," WM, 90; AMT, September 4, 1907, 3:130; quotations in that order.

78. SLC to Orion Clemens, May 14, 1877, MTLE, 2:70; Twain, "Taxes and Morals," January 22, 1906, *Mark Twain's Speeches*, ed. Albert Bigelow Paine (New York: Harper and Brothers, 1923), 279; AMT, January 23, 1906, 1:308; July 4, 1898, MTN 345; quotations in that order.

79. Mark Twain, "The Descent of Man from the Higher Animals," CT, 2:207. See also Twain, "Man's Place in the Animal World" (1896).

80. MTN, May 1, 1885, 181 (first and second quotations); Twain, "Three Statements of the Eighties," WM, 58–9; MTMS, 164 (third quotation).

81. SLC to WDH, January 25, 1900, MTL, 2:693; Twain, "The Czar's Soliloquy," *North American Review* 180 (March 1905), 326.

82. MTN, early February 1896, 276; marginalia in a book by Charles Darwin, "Hartford Museum Purchases Barrels Full of Twain's Old Books," *New York Times*, July 31, 1997; quotations in that order.

83. SLC to WDH, May 12–13, 1899, MTHL, 2:695.

84. AMT, June 19, 1906 2:128. Cf. *Letters from the Earth*, in *Bible According to Mark Twain*, ed. Baetzhold and McCullough, 231.

85. PW 26; MTB, 1567.

86. SLC to OL, January 7, 1869, LTR, 3:13; Mark Twain, *The Adventures of Huckleberry Finn* (Hartford, CT: American Publishing Company, 1885), 271–2; quotations in that order.

87. MTA, 2:134.

88. MTB, 1513.

89. Quoted in Harold Baetzhold, *Mark Twain and John Bull: The British Connection* (Bloomington: Indiana University Press, 1970), 138.

90. MTSC, 1.

91. MTSC, 109–10, 113.

92. Twain, "The Indignity," 53 (first quotation); Twain, Tuskegee Institute speech, January 22, 1906, MTS, 479 (second and third quotations); Twain, "Three Statements of the Eighties," WM, 57 (fourth quotation).

93. MTSC, 130–1; Franklin Walker and Ezra Dane, eds., *Mark Twain's Travels with Mr. Brown* (New York: Knopf, 1940), 162; (first quotation); Twain, "The Indignity," 54 (second quotation).

94. MMT, 31; William Dean Howells, "My Memories of Mark Twain," *Harper's Magazine* 121 (July 1910), 177; quotations in that order.

95. See his parody of the Apostles' Creed in an April 16, 1867 letter to the *Alta California* (*Mark Twain's Travels*, ed. Walker and Dane, 142–3).

96. Daniel Pawley, "The Hound of Hannibal," *Christianity Today*, November 8, 1985, https://www.christianitytoday.com/ct/1985/november-8/books.html; Twain, "Taxes and Morals," 479–80.

97. Dwayne Eutsey, "God's 'Real' Message: 'No. 44, The Mysterious Stranger' and the Influence of Liberal Religion on Mark Twain," *Mark Twain Annual* 3 (2005), 57.

98. AMT, June 22, 1906, 2:134 (quotation); MTN, July 18, 1897, 332.

99. RV, 182–3; CS, 142 (quotation).

100. Mark Twain, *A Tramp Abroad* (New York: Harper and Brothers), 2:80 (first quotation); MTN, December 25, 1896, 313 (second quotation); Twain, "Bible Teaching and Religious Practice," WM, 75 (third quotation); MTB, 1534 (fourth quotation), 1535 (fifth quotation).

101. Alan Gribben, *Mark Twain's Library: A Reconstruction* (Boston: Hall, 1980), 760, marginalia, on 1:204–5 of Andrew Dickson White, *A History of the Warfare of Science with Theology in Christendom*, 2 vols. (New York: D. Appleton, 1901); SLC to OL, January 8, 1870, MTLE.

102. AMT, March 30, 1906, 1:361 (first quotation); AMT, June 22, 1906, 2:132–3 (second and third quotations).

103. SLC to JHT, March 14, 1905, MTL 2:768–70; first quotation from 768; second quotation from 770.

104. MTN, May 18, 1897, 328 (first quotation); July 4, 1898, 346 (third quotation); September 9, 1902, 376 (fourth quotation); Twain, "Three Statements," 58 (second quotation).

5

The 1880s

In Hartford as in Heaven

The 1880s were a productive decade for Twain as four of his books—
The Prince and the Pauper (1881), *Life on the Mississippi* (1883), *Adventures of
Huckleberry Finn* (1885), and *A Connecticut Yankee in King Arthur's Court*
(1889)—were published. *Huckleberry Finn* is especially replete with
religious themes. During this decade, Twain promoted social reform
through his writing, speaking, and other activities in Hartford and his
condemnation of racial discrimination. During the 1870s and 1880s,
his friend and pastor Joseph Twichell's sermons and their frequent
theological discussions helped Twain view favorably the Social
Gospel's quest to reform society. From the 1870s to the 1910s,
hundreds of thousands of advocates of social Christianity used pulpits,
platforms, and publications to attack materialism, racism, imperialism, and political corruption, support women's rights, and champion
unions. Through churches, synagogues, and reform organizations
Social Gospelers worked to curb industrial ills, reduce poverty, and
assist immigrants.

Twain addressed many of these issues in his writing and lectures.
He also funded the education of several African American students,
spoke at numerous black churches, served for many years on the
board of Atlanta University (a leading African American institution),
enthusiastically supported Booker T. Washington, attacked racial
discrimination in several essays, and argued that the United States
should pay reparations to black Americans. Under the leadership of
Congregational ministers Twichell, Horace Bushnell, Nathaniel Burton, and Edwin Parker, Hartford became a hotbed of both liberal
Christianity and the Social Gospel in late nineteenth-century America

as many Christians worked energetically, as instructed by the Lord's Prayer, to bring God's kingdom on earth as it is in heaven.[1]

"The Week-day Preacher"

Mark Twain, the *Philadelphia Daily Evening Bulletin* declared in 1869, abhorred "sham, hypocrisy and cant." The editors lauded his formidable assault on the religious, social, and political "follies of the times" and predicted that he would have "a very considerable influence as a reformer." Twain cleverly employed ridicule in his screeds and speeches as a "powerful weapon against pretension and humbug" because it appealed to a popular audience.[2] As a journalist and author in the 1860s, Twain attacked social abuses so fervently, Progressive activist Edith Wyatt declared, that he became known as "The Moralist of the Main." For the next four decades, he relentlessly denounced social injustices around the globe in short stories, lectures, and essays.[3]

In his copy of William Thackeray's essay on Jonathan Swift, Twain underlined a comment that "the humorous writer" assumed the mantle of "the week-day preacher" to awaken people's love, pity, and kindness, their scorn for untruth and pretension, and their tenderness for the weak, poor, and oppressed, and unhappy.[4] Functioning as a preacher and prophet, Twain condemned numerous social ills including racism, sexism, economic exploitation and inequality, poverty, political corruption, and corporate and personal greed throughout his long writing career. He strove to reduce discrimination against African Americans, Asian Americans, Jews, women, and blue-collar workers. Although not considered one of the muckrakers—investigative journalists who denounced various injustices in government, business, and society beginning around 1900—Twain, during the last decade of his life, shared their concerns. Accordingly, the *Louisville Courier-Journal* called him "a vigorous reformer, a sort of knight errant who does not hesitate to break lance with either Church or State."[5]

In *Mark Twain: Social Critic*, Philip Foner contends that he aided the defenseless and oppressed and fiercely combatted "corruption, privilege and abuse."[6] Little evidence supports "the once-popular view that Mark Twain was a social critic who hid his light under a bushel,"

Edward Wagenknecht claims. He spoke out, often aggressively, on more major social issues than any other prominent author of his era.[7] Twain, Jeanne Reesman argues, "does not spare Americans' most cherished institutions: banks, police, courts, Congress, clergy, colonialism, the bourgeois class he married into, Sunday Schools, [or] universities."[8]

Improving Politics

Throughout his literary career, Twain deplored political corruption and urged Americans to back honest candidates who worked to advance the nation's best interests. Twain often lampooned politicians. "Judas Iscariot," he declared, "was nothing but a low, mean, premature Congressman."[9] "There is no distinctly native American criminal class," he quipped, "except Congress."[10] In 1908, two men were caught trying to rob Twain's house. At their arraignment, Twain joked, "If you keep this up, one day you'll end up in the United States Senate."[11]

As previously noted, Twain decried the disjunction between American Christians' private and public morality. Most of them were honest and faithfully followed religious norms in their private relationships. In nine cases out of ten, however, they betrayed the public trust to support their political party. Most Christians, Twain complained, did not hesitate to vote for "notorious blatherskites and criminals" rather than honest candidates if party loyalty required it. Many Christians had "sound and sturdy private morals," but their faith had no influence on them when they acted in a public capacity. During the 1906 municipal election in New York City, Twain claimed, almost half the votes were cast, many by Christians, for men who belonged in jail. These Christians went to church the next Sunday without recognizing the duplicity of their deed. Moreover, the US Congress consisted largely of Christians who behaved honorably in private life but shamelessly violated all their principles in performing their political roles.[12]

Twain used his lecture platform and pen to influence American politics. Twain's widely printed and quoted speeches on behalf of Grover Cleveland in 1884 helped the Democrat win the presidency. In January 1901 Twain denounced New York City's political corruption at a meeting of the City Club, and that fall he spoke at a dinner sponsored by opponents of Tammany Hall.[13] In "Christian Citizenship," published in *Collier's Weekly* in September 1905, Twain exhorted voters to repudiate Tammany Hall, the crooked Democratic political machine. Because "a Christian's first duty is to God," Twain argued, he must take his "Christian code of morality to the polls." "God," he insisted, "is an issue in every election"; every morally upright candidate represented God. "No fealty to party," Twain maintained, could absolve God's servants from their "higher and more exacting" loyalty to the Lord. If Christians did "their duty to God at the polls," upstanding men would be elected, unprincipled men would stop running for office, and graft would cease. Members of every Christian congregation in the country, however, helped elect "foul men to public office," even though they knew this was "an open and deliberate insult to God" who deplored "placing the liberties and well-being of His children" in the hands of disreputable men.[14]

Many pastors, Twain protested, supported unsavory candidates either to enhance their own reputations or to provide financially for their families. He used a Hartford clergyman as an example. The minister told Twain privately that a certain candidate was an "unscrupulous scoundrel." Forty days later, however, the minister described this candidate at a political gathering as the Cid, Great-heart, Sir Galahad, and Bayard the Spotless "all rolled into one," showing how one could convince himself of a lie if it were "the popular thing to do." "The preacher who casts a vote for conscience'[s] sake," Twain lamented, "runs the risk of starving."[15] He could not fault Joseph Twichell "for voting his infernal Republican ticket" because he had a large family to support, which was his primary duty. To provide for his family, however, the minister had to sacrifice his "political conscience." Only twenty of the nation's 80,000 pastors, Twain complained, were politically independent. For pragmatic reasons, the rest felt compelled to vote as did their congregants.[16]

Slavery and Racism

Twain has often been called a racist because he frequently used the N-word in *Huckleberry Finn*. Many libraries and schools have banned the book. The novel, however, expresses Twain's view of racial equality. Huck refuses to turn runaway slave Jim in to the authorities despite the temporal and eternal threats this decision poses, because he recognizes their shared humanity. Moreover, Twain's hideous portrait of Huck's racist father powerfully exposes "the moral bankruptcy of white supremacist claims."[17]

Twain's experiences as a youth—his family owned several slaves during his childhood and a couple hundred slaves lived in the Hannibal area—and the prejudices of his era made racist attitudes seem acceptable. But Twain married into a fervently abolitionist family that had helped numerous slaves escape before the Civil War. In his writings and lectures, Twain condemned slavery, deplored discrimination, and called for reparations for blacks. He also developed relationships with some of the black Americans who founded the NAACP in 1909.

After the Civil War, Twain strongly denounced Southerners' use of the Bible to defend slavery and the horrors of the slave trade. "In my schoolboy days," he stated, "I was not aware that there was anything wrong" with slavery. Ministers in Hannibal, he reported, "taught us that God approved" of slavery, that "it was a holy thing," and then read biblical texts to prove it.[18] His mother did not recognize until the Civil War, Twain asserted, that "slavery was a bald, grotesque, and unwarrantable usurpation." She had heard slavery "defended and sanctified in a thousand" sermons and was "familiar with Bible texts that approved it." In her experience, the wise, good, and holy unanimously argued that "slavery was right, righteous, sacred, the peculiar pet of the Deity and a condition" for which slaves should be thankful.[19] His acceptance of slavery before the Civil War, Greg Camfield argues, "partly explains the tortured conscience that bedeviled Clemens all his life."[20]

For 250 years, Twain lamented, Christians had monopolized the "bloody and awful" slave trade that had separated countless families and broken millions of hearts. They did this so that "Christian nations might be prosperous and comfortable, Christian churches be built, and the gospel of the meek and merciful Redeemer be spread abroad in the earth."[21] In *Life on the Mississippi*, *Huckleberry Finn*, and *Pudd'nhead Wilson* (1894), Twain portrays Christianity as justifying chattel slavery and depicts basically upright characters such as Widow Douglas, Percy Driscoll, and David Wilson as failing to recognize the horrors of this evil institution.[22] No one, William Dean Howells argued, abhorred slavery more than Twain, and no one ever "poured such scorn" on the "pseudochivalry of the Southern ideal."[23]

Twain provided scholarships for African American students at Lincoln University near Philadelphia, paid for the education of a black ministerial student, and gave numerous lectures in black churches.[24] In the mid-1880s, he helped pay the expenses of Warner McGuinn, one of Yale Law School's first African American students. Explaining his motivation, Twain told the law school dean that "we have ground the manhood out" of blacks, and "we should pay for it." McGuinn had an illustrious career as an attorney; Thurgood Marshall called him "one of the greatest lawyers who ever lived."[25] Twain became friends with Booker T. Washington, chaired Tuskegee Institute's Silver Jubilee fundraiser at Carnegie Hall in New York City in 1906, and effusively praised its work. Washington, Twain asserted, was "worth a hundred [Theodore] Roosevelts"; Roosevelt "is not worthy to untie" Washington's shoes.[26]

Harold Bush, Jr. argues that Twain's view of blacks and his efforts to improve race relations and secure black rights grew out of his belief, developed through his friendship with proponents of the Social Gospel and African Americans including Frederick Douglass, that God equally valued people of all races.[27] Twain was deeply affected by his relationship with three blacks: his butler George Griffin; John Lewis, a farmer in Elmira, New York; and Mary Ann Cord, a cook who worked for his in-laws Theodore and Susan Crane in Elmira. Twain admired the faith and conduct of Griffin, whom he employed for fifteen years. The African Methodist Church deacon "was strenuously religious," Twain wrote; no profanity "ever soiled his speech, and he neither drank nor smoked." In some ways, Twain stated, Griffin was "my superior."[28] Lewis, who served as a model for Jim in *Huckleberry Finn*, was an exemplar of integrity and courage.[29] Lewis saved the lives of the wife and child of Twain's brother-in-law Charles Langdon in 1877 by stopping their out-of-control buggy. Twain sometimes eavesdropped on the theological debates between Lewis, a Baptist, and Cord, a Methodist.[30]

Twain was deeply moved by Cord's heartbreaking story of slave traders taking her children, which he used as the basis for an 1874 *Atlantic Monthly* article. In his story, the narrator angers Aunt Rachel, a black domestic servant, by asking her how she had "lived sixty years and never had any trouble." This prompts Rachel to recount her personal pathos as she witnessed all her children being sold at a slave auction in Richmond. Twenty-two years later, she is reunited with her son Henry, who had escaped from slavery, served in the Union Army, and been searching for his mother for several years.[31] Twain's tale depicts slavery's tragic toll on families, especially mothers who were separated from their children. Twain was deeply moved by Cord's ability to maintain her faith in God despite her ordeal. He went on to write numerous short stories and novels, including *Huckleberry Finn* and *Pudd'nhead Wilson*, that portrayed the plight and resolve of African Americans. In these tales, Shelley Fisher Fishkin claims, Twain "subverted and challenged his culture's ingrained pieties with a boldness and subtlety that readers are still struggling to appreciate fully" today.[32]

Pudd'nhead Wilson takes place in a Southern village on the banks of the Mississippi River during the three decades prior to the Civil War. Roxy, a slave who is 15/16ths white, is impregnated by her owner, Percy Driscoll, and gives birth to a blond, blue-eyed, white-skinned son. While serving as a nanny for Percy's infant son Thomas, she secretly switches her son Chambers with Thomas. "Chambers" is then raised as a slave by his uncle Judge Driscoll after Percy dies. "Chambers" is kind, respectful, and docile but is treated brutally by the self-centered, mean-spirited, and malicious "Thomas," even though "Chambers" had rescued "Thomas" from drowning. "Thomas" robs houses to help pay his gambling debts and murders a judge. He mistreats his biological mother, viewing her as "his cringing and helpless slave," and sells her back into slavery after she becomes free.[33] Attorney Pudd'nhead Wilson eventually discovers that the men had been swapped as infants. As a result, "Thomas" is sold into slavery, while "Chambers" is restored to his proper position as the Driscoll heir, but because of his socialization and speech pattern, he does not fit into white society.

Pudd'nhead Wilson attacks miscegenation and identifying people racially by their bloodlines. Although the celebrated author does not totally escape the racial and gender stereotyping of his era, his story shows that the distinction between free people and slaves based on their parentage was an arbitrary "fiction of law and custom."[34] Not surprisingly, the Southern reaction to Twain's story was hostile. In *Southern Magazine*, for example, Martha McCulloch Williams castigated the book as "incredibly stupid," "malicious," and "misleading" and accused Twain of falsifying history.[35]

In 1869 Twain published an essay titled "Only a Nigger," a satirical denunciation of lynching, in the Buffalo *Express*, which he co-owned and edited. "What if the blunder of lynching the wrong man does happen once in four or five cases!" Twain sarcastically declared. "Is that any fair argument against the cultivation and indulgence of those fine chivalric passions and that noble Southern spirit which will not brook the slow and cold formalities of regular law, when outraged white womanhood appeals for vengeance?"[36] In 1901 Twain penned another attack on this horrific practice, titled "The United States of Lyncherdom." However, in an era of intensifying racism, discrimination, and Ku Klux Klan activity, Twain decided not to publish the essay. Finally published in 1923, the essay condemned the public execution of black men without a trial. Twain was prompted to write the article by the lynching of three African Americans, the burning of five black houses, and the driving of thirty black families into the woods by residents of a small town in southwest Missouri after a white woman was murdered on her way to church. Twain censured the town's residents for taking "the law into their own hands." He urged missionaries to return from China and work to stop this barbaric practice.[37]

Women

Twain claimed in 1909 that he had advocated women's suffrage "earnestly for the last fifty years."[38] The historical record indicates, however, that Twain was initially ambivalent about women's suffrage. However, through his relationship with Livy and friendship with Julia Beecher, the wife of Thomas Beecher (pastor of Park Church in Elmira), he eventually became a strong supporter of women's rights. He wrote essays, spoke at suffragists' rallies, and donated money to promote their cause. He also endorsed women's acts of civil disobedience to secure their rights.

Women, Twain insisted in 1874, deserved the same voting rights as men, including African Americans, recently arrived immigrants, or released convicts. Extending suffrage to women "could lose absolutely nothing & might gain a great deal." Despite being intelligent, born in the United States, well educated, and "having large interests at stake," suffragists, Twain protested, currently had no voice in electing political officials and passing laws. They and other women found "their tongues tied & their hands fettered, while every ignorant whisky-drinking foreign born savage in the land" could hold office and help devise laws. Women watched their fathers, husbands, and brothers "sit inanely at home & allow the scum of the country" to select and elect candidates. If women were enfranchised, "they would vote on the side of morality" and would not allow "loafers, thieves, & pernicious little politicians" to control party primaries. Refusing to "sit indolently at home as their husbands & brothers do now," they "would hoist their praying banners, take the field in force, pray the assembled political scum back to the holes & slums where they belong," and nominate worthy candidates. History had shown, Twain contended, that women were undaunted "in a moral fight." "We all know," Twain proclaimed, that "from the day that Adam ate of the apple & told on Eve down to the present day," in moral battles almost all men had been cowards. Women would end the nation's political corruption and expel robbers and perjurers from Congress.[39]

Three decades later, Twain praised four "powerful sisters"—Susan B. Anthony, Elizabeth Cady Stanton, Mary Livermore, and his former neighbor Isabella Beecher Hooker—for their effective crusade to procure women's rights. When suffragists began their work in 1848, he explained, women, as they had been in every country and under all religions, were subject to disgraceful laws and treated like slaves. "Those brave women besieged the legislatures of the land, year after year, suffering and enduring all manner of reproach, rebuke, scorn and obloquy, yet never surrendering, never sounding a retreat." The campaign of these women and many others, Twain declared in 1907, had "achieved a revolution," emancipating half the nation without shedding "a drop of blood." Suffragists "broke the chains of their sex" and set women free.[40] Given that women would not receive the right to vote for another thirteen years and continued to be discriminated against in politics, society, the workplace, the church, marriage, and the home, many of them may have cringed at Twain's glowing appraisal.

Materialism, Greed, and Business Malpractice

Twain also denounced materialism, avarice, and fraudulent business practices. Throughout his literary career, beginning with his 1869 "Open Letter to Commodore Vanderbilt," he accused American tycoons of greed, self-glorification, perversion of biblical teachings, and immoral business actions. Twain pitied Cornelius Vanderbilt because he was not satisfied with his $70 million fortune; the railroad magnate was so preoccupied with enlarging his wealth that he could not enjoy what he had.[41] Many of Twain's stories written during the 1890s, when he was struggling with financial problems, focus on "the meaning of money as romance, fairy tale, delusion, disease and nightmare."[42] Numerous Twain tales also lampoon the negative impact of trusts and monopolies.

Twain ridiculed the Sunday school lessons prepared by John D. Rockefeller, Jr. and his father, which were published in newspapers throughout the nation. If the son's lessons were based on his "mental merit" instead of his father's money, the public would have never heard his explanations of Scripture. "With admirable solemnity and confidence," John Jr. discussed "the Bible with the inspiration and the confidence of an idiot." Many laughed at his analysis of Scripture, Twain contended, but hundreds of pulpits preached the same foolishness every Sunday.[43] John Sr., the world's richest man, was worth a billion dollars but paid taxes on only $2.5 million. This "earnest, uneducated Christian" had taught a Sunday school class in Cleveland for many years. His class, Twain protested, "has listened in rapture and has divided its worship between him and his Creator—unequally." His Sunday school talks were "as eagerly read" as those of his son.[44]

Twain aimed his greatest venom at Jay Gould, whom he called "the mightiest disaster" to ever befall this country. Gould taught people "to fall down and worship" money. His gospel was "Get money. Get it quickly. Get it in abundance. Get it in prodigious abundance. Get it dishonestly if you can, honestly if you must."[45] Twain complained that newspapers and pulpits had praised Gould, the "most infamous corrupter of American commercial morals," for giving $5,000 in 1878 to aid Memphis residents suffering from yellow fever while "wallowing in uncountable stolen millions." Gould's donation required "no sacrifice; it was only the income" of an hour—which he daily spent in prayer "for he was a most godly man," Twain added sarcastically.[46]

Twain simultaneously admired and detested capitalism and affluence, as his anxiety and ambivalence about them in his personal life and writing displayed.[47] On one hand, he desperately wanted to avoid the financial woes his family of origin experienced. When his life circumstances permitted, he lived lavishly in his Nook Farm mansion, posh European villas and hotels, and sumptuous quarters in New York City and Redding, Connecticut. Twain spent extravagantly, participated in elite social networks, deplored social disorder, and valued intellectual over manual labor. He developed a friendship with Andrew Carnegie, who overlooked Twain's earlier criticisms. Moreover, another wealthy friend, Henry Huttleston Rogers, an executive at Standard Oil, helped save Twain from financial ruin by devising a schedule to pay his creditors.[48]

Nevertheless, anticipating economist Thorstein Veblen's critique of conspicuous consumption in *The Theory of the Leisure Class* (1899), Twain frequently assailed Americans' passionate pursuit of prosperity. The California gold rush's relentless quest for lucre, Twain asserted in *Roughing It*, had sacrificed thousands of people "upon the altar of the golden calf." Its victims constituted "the noblest holocaust that ever wafted its sacrificial incense heavenward."[49] Parodying the Westminster Shorter Catechism, Twain wrote in 1871, "What is the chief end of man?—to get rich . . . . Money is God. God and Greenbacks and Stock—father, son, and the ghost of same—three persons in one; these are the true and only God, mighty and supreme."[50] Twain also attacked the worship of money in *The Gilded Age* (1873). He called for removing "In God We Trust" from US coins because this motto was a lie. Americans actually placed their trust in "the Republican party and the dollar—mainly the dollar."[51] "How unfortunate and how narrowing a thing it is," he maintained, for people to make money a god "instead of a servant."[52] In his 1900 burlesque of "The Battle Hymn of the Republic," Twain wrote, "As Christ died to make men holy, let men die to make us rich." "Greed," he lamented, "is marching on."[53]

In an 1895 essay, Twain refuted the widely accepted idea that "the love of money" and "the mad desire to get suddenly rich" were exclusively American, calling them "natural to all nations." He insisted that this love "has existed everywhere, ever since the Bible called it the root of all evil." Americans were especially "addicted to trying to get rich" quickly because their opportunity to do so was greater than elsewhere.[54] Although the lust for money had always existed, Twain argued, in the United States money was "the supreme ideal"; gaining it had become "a craze, a madness."[55] Some people, he avowed, worship status, heroes, power, or God, but above these, "all worship money." Tom Sawyer expresses Twain's most negative assessment of affluence: "Being rich ain't what it's cracked up to be. It's just worry and worry, and sweat and sweat, and a-wishing you was dead all the time."[56]

In many Twain tales, people's greed seriously harms or even destroys them. *The Man That Corrupted Hadleyburg* (1900) portrays the devastating impact of greed on a town that had been famous for its moral virtue and "commercial integrity." Nineteen of the town's most prominent residents receive a letter, promising a large gift, from a stranger who had been kindly treated when visiting the town. Each one thinks that only he has received the letter. All of them embark on a spree of imaginary spending; a local architect is deluged with requests to design opulent houses for them. The promise of this "deadly money" destroys "the town's social fabric and all its personal relations."[57] Similarly, "The Esquimau Maiden's Romance" (1893) describes the corrupting influence of wealth on Eskimo society.

In "The $30,000 Bequest" (1904), two devout Presbyterians, a bookkeeper and his wife, receive a letter from a relative who tells them he will soon die and leave them $30,000. The spouses become preoccupied with how they will use this inheritance. Several years later, they learn that their relative had died a pauper. Reflecting on their obsession with the anticipated bequest, the bookkeeper declares, "Vast wealth, acquired by sudden and wholesome means, is a snare. It did us no good, transient were its feverish pleasures; yet for its sake we threw away our sweet and simple and happy life—let others take warning by us."[58] The story teaches that the pursuit of wealth, even in people's dreams, prevents them from enjoying life. Twain believed that most Americans, like the story's protagonists, did not recognize that they worshipped money. His tale warns readers that the insidious acquisitiveness promoted by the "American dream of upward mobility" can destroy them.[59]

Twain also denounced business practices that he deemed unfair or contrary to the public good. The Golden Rule is "exhibit A in the Church's assets, but it is strictly religious furniture," he complained. "It has never been intruded into business."[60] While valuing capitalism and technology, Twain critiqued their misuse by businessmen who valued profits over people.

Unlike most of his Protestant Republican friends in Hartford, Twain supported labor unions,[61] lamenting that workers had been "the bleeding grist of our great financial machine."[62] Albert Bigelow Paine argued that Twain defended unions as the only means workers could use to obtain their rights.[63] An illustration in Twain's *A Connecticut Yankee in King Arthur's Court* (1889) depicts a post-bellum American industrialist subjugating a worker and declares instead that they are brothers.

Huckleberry Finn

In the mid-1880s, as Twain was writing *The Adventures of Huckleberry Finn*, Livy and his daughters were afflicted with various diseases including scarlet fever and diphtheria. As Twain struggled with his family's large living expenses, he was drained financially and emotionally and had little personal peace. Despite his strong support of Social Gospel activities, he was developing a gloomier view of humanity, Christianity, and civilization as his religious views became less orthodox. At the pinnacle of his creative powers, Twain wrote his magnum opus, working more intensely than at any other time in his literary career.[64] *Huckleberry Finn*, the product of his strenuous efforts, is sometimes called "the greatest novel ever written by an American."[65]

Few novels have provoked more controversy and censorship in the United States than *Huckleberry Finn*. Although the book is better known for its racial motifs and allegedly racist language, its numerous religious subjects—prayer, providence, church services, revival meetings, human nature, heaven, and hell—reflect both Twain's childhood religious socialization in Hannibal and his adult understanding of God and Christianity.

Huckleberry Finn asserts that society is replete with "empty rules, vacant prejudices, gross inequalities," and phony piety. Civilization furnishes people "with a false morality"—a warped conscience that often leads them to think they are acting morally when they are not. Twain challenged the Gilded Age's social system that pressured people to adhere blindly to detrimental norms and customs promoted by governments, churches, families, and community organizations.[66] In some ways, the novel parodies the spiritual-adventure autobiographies many Protestants found inspiring. Despite their many flaws, Huck and Tom Sawyer strive to triumph over their society's lies, sham, and perverted orthodoxy. Twain exposes the chasm between society's allegedly biblical ideals and its debauched and oppressive structures and practices. He also challenges the widely held view among both Protestants and Catholics that the United States had a divine mission to expand its territory and spread Christianity, liberty, and civilization to the world.[67]

Finding a raft, Huck and Jim, an escaped slave, begin their own version of *Pilgrim's Progress* (of which Huck had read a "considerable" portion). When they go ashore at various places with the king and the duke—two swindlers who join them on their journey—they confront various religious, cultural, and family conflicts, including the feuding Grangerfords and Shepherdsons who cannot remember what caused their animosity. Both Jim and Huck are fighting for their freedom—Jim from the bondage of slavery and Huck from the fetters of social norms and values that have constrained his moral development.

"No American of Northern birth or breeding," William Dean Howells contended, "could have imagined the spiritual struggle" Huck Finn faced in deciding to help Jim obtain his freedom. Huck was torn between his conscience and his fear of being despised by his hometown residents as "a low-down Abolitionist" and eternally damned. The most significant passages in Twain's fiction, Howells argued, are ones that discuss how people's character is affected for good or evil by their Sunday school and church experience.[68]

Huckleberry Finn often portrays Christianity as malign, self-contradictory, and incapable of fulfilling people's "basic spiritual and emotional needs." Jeanne Campbell Reesman avers that the novel depicts "bad fathering both on the human and divine levels"; Huck's sadistic father Pap can be seen as a model for Twain's conception of God as "fickle, jealous, cruel, uncaring, [and] murderous." "Pap's fecklessness, neglect, abuse, jealousy, [and] self-aggrandizement,"

Reesman adds, are all faults Twain attributed to God.[69] Several characters—the Widow Douglas who becomes Huck's guardian, her spinster sister Miss Watson, and Tom Sawyer's Uncle Silas Phelps and his wife Polly—are pious, but they own slaves or support slavery and devalue black lives. St. Petersburg, populated by many Christians, sends Huck back to his abusive father. In Twain's novel, Christianity is characterized more by rules, regulations, pseudo-spirituality, and eternal judgment than by love, grace, and forgiveness.

Huck struggles to believe in God but finds it very difficult. Prayer appears to work for Widow Douglas and Miss Watson, but not for him. Once Miss Watson took Huck into "the closet and prayed, but nothing come of it." She promised him that he would get whatever he prayed for, "but it warn't so." He receives the fishing line he requested, but repeated petitions for hooks are not granted, so the line is worthless. Huck also questions the Bible's relevance to his life; he tells Miss Watson that he has no interest in what Moses did eons earlier because "I don't take no stock in dead people." Later, Jim similarly dismisses the widow's claim that the instructions of Solomon, the wisest man in the world, are valuable.

Huck concludes that prayer is also ineffective for many other people. If individuals could receive anything they prayed for, why did Deacon Winn not get back the money he lost on pork? Why was Widow Douglas's stolen snuffbox not returned? Why could Miss Watson not gain weight? When he tells the widow that prayer does not work, she replies that God gives people "spiritual gifts," rather than material things, in response to their prayers. These gifts enable their recipients to help others, continually promote others' interests, and never think of themselves. Because Huck could see no personal advantages in such behavior, he decides not to pray anymore.

Jim expresses a similar perspective on prayer when he describes the unfulfilled promises of a minister's prosperity-gospel message. Jim's friend lent some money to the poor, motivated by a pastor's guarantee that anyone who did so would receive his money back one hundred-fold. This did not happen, and his friend could not even recover his loan.

Later, however, when a hungry Huck and Jim obtain much-needed bread, Huck reaches a different conclusion about the efficacy of prayer. "I reckon the widow or the parson or somebody prayed that this bread would find me," Huck declares. When a godly person like the widow or the parson prays, "there's something in it." Prayer worked only for the right kind of person, Huck reasons; "it don't work for me." On their trip down the Mississippi River, Huck meets nineteen-year-old Mary Jane Wilks, who promises to pray for Huck, prompting him to exclaim that if she truly knew him, "she'd take a job that was more nearer her size." However, since she "had the grit to pray for Judus if she took the notion," he gratefully assumes that she had prayed for him. And, Huck adds, "if ever I'd a thought it would do any good for me to pray for her," he would do it.

Perhaps reflecting Twain's own inner struggle, Widow Douglas and Miss Watson present Huck with contrasting views of God's providence. The kind, gentle, patient Douglas explains it in a way that made his "mouth water," whereas the stern and disagreeable Watson portrays providence rather bleakly. Huck concludes that there are two providences; the widow's providence is very desirable, but if Watson's providence "got him there warn't no help for him any more." Later, Huck decides that providence has indeed been blessing him. He did not devise plans, he declares, but simply trusted providence to enable him to say the right things because "I'd noticed that Providence always did put the right words in my mouth if I left it alone." He also testifies that "Providence had stood by me this fur."

The duke and king, two rapscallions pretending to be royalty, claim that providence is directing their efforts to fleece people. The king declares that rather than making any plans, he will "trust in Providence to lead him the profitable way," which Huck reasons, based on his character, meant he would follow the devil. The king later asserts disingenuously that he has tried all paths and "the best way, in the long run" is to place faith in providence.

Jim frequently looks to the occult realm of spirits and omens rather than Christianity for guidance.[70] Huck and Jim repeatedly use various rituals to try to ward off witches, evil spirits, the devil, and bad luck. On the other hand, they seek to use other spirits, magic, and the knowledge supplied by fortune tellers to assist them. Jim claims that two angels are hovering around Huck's derelict, dysfunctional, often drunken and abusive father—a white one and a black one. Sometimes the white one prompted Pap to act properly for a while, but then the black one tempted him to misbehave.

Throughout the book, Huck battles his conscience, which has been shaped by Southern society's advocacy of slavery. For example, his conscience asks him why he had not told Miss Watson that Jim had escaped. She had tried to educate him, teach him manners, and be good to him, and he had repaid her by helping her slave abscond.

Ridiculing the inconsistency between the profession and practice of many Christians, Twain describes a feud between two Arkansas families—the Grangerfords and the Shepherdsons. Their conflict, which had begun thirty years earlier for reasons that were unclear to their children, had produced numerous deaths. Both families worshipped at the same Presbyterian church, and Huck accompanies them to a service one Sunday. All the men brought their guns to church and "kept them between their knees or stood them handy against the wall." The minister preaches about brotherly love, and "everybody said it was a good sermon." On the way home, both families discuss the sermon and the biblical themes of "faith and good works and free grace and preforeordestination," but their senseless feud continues.

Huckleberry Finn also depicts a camp meeting, which were common during the antebellum era. An evangelist exhorts people to be converted immediately despite the devil's efforts to prevent them from being saved. Most of the area's residents, about a thousand souls, attend a service in the woods. Whipped into an emotional frenzy, worshippers sing loudly, and some begin to groan and shout. The evangelist preaches "with all his might." Holding up his Bible, he shouts, "It's the brazen serpent in the wilderness! Look upon it and live!" He urges his listeners not to resist the Holy Spirit, who is working in their hearts. "The devel's hold is a wekenin' on you, sister," he proclaims, "shake him loose." The evangelist invites those "black with sin" to "come with a contrite heart" to the mourners' bench. "The door of heaven" stands open; those who enter will receive rest. Many come forward with tears streaming down their faces; they sing, shout, and fling themselves "down on the straw, just crazy and wild." At the end of the service, the king testifies that he had been a pirate for thirty years, but he is now a changed man and "happy for the first time in his life." He vows to work to convince other pirates to take "the true path," prompting the gullible crowd to give the charlatan eighty-seven dollars.

During their time with Huck and Jim, the king and duke also lecture about temperance (while failing to earn enough money to get drunk), mesmerizing, doctoring, and fortune telling, all with little financial success. Critiquing the foolishness of Christians, Twain has the king say, "Folks will plank out cash for the heathen mighty free, if you locate your heathen fur enough off." The king and duke's attempts to procure money from naive people makes Huck "ashamed of the human race." Nevertheless, when a crowd tars and feathers the two after they are exposed as con artists, Huck calls it a dreadful sight. "Human beings," he adds, "can be awful cruel to one another."

After the king and duke resell Jim into slavery to the Phelpses, Huck considers telling Miss Watson where Jim is. He decides against doing so, however, recognizing that angered by Jim's "rascality and ungratefulness for leaving her," she will "sell him down the river again," making Jim "feel ornery and disgraced." However, the more Huck studies this problem, the more his conscience, shaped by the Southern argument that slavery is a positive good, bothers him and "the more wicked and low-down" he feels. It suddenly hits him that "the plain hand of Providence" was "slapping me in the face and letting me know my wickedness" was being continually watched in heaven. The "One that's always on the lookout" would punish him for stealing the slave of an old lady who had treated him so kindly. Frightened, Huck tries to devise a defense for his actions to prevent St. Petersburg residents from condemning him. He decides to claim that he had been "brung up wicked, and so I warn't so much to blame." But, he adds, "something inside of me kept saying" that he could have gone to Sunday school and learned that people who did such things went "to everlasting fire." Huck tries to ask God to help him act morally. He kneels, "but the words wouldn't come" because his "heart warn't right." He was not being honest with God. Huck was promising to stop sinning, but he was unwilling to repent of his biggest sin—helping Jim escape. Huck wanted to promise to "do the right thing" and write to Miss Watson to tell her where Jim was, but deep down both he and God knew that this was a lie. Huck concludes that "you can't pray a lie."

Huck writes a letter to Miss Watson, informing her that Jim is on the Phelps farm near Pikesville, Arkansas, and that she can retrieve him by sending the Phelpses the reward money she had advertised. After writing the letter, Huck feels "washed clean of sin for the first time" in his life, "and I knowed I could pray now." He remembers "how near I come to being lost and going to hell." Nevertheless, Huck quickly decides that he cannot live with himself if he discloses Jim's location. His good heart triumphs over his perverted conscience, and he tears up the letter, declaring, "All right, then, I'll go to hell." Ironically, Miss Watson, ashamed that she had planned to sell Jim "down the river," had died two months earlier and had set him free in her will, so Jim had been a free man during most of his journey with Huck.

Huck thinks he can obtain peace with God only by admitting that God had ordained the institution of slavery. Huck prays for "the moral strength to betray Jim," which he ironically considers an immoral act. He seems to strongly desire to do God's will, even though he believes that aiding Jim's escape is an unpardonable sin.[71] By refusing to follow Southern Protestant teachings about slavery, Huck unwittingly acts as Jesus would have. Huck, the untutored youngster, behaves more morally than the adults who allege that the Bible endorsed slavery.[72]

Huck's decision to violate his conscience, risk condemnation by his community, and potentially suffer eternal damnation expresses Twain's disgust with a Southern "white Christian culture and religion where church bulletin boards advertised slave auctions and where sermons licensed their listeners to hold other human beings in bondage or, following Emancipation, to terrorize them into a captive docility."[73] Christianity is strongly tarnished by its support for slaveholding. *Huckleberry Finn* never mentions the existence of Christian abolitionists.

Further criticizing Christianity, Twain lampoons Silas Phelps and other Southern preachers. Phelps never charged anything for his preaching, "and it was worth it, too." The sermons of other Southern farmer-preachers, Twain insisted, also had no positive impact.

As noted, many factors undermine the characterization of *Huckleberry Finn* as a racist novel. Throughout the book, Jim is portrayed as the hero and the story's moral center. Near the end, Jim, jeopardizing his freedom and his life, emerges from hiding to help the injured Tom Sawyer, who had mistreated him. Bernard DeVoto argues that Jim possessed many of the virtues Twain most admired, including kindness, faithfulness, fortitude, and the willingness to risk his life and sacrifice his freedom for another.[74] Jim, Booker T. Washington contended, exhibited Twain's interest in and sympathy for blacks.[75]

Whereas at the end of *Tom Sawyer*, Huck capitulates to the efforts of some St. Petersburg inhabitants to reform his uncouth ways, at the conclusion of *Huckleberry Finn* he proclaims, "I reckon I got to light out for the Territory" so that Aunt Sally does not "adopt me and sivilize me." Life in "the Territory," beyond the constrictions of religious orthodoxy and traditional social norms, would be freer and presumably more satisfying for Huck.

Huckleberry Finn and Its Critics

Twain's contemporaries both lambasted and lauded *Huckleberry Finn*. Numerous reviewers agreed with Twain's claim that his novel had no motive, moral, or plot (although Twain was being sarcastic), but others insisted that its moral was both plain and salutary. One Boston newspaper called the book "wearisome" and "monotonous," while another labeled it "extraordinarily senseless," concluding that nothing "short of the point of the bayonet" would compel people to read it.[76] Louisa May Alcott, whose seven moralistic children's novels published before 1885 made her America's best-selling author of this genre, allegedly declared that if Twain could not "think of something better to tell our pure-minded lads and lasses he had better stop writing for them."[77] The *New York World* protested that Twain's "cheap and pernicious" novel made good parents look ridiculous. This "piece of careless hackwork" contained "a few good things" amidst "a mass of rubbish." Moreover, Twain confined Huck's spiritual understanding "to an unwavering belief in signs of bad luck." The *Hartford Courant*, by contrast, praised Twain's perceptive analysis of human nature and morality. Literary critic Brander Matthews argued that *Huckleberry Finn*'s portrait of Jim ranked with the best recent depictions of blacks in American fiction. No author had displayed the kindness and generosity of Southern blacks better than Twain.[78]

The novel provoked a firestorm as some libraries declined to purchase it, a decision some newspapers denounced. In defending its choice not to shelve the book, members of the board of the Concord Public Library near Boston criticized its bad grammar and "inelegant expressions" and called the novel frivolous "trash."[79] The *Springfield*

(Massachusetts) *Republican* castigated *Huckleberry Finn* as "trashy and vicious" and contended that Twain had no "sense of propriety."[80] The *Atlanta Constitution* wondered whether critics who "condemned the book as coarse, vulgar and inartistic" had actually read it and countered that the novel "teaches the necessity of manliness and self-sacrifice." The *San Francisco Chronicle* called the decision to exclude Twain's novel on the grounds that it is "flippant and irreverent" absurd. Only those who had no sense of humor would find the book "dreary, flat, stale and unprofitable." It would furnish most readers with "much hearty, wholesome laughter" and contained nothing to offend "a pure-minded woman." Twain was "the Edison of our literature," the newspaper declared; "there is no limit to his inventive genius."[81]

From its publication to the present, *Huckleberry Finn* has often been censured for its "racial slurs" and "belittling racial designations."[82] African American educator John Wallace calls the novel "the most grotesque example of racist trash ever written."[83] It should be burned, Wallace argues, because it depicts blacks as subhuman and less intelligent than whites and had "caused a great deal of trauma for black children." Many critics, however, accept the "irony defense." Black actor Meshach Taylor maintains that *Huckleberry Finn* is a powerful statement against racism, while others contend that the book displays Jim's humanity and heroism and exposes the folly of antebellum Southern views of blacks and slavery.[84]

Conclusion

In 1884–1885, Twain went on a four-month lecture tour with George Washington Cable, an elder, Sunday school superintendent, and choir member at a Presbyterian church in New Orleans who attended two worship services plus Sunday school every sabbath day. Cable's father had owned slaves and fought to preserve the Confederacy, but the son had become a leading critic of racism and Jim Crow laws, and he based his activism on biblical principles.[85] Twain greatly admired Cable's staunch advocacy of black rights in his numerous books, articles, and lectures despite the invective and abuse fellow Southerners showered on him.[86]

Twain, however, despised many of Cable's religious practices. In the early days of their tour, Cable read the Bible aloud to Twain every evening. This, coupled with Cable's unwillingness to travel on Sundays, prompted Twain to dub him a "pious ass" and a "Christ-besprinkled psalm-singing Presbyterian."[87] On the final day of their tour, Twain wrote to William Dean Howells, "You will never know" how loathsome Christianity "can be made until you" observed Cable daily. They got "along happily," but Cable had caused Twain "to hate all religions. He has taught me to abhor & detest the Sabbath-day & hunt up new & troublesome ways to dishonor it."[88] Mocking strict sabbath observance, Twain later wrote, "My ancestors used to roast Catholics and witches," but they would have "blanched with horror" at the mere "thought of breaking the Sabbath."[89]

Some of his correspondence during the 1880s also illuminates Twain's religious mindset In 1883, Bessie Stone of Auburndale, Massachusetts, wrote Twain that Jesus "has just come to several of my friends, and found an entrance; and I, who have not ceased to pray for you these [last] twelve years, am expecting Him to come to you now." In response, Twain wrote on the envelope "D—d fool." Continuing her prayers for Twain's salvation, Stone, in an 1890 letter, alluded to Mary Jane Wilks's vow to Huckleberry Finn that she would pray for him and added, "As you sent that extraordinary passage out into the world, weren't you hiding in it a hint to your small friend that you still cared for my prayers."[90] Twain did not respond.

Twain had a very high regard for Charles Warren Stoddard, his former secretary. In 1885, Stoddard asked Twain to read his spiritual autobiography, *A Broken Heart*, which described his conversion to Catholicism. Stoddard had been a Catholic for ten years, and he and Twain probably had previously discussed their differing religious views. Twain affirmed Stoddard's book, arguing that "there are all sorts of people, & they require all sorts of comforting," and some people found comfort in religion. "Peace of mind is a most valuable thing. The Bible has robbed the majority of the world of it during many centuries," Twain averred, but it had provided serenity for a few individuals. He warned Stoddard not to think that "absolute peace of mind is obtainable only through some form [of] religious belief," declaring, "On the contrary, I have found that as perfect a peace is to be found in absolute unbelief." Twain looked back with "shuddering horror" on the days when he believed in orthodox Christianity, as Stoddard currently did. "Both of us are certain now," Twain declared, "& in certainty there is rest. Let us be content. May your belief & my unbelief never more be shaken in this life!" Stoddard argued persuasively, Twain maintained, but he began with "false premises" and used "false history." Nevertheless, Twain concluded, "I love you just the same!"[91]

This letter testifies to Twain's "need of certainty, and probably also to the terrors he experienced" as a youth "when, like Tom Sawyer, he read God's personal wrath against him into every disturbance of nature." However, if comfort can be "derived from 'absolute unbelief,' he never achieved it."[92] Despite Twain's profession, for the remainder of his life he would search for a belief system that truly provided certainty, comfort, and meaning.

Notes

1. See MTSC, 126–60.
2. "Mark Twain," *Philadelphia Daily Evening Bulletin*, December 8, 1869, https://twain.lib.virginia.edu/onstage/sandrev2.html.
3. Edith Wyatt, "An Inspired Critic," *North American Review* 205 (April 1917), 604 (quotation), 605–6, 615.
4. Paul Carter, "Mark Twain: 'Moralist in Disguise,'" *University of Colorado Studies* 6 (January 1957), 65.
5. *Louisville Courier-Journal*, early 1901, as quoted in MTL, 2:703.
6. Philip Foner, *Mark Twain: Social Critic* (New York: International Publishers, 1975), 400.
7. MTMW, 243.
8. Jeanne Campbell Reesman, "Mark Twain vs. God: The Story of a Relationship," *Mark Twain Journal* 52 (Fall 2014), 120.
9. Mark Twain, letter to the editor of the *New York Daily Tribune*, March 10, 1873, 5.
10. FE, 99.
11. Michael Shelden, "'Man In White' Reveals Twain's Haunted Final Years," https://www.npr.org/transcripts/123336585.
12. CS, 251–2; quotation from 251.
13. Mark Twain, "The Causes of Our Present Municipal Corruption," January 4, 1901, MTS, 370.
14. Mark Twain, "Christian Citizenship," *Colliers Weekly*, September 2, 1905, in *What Is Man and Other Irreverent Essays*, 185.

15. AMT, January 23, 1906, 1:314.
16. AMT, February 1, 1906, 1:320.
17. ILR.
18. "Random Extracts," AMT, 1:212. See also MTN, January 20, 1896, 271.
19. MTA, 1:123.
20. Gregg Camfield, *The Oxford Companion to Mark Twain* (New York: Oxford University Press, 2003), 114.
21. Mark Twain, "Bible Teaching," WM, 73–4; quotations in that order.
22. RV, 182.
23. MMT, 35.
24. MTB, 701; MTL, 1:394.
25. SLC to Francis Wayland, December 24, 1885 and Marshall, both quoted in Edwin McDowell, "From Twain, A Letter on Debt to Blacks," https://www.nytimes.com/1985/03/14/books/from-twain-a-letter-on-debt-to-blacks.html.
26. AMT, July 14, 1908, 3:579.
27. MTSC, 151–2.
28. Mark Twain, *A Family Sketch and Other Private Writings*, ed. Benjamin Griffin (Berkeley: University of California Press, 2001), 20, 26; quotations in that order.
29. Jocelyn Chadwick-Joshua, *The Jim Dilemma: Reading Race in Huckleberry Finn* (Jackson: University Press of Mississippi, 1998), 20.
30. MTB, 599–600, 515.
31. Mark Twain, "A True Story, Repeated Word for Word as I Heard It," *Atlantic Monthly* 34 (November 1874), 591–4; quotation from 592.
32. Shelley Fisher Fishkin, "Mark Twain and Race," in *A Historical Guide to Mark Twain*, ed. Fishkin (New York: Oxford University Press, 2002), 154.
33. PW, 37.
34. Susan K. Harris, "Mark Twain and Gender," in *A Historical Guide*, ed. Fishkin, 187.
35. Martha McCulloch Williams, "In Re 'Pudd'nhead Wilson,'" *Southern Magazine*, February 1894, https://twain.lib.virginia.edu/wilson/pwsouthn.html.
36. *Buffalo Express*, August 26, 1869.
37. Mark Twain, "The United States of Lyncherdom," E&E, 241.
38. "Mark Twain Comes Home Ill," *Chicago Daily Tribune*, December 21, 1909, 5.
39. Mark Twain, "To the Editors of the London Standard," March 12, 1874, LTR, 6:68–70; first two quotations from 68; the remainder from 69.
40. AMT, March 1, 1907, 3:4.
41. Mark Twain, "Open Letter to Commodore Vanderbilt," *Packard Monthly* 1 (March 1869), 89–90.

42. MTAP, 199.

43. Mark Twain, "Mr. Rockefeller's Bible Class," MTE, March 20, 1906, 83–4.

44. AMT, March 20, 1906, 421 (all quotations except "with admirable solemnity" which is from AMT, February 16, 1906, 1:365).

45. Mark Twain, "The Teaching of Jay Gould," February 16, 1906, MTE, 77.

46. AMT, January 28, 1907, 2:388.

47. Harold K. Bush, "'A Moralist in Disguise': Mark Twain and American Religion," in *Historical Guide*, ed. Fishkin, 61.

48. Robert Weir, "Mark Twain and Social Class," in *Historical Guide*, ed. Fishkin, 208 (quotation), 212.

49. RI, 132.

50. Mark Twain, "The Revised Catechism," *New York Tribune*, September 27, 1871.

51. Mark Twain, "Andrew Carnegie," December 2, 1907, MTE, 50.

52. Twain, "Commodore Vanderbilt," 90.

53. Mark Twain, "Battle Hymn of the Republic (Brought Down to Date)," http://www.bachlund.org/The_Battle_Hymn_of_the_Republic_Updated.htm.

54. Mark Twain, "What Paul Bourget Thinks of Us," *North American Review* 160 (January 1895), 57.

55. SLC to JHT, March 14, 1905, MTL, 2:770.

56. MTN, July 4, 1898, 343; TS, 273.

57. MTAP, 195–9; quotation from 196.

58. Mark Twain, "The $30,000 Bequest" (1904), *CSS*, 522.

59. Elizabeth McMahan, "Finance and Fantasy as Destroyers in Twain's 'The $30,000 Bequest,'" *Mark Twain Journal* 21 (Summer 1982), 26.

60. Mark Twain, "Concerning the Jews," in *The Man That Corrupted Hadleyburg and Other Essays and Stories* (New York: Collier, 1917), 152.

61. Paul Carter, "Mark Twain and the American Labor Movement," *New England Quarterly* 30 (September 1957), 352–8.

62. Quoted in Milton Rugoff, *The Beechers* (New York: Harper, 1981), 559.

63. MTB, 1557.

64. Jeffrey Holland, "Soul-Butter and Hogwash: Mark Twain and Frontier Religion," March 8, 1977, https://speeches.byu.edu/talks/jeffrey-r-holland/soul-butter-hogwash-mark-twain-frontier-religion/.

65. Two great writers who expressed this view were English novelist and historian Walter Besant, quoted in "Mark Twain," *Baltimore American*, April 22, 1910, https://twain.lib.virginia.edu/sc_as_mt/mtobit1.html, and American journalist H. L. Mencken, "The Burden of Humor," *The Smart Set* 38 (February 1913), 151–4.

66. Daniel Pawley, "The Hound of Hannibal," *Christianity Today*, November 8, 1985, https://www.christianitytoday.com/ct/1985/november-8/books.html.

67. Stanley Brodwin, "Mark Twain in the Pulpit: The Theological Comedy of *Huckleberry Finn*," in *One Hundred Years of Huckleberry Finn: The Boy, His Book, and American Culture*, ed. Robert Sattlemeyer and J. Donald Crowley (Columbia: University of Missouri Press, 1985), 379 (quotation), 385.

68. William Dean Howells, "Mark Twain: An Inquiry," *North American Review* 172 (February 1901), 311.

69. Reesman, "Mark Twain vs. God," 123, 126; quotations in that order. See also Jeanne Campbell Reesman, "Bad Fathering in Huckleberry Finn," in *The Turn Around Religion in America: Literature, Culture, and the Work of Sacvan Bercovitch*, ed. Nan Goodman and Michael Kramer (New York: Rutgers Transactions Press, 2011), 157–82.

70. RV, 183.

71. Dwayne Eutsey, "'Be Never Afraid of Doubt': Mark Twain, Liberal Religion, and Huck Finn," October 7, 2018, http://uufeaston.org/services/never-afraid-doubt-mark-twain-liberal-religion-huck-finn/.

72. Edward Wagenknecht, *Cavalcade of the American Novel* (New York: Henry Holt, 1952), 124.

73. CAR, 138.

74. Bernard DeVoto, *Mark Twain at Work* (Cambridge, MA: Harvard University Press, 1942), 96.

75. "Tributes to Mark Twain," *North American Review* 191 (June 1910), 829.

76. *Boston Daily Advertiser*, March 12, 1885, https://twain.lib.virginia.edu/huckfinn/bosdail3.html; *Boston Evening Traveler*, March 5, 1885, https://twain.lib.virginia.edu/huckfinn/bosttrav.html.

77. Quoted in Frank Luther Mott, *Golden Multitudes: The Story of Best Sellers in the United States* (New York: Bowker, 1966), 249.

78. *New York World*, March 2, 1885, https://twain.lib.virginia.edu/huckfinn/nyworld.html; *Hartford Courant*, February 20, 1885, https://twain.lib.virginia.edu/huckfinn/harcour2.html; Brander Matthews, *Saturday Review*, January 31, 1885, https://twain.lib.virginia.edu/huckfinn/satrev.html.

79. "'Huckleberry Finn' in Concord," *New York Herald*, March 18, 1885, https://twain.lib.virginia.edu/huckfinn/nyherald.html.

80. As quoted in *The Critic: A Literary Weekly, Critical and Eclectic*, March 28, 1885, https://twain.lib.virginia.edu/huckfinn/concordcon.html.

81. "'Huckleberry Finn' and His Critics," *Atlanta Constitution*, May 26, 1885, https://twain.lib.virginia.edu/huckfinn/atlanta.html; *San Francisco Chronicle*, March 29, 1885, https://twain.lib.virginia.edu/huckfinn/sfchron2.html; *San Francisco Chronicle*, March 15, 1885, https://twain.lib.virginia.edu/huckfinn/sfchron.html.

82. Leonard Buder, "'Huck Finn' Barred as Textbook by City," *New York Times*, September 12, 1957, 29, quoting an NAACP spokesperson.

83. John Wallace, "The Case Against Huck Finn," in *Satire or Evasion? Black Perspectives on Huckleberry Finn*, ed. James Leonard, Thomas Tenney, and Thadious Davis (Durham, NC: Duke University Press, 1992), 16.

84. Quotations from E. R. Shipp, "A Century Later, Huck's Still Stirring Up Trouble," *New York Times*, February 4, 1985, A8. See also William Styron, "Huck, Continued," *New Yorker*, https://www.newyorker.com/maga zine/1995/06/26/huck-continued-3; and Jonathan Arac, *Huckleberry Finn as Idol and Target: The Functions of Criticism in Our Time* (Madison: University of Wisconsin Press, 1997). Shelley Fisher Fishkin defends the book against charges of racism in *Lighting Out for the Territory: Reflections on Mark Twain and American Culture* (New York: Oxford University Press, 1997).

85. E.g. George Washington Cable, "The Freedman's Case in Equity," *Century Magazine* 29 (January 1885), 409–18.

86. E.g. Mark Twain, "Introducing George W. Cable," April 4, 1883, MTS, 176.

87. Quoted in Edward Tinker, "Cable and the Creoles," *American Literature* 5 (January 1934), 322.

88. SLC to WDH, February 27, 1885, MTL, 2:520.

89. Mark Twain, "O'Shah," E&E, 58.

90. Bessie Stone to SLC, February 13, 1883, MTP; Stone to SLC, November 30(?), 1890, AMT, 2:609.

91. SLC to Charles Stoddard, June 1, 1885, in Seymour Gross, "Mark Twain on the Serenity of Unbelief: An Unpublished Letter to Charles Warren Stoddard," *Huntington Library Quarterly* 22 (May 1959), 161–2.

92. MTMW, 179.

6

The 1890s

A Troubled Time

The 1890s were a difficult decade for the Clemenses as they dealt with the death of their beloved daughter Susy at age twenty-four and financial struggles that brought them near bankruptcy and led Twain to undertake a world lecture tour in 1895–1896 to pay off their debts. More positively, by the mid-1890s, Twain was a global celebrity whose opinions were solicited on a wide variety of matters and who enjoyed friendships with numerous political, business, and literary luminaries.[1]

Twain had previously spoofed religious tracts, pompous preachers and grandstanders, and pretentious moralizing, but during the 1890s, his criticism of Christianity became harsher. In 1896, however, Twain published his most enigmatic book: *Personal Recollections of Joan of Arc*, a glowing portrait of the fifteenth-century French warrior-saint who played a pivotal role in liberating France from long-standing British domination but was captured and burned at the stake for her alleged heresy. Twain's celebration of her exploits and faith appeared to conflict with his personal religious beliefs and his increasingly acrimonious attacks on Christianity. Twain's view of the Bible and God also highlights this contrast.

Troubles, Tragedy, and a World Tour

The Clemenses experienced substantial stress during the 1890s. The year 1890 was especially traumatic. The family faced onerous financial problems; Twain greatly missed his favorite daughter Susy when she began college at Bryn Mawr in Philadelphia; Twain's mother Jane died in October, and Livy's mother died the next month.

A despondent Twain sketched a story about a desolate Tom Sawyer and Huck Finn dying together at age sixty, seeing their lives as failures.[2] The next year, Twain's publishing company sank deeper into debt; a homesick and distraught Susy left college midway through her second semester; Twain suffered from chronic back pain and rheumatism in his arm; Livy's heart problems intensified; and their financial woes prompted the Clemenses to spend most of the next nine years in Europe. The family initially stayed for five weeks in Aix-les-Bains, Switzerland, where the parents both soaked in sulfuric baths every day—Livy to help her heart condition and alleviate her head-aches and Twain to help his right arm, which ached from his constant writing. During the next nine years, the Clemenses would also live in Berlin, Bad Nauheim, Florence, Vienna, London, and other European locales.

Twain had a substantial income from the royalties from his books, writing articles for popular magazines, lecturing, and owning a publishing house, but he made unwise investments that caused his family financial misfortune. On a trip from Europe to the United States in 1893, Twain met Henry Rogers, who would help him eventually pay off his debts and achieve financial stability. In 1894, however, he teetered on the edge of bankruptcy when the company manufacturing the Paige typesetter, in which Twain, before he met Rogers, had invested as much as $300,000, was dissolved. As he contemplated a year-long world lecture tour in 1895, Twain, who was nearly sixty, described himself as "almost an old man, with ill health, carbuncles, bronchitis and rheumatism."[3] Because of his poor health, Twain was very reluctant to undertake a global tour, but he could think of no other way to pay off his $100,000 debt.

Twain's tour, which began on July 15, 1895, started splendidly. After giving twenty-three lectures in twenty-two American and Canadian cities, he declared that he had not "had a blue day" in a month.[4] Following his North American performances, Twain, Livy, and their middle daughter Clara spent eight weeks in Australia, six in New Zealand, eight in India, and seven in South Africa, as he gave more than a hundred lectures to large, enthusiastic, appreciative audiences. When his tour ended on July 15, 1896, Twain was exhausted but had earned enough money to pay off about half his debts.[5] His travels exposed him to a variety of religious groups, prompting him to ask additional questions about religious issues.

Soon after the tour ended, tragedy struck. The three Clemenses were resting in England and looking forward to the arrival of Susy and their youngest daughter Jean. A telegram in early August informed them, however, that Susy was ill. A second telegram indicated that she would recover, so Twain stayed in England while Livy sailed home to be with their daughter. After several days of delirium, Susy died of spinal meningitis on August 18, while Livy was still en route to Hartford. Twain's decision not to return to America was one of the numerous ones he greatly regretted for the remainder of his life.

Susy's death was a crushing blow to both her parents. She was their "favored daughter, their most prized production." Her death, Harold Bush, Jr. contends, was "the crucial event of the final fourteen years of Twain's life"; it deeply affected him as a parent, an author, and a public figure. Housekeeper Katy Leary claimed that Livy "never really got over losing Susy," and Clara observed that her father not only had "to bear his own sorrow but the moving sight of Mother's grief."[6]

To commemorate Susy's death, Twain wrote "In Memoriam" in August 1897, which was published in *Harper's Monthly* in November. On the second anniversary of her death, he penned another tribute, titled "Broken Idols." Both pieces express Twain's profound sense of loss. About the same time Twain composed "In Memoriam," he also wrote a short diatribe against God called "In My Bitterness." God had taken Susy, Twain complained, "to drive one more knife into my heart." God "never does a kindness. When he seems to do one," he is setting a trap. If "He gives riches," Twain avowed, it is merely "to quadruple the bitterness of the poverty He has planned for you. He gives you a healthy body," but later God "rotted it with disease and made it a hell of pains." God "gives you a wife and children whom you adore," Twain cried, so that by inflicting misery on them, "He may tear the palpitating heart out of your breast and slap you in the face with it." A month later, however, Twain insisted that he "had been out of his right mind when he expressed those blasphemous feelings."[7]

About the same time, though, Twain protested to Livy that "as a reward" for taking a "lecture trip around the world" to maintain their honor by paying off debts that "were not even of my own making," while he suffered from carbuncles, bronchitis, rheumatism, and other health problems, "we were robbed of our greatest treasure, our lovely Susy in the midst of her blooming talents and personal graces. You want me to believe" that "a judicious, a charitable God" oversees this world, he continued; "Why, I could run it better myself." Expressing his grief, Twain declares in "Broken Idols," "This child was all the world to me." Her "wonder-working intellect," he laments, has been quenched; "The sun that lit my life went out."[8]

Bush argues that Susy's death inspired Twain to write *A Dog's Tale* (1903), *What Is Man?* (1906), *Christian Science* (1907), and the *Mysterious Stranger Manuscripts* (written between 1897 and 1908 but not published until 1969), all of which challenge conventional Christian beliefs. Her death also increased Twain's compassion for the downtrodden, "exacerbated Twain's sense of moral outrage," and contributed to his attacks on imperialism and support for social reforms.[9]

Twain's growing religious skepticism and disillusionment are evident in a May 1899 letter he sent to William Dean Howells after speaking with Austrian Baroness Amelie von Langenau at a tea in Vienna. "She has religious beliefs & feelings," Twain stated, "& I have none)." A description of a Wagner opera he attended in Nuremberg, Germany in 1891 probably captured Twain's reaction when he occasionally attended church services during the 1890s: "I feel like the one blind man where all others see; the one groping savage in the college of the learned," and "a heretic in heaven."[10]

Personal Recollections of Joan of Arc

"I like *Joan of Arc* best of all my books," Twain declared in 1908, "& it *is* the best."[11] Moreover, he insisted, producing it furnished "seven times the pleasure afforded" by any of his other novels. *Joan of Arc* required twelve years to research and two years to write, whereas his other books required no preparation. He was working arduously to pay off his debts and recognized that this book might have limited sales, "but that is nothing—it's written for love & not for lucre."[12]

Imagine a question on a standardized test: which of Mark Twain's novels is least like the others? The answer is indisputably *Joan of Arc*. "Twain's obsession with Joan of Arc," writes Daniel Crown, is "among the most baffling...enigmas in American literature." In his account of Joan, Twain abandons satire and humor and appears to contradict his stated views of Christianity, the Catholic Church, the likelihood of miracles, and the dangers of undiscerning patriotism. By the time Twain penned *Recollections*, Susan K. Harris asserts, "he's not a believer. He is anti-Catholic, and he doesn't like the French." Writing a book about a French Catholic martyr therefore "doesn't make a lot of sense."[13] Twain spent countless hours working on a narrative about a teenage woman who claimed to regularly communicate with God, profusely praising her character and exploits and saying not a single disparaging word about her.

Twain first encountered the story of Joan of Arc at age thirteen, when a random page of a biography describing her persecution in an English prison blew across his path. In an 1869 letter, Twain compared Livy's work with Joan of Arc's heroic efforts. In an 1872 speech in London, Twain expressed his admiration for the French martyr, asking, "Who was more patriotic than Joan of Arc? Who was braver? Who has given us a grander instance of self-sacrificing devotion?"[14]

Twain's book, the most historical of all his novels, is based on nine biographies (eight of which he lists in his preface to verify the veracity of his narrative), most notably Jules Michelet's *Jeanne D'Arc* (1858), and extensive archival research. None of his previous works required so much thinking, weighing, planning, or "painstaking execution."[15]

Twain wrote *Joan of Arc* from 1893 and 1895, while dealing with major financial problems and weighty personal disappointments. Although Twain questioned many aspects of Christian orthodoxy during this time, his historical novel clearly displays his "continued spiritual sensibility" as well as his "outrage toward social injustice" that was so prevalent during his later years. Twain was especially attracted to Joan because she opposed two institutions that had long oppressed common people—the crown and the church. He seems to accept Joan's resilient faith in God, sterling character, numerous miracles, and frequent prophecies as genuine.[16] Twain presents positively Joan's claims that God spoke to her, that the Bible was worth more than all the books her examiners cited, and that God would grant France victory over England.

Clearly influenced by his admiration for Livy and Susy, Twain depicts Joan in hagiographic style. In his reverential account, Joan is a faultless, sensitive, inspiring warrior and a defender of the true faith.

In her gallant battle to topple a decrepit political, social, and religious order, Joan is a "transcendent figure" who possesses "Huck Finn's purity of heart and Jim's intuitive religious faith," incarnating youth, purity, and power.[17]

During the fifteenth century, near the end of the Hundred Years' War when England controlled most of France, Joan of Arc miraculously arose to liberate the nation. The daughter of a tenant farmer, Jacques d'Arc, and his pious wife Isabelle, who lived in a small village in northeastern France, Joan had an "ideally perfect" character, loftier than that of "any other mere mortal." She stood, Twain maintained, as a sharp contrast to her era: she was honest when lying was common; she focused on weighty issues while others thought only about petty matters; she was merciful when "cruelty was the rule," honorable while dishonesty reigned, and courageous when fear paralyzed her nation; she was "spotlessly pure in mind and body" when French political officials were degenerate and the highest church leaders engaged in "unimaginable treacheries, butcheries, and beastialities [sic]"; and she was "a rock of convictions" when others "believed in nothing and scoffed at all things."

Joan's accomplishments, Twain asserted, were the most impressive in recorded history considering the conditions in which they occurred, the obstacles she confronted, and the means she possessed. An uneducated, unknown village teenager, inspired by angelic visions and voices, rescued "a great nation lying in chains, helpless and hopeless under alien domination, its treasury bankrupt, its soldiers disheartened," and its dauphin cowed and ready to flee the country. "France was a wreck, a ruin, a desolation." "Half of it belonged to England," while "the other half belonged to nobody." To liberate France, Joan conducted the "most amazing campaign" in history. In a mere seven weeks, Joan ended the siege of Orléans and led France to 30 battlefield victories; in many cases, British troops surrendered rather than fight against a young woman who appeared to have either a mandate from God or satanic assistance. She turned "the tide of the Hundred Years' War," fatally damaged England's power in France, and earned the "title of DELIVERER OF FRANCE." And as a reward for her exploits, the most innocent, lovely, and adorable person in history was burned at the stake. According to Twain's eighty-two-year-old narrator, a fictionalized version of Joan's page Louis de Contes, only

Jesus was more noble than her. Joan's deep faith "made her inwardly content and joyous."

Joan insisted that the archangel Michael, the "lord of the armies of heaven," had appeared to her many times and had chosen her to free France from English bondage and crown Charles VII as king. She was convinced that God would accomplish this even though France's situation seemed bleak: its dauphin was surrounded by fools and lived "in inglorious idleness and poverty" possessing no authority anywhere, no money, and not a single regiment of soldiers. Joan convinced the dauphin that she had been sent by God, persuaded the illustrious doctors of the University of Poitiers that her supernatural help came from heaven rather than hell, was named the leader of the French army, won a series of victories over the British, and facilitated Charles VII's coronation at Rheims. Joan had no military training or experience, but she had great courage, endurance, and conviction and a remarkable ability to inspire the French troops. The French generals developed a deep reverence for Joan, believing that she was "endowed with a mysterious supernatural" gift that enabled her to "blow the breath of life and valor into the dead corpses of cowed armies and turn them into heroes." Whereas French soldiers "were full of courage, enthusiasm, and zeal," their English counterparts were terrified and demoralized by their belief that Joan "was in league with Satan" and, in several cases, fled in panic without fighting.

Joan of Arc contains little of the jesting or sarcasm characteristic of Twain's other works, but he does ridicule the theological nitpicking of the priests and monks at Poitiers who examine Joan's suitability to serve as France's chief military leader. Instead of using a military commission to determine Joan's fitness to vanquish the English, a group of "holy hair-splitters and phrase-mongers" was assigned to evaluate her piety and doctrine. After Joan was harried and pestered with arguments, objections, and "other windy and wordy trivialities," she protested that the matters the inquisitors were "puttering over are of no consequence!"

To defeat the British, Joan morally cleansed the French army, created an orderly camp, and evangelized. She required all her soldiers to confess their sins before a priest and attend worship services twice daily, and she banned gambling, profanity, and prostitutes. Perhaps describing his own spiritual struggle, Twain notes that

"Joan worked earnestly and tirelessly to bring" Étienne de Vignolles, better known as La Hire, "to God—to rescue him from the bondage of sin—to breathe into his stormy heart the serenity and peace of religion." When she implored La Hire to pray; he said that "he would go through the fire for her" but asked her not to require him to pray; eventually, though, he relented.

Twain stresses Joan's "loving and merciful nature" and contrasts her magnanimity with what he considered the Old Testament God's harsh insistence that the Israelites exterminate their enemies. She offered her opponents the opportunity to surrender and peacefully retreat and always strove to save her enemies' lives.

After winning a series of battles en route to trying to capture Paris, Joan was wounded and taken prisoner by the Duke of Burgundy. Despite all she had done for him, Charles VII refused to ransom her, and the duke eventually sold the savior of France to her enemies, the British. French bishop Pierre Cauchon, who was working for the British, arranged four trials, seeking to prove that Joan was a heretic sent by Satan. Joan had no legal counsel, friends, or witnesses to testify on her behalf. Twain portrays Joan's eloquence, acumen, ingenuity, and courage during these interrogations as powerfully exhibiting her character and convictions, as did her miracles and victories over the English. Joan resisted various efforts to trick or trap her and continued to assert, "I have done nothing but by revelation." "I believe the Christian faith and that God has redeemed us from the fires of hell," she declared, and "that God speaks to me." When Cauchon asked Joan, "Are you in a state of Grace?" she seemed to have no good way to respond, because the Catholic Church taught that people could not know whether they were or not. Joan's "immortal answer" enabled her to escape this formidable snare: "If I be not in a state of Grace, I pray God place me in it; if I be in it, I pray God keep me so." Some of her judges, Twain maintained, were softened by Joan's fortitude, piety, purity, intelligence, and character.

Cauchon tried to set another trap by asking Joan, "Will you submit to the determination of the Church all your words and deeds?" Saying yes would put her mission on trial; saying no could expose her to a charge of heresy. Joan replied shrewdly that "she loved the Church and was ready to support the Christian faith with all her strength," but that her mission "must be judged by God alone" who had commanded her to undertake specific tasks.

For Joan's third trial, Cauchon selected twelve judges to examine sixty-six charges against her. She was accused of being "a sorceress, a false prophet, an invoker and companion of evil spirits, a dealer in magic," a "schismatic," an "apostate, a blasphemer of God," and a scandalous, seditious, "disturber of the peace" who irreverently dressed as a man and improperly assumed a soldier's vocation. When this trial, like its two predecessors, ended with no verdict, a commission reduced the charges to twelve. Joan was accused of asserting that she had found salvation, refusing to submit to the church, and claiming to have never sinned. When Joan became sick, her enemies feared that she might die without being condemned by the church. If that occurred, the pity and the love of the French people would turn her suffering and death "into a holy martyrdom" and she would become an even "mightier power in France dead than she had been when alive." Fortunately for her enemies, Joan recovered.

Cauchon claimed that at her four trials Joan had declined to answer some questions and had lied in responding to others. If she did not submit to the church, he warned, she would be burned at the stake. Joan's continual bafflement of the "cunningest schemes" of France's master intellects, Twain argued, displayed her greatness. She defeated their cleverest plans, avoided their secret traps and pitfalls, "repelled their assaults," and remained "true to her faith and her ideals," defying torture, the stake, and the threat of "eternal death and the pains of hell."

Despite her ingenious responses, a jury of University of Paris theological faculty found Joan guilty of heresy, sorcery, and the other ten counts; unless she renounced her errors, she would be remanded to the secular government to be punished. The faculty lauded Cauchon for hunting down a woman "whose venom had infected the faithful of the whole West." Joan's voices told her, "Submit to whatever comes; do not grieve for your martyrdom; from it you will ascend into the Kingdom of Paradise." "The knowledge that I shall be saved," she declared, "is a great treasure."

In a passage where Twain unsheathes his biting irony, his narrator declares, describing Joan's situation, "Think of being abandoned by the Church!—that august Power" that controlled "the fate of the human race." It had authority "over millions that live and over the billions that wait trembling in purgatory for ransom or doom"; its "smile opens the gates of heaven to you," whereas its "frown delivers you to the fires of everlasting hell."

Her fear of the fire prompted Joan to sign a paper she did not properly understand, confessing that she was "a sorceress, a dealer with devils, a liar, a blasphemer of God and His angels, a lover of blood, [and] a promoter of sedition" commissioned by Satan. The "Deliverer of France," however, quickly recanted her confession and "lay down her life for the country she loved" and the king who had abandoned her. Wearing a miter-shaped cap stating that she was a heretic, apostate, and idolator, Joan went to her martyrdom at peace with God and with "endearing words and loving prayers" for the contemptible king "she had crowned and the nation of ingrates she had saved." Throughout his novel, Twain praises Joan's keen mind and her ability to outwit her male ecclesiastical opponents. Nevertheless, he portrays her as fulfilling a very conventional female role by sacrificing her life for God, the king, and the people of France.[18]

Twain's account ends with Joan's rehabilitation by Pope Callixtus III in 1456. Twenty-five years after Joan's execution, the pope assembled an ecclesiastical court that reexamined her case and cleared "her illustrious name from every spot and stain." Twain concludes with another paean to the greatness of "that sublime personality" who alone in profane history engaged in no "self-seeking, self-interest, [or] personal ambition."

Many American Catholics were delighted by Twain's depiction of Joan. Reviewing *Joan of Arc* in *America*, Michael Kenny asserted that Twain's "admiration of the Maid is absolute." Even his depiction of the religious aspects of her character was "warm." Similarly, Father Daniel Hudson, who had decried *A Connecticut Yankee* as "an insult to Catholics" and "irreverent, vulgar, and stupid," praised Twain for portraying Joan's "beauty of character" more powerfully and sympathetically than other authors writing in English."[19]

Twain was unhappy with suffragists' appropriation of Joan as a symbol of female empowerment as they displayed her image on buttons, posters, and banners in the early twentieth century. Attacking these depictions in a 1904 essay in *Harper's Magazine*, Twain called Joan "the Wonder of the Ages," given her origin, early life, and sex.

The incredible talent of William Shakespeare, Napoleon, Richard Wagner, or Thomas Edison, Twain argued, was only part of their story; their training, the knowledge gained by reading and studying, and the recognition they received all enabled their talent to develop. Joan, by contrast, had none of these benefits. She was born with military genius, incomparable fortitude, a lawyer's aptitude for detecting "cunning and treacherous" traps, and a judge's ability to sort and weigh evidence. But how she managed to apply these talents without "instruction, study, years of practice and the help of making a thousand mistakes" was incomprehensible.[20]

Twain also reemphasized Joan's spirituality, which most suffragists ignored. The deeply religious woman believed that she spoke daily with angels; "they counseled her, comforted and heartened her, and brought commands to her directly from God. She had a childlike faith in the heavenly origin of her apparitions and her Voices," which the threat of death could not destroy. Moreover, Joan was the only prophet who daringly specified the precise nature of future events and the time and place when they would occur; Twain listed numerous instances of her fulfilled prophecies.[21]

Joan was beatified by Pope Pius X in 1909, formally acknowledging that she was in heaven. In 1920, as American women finally gained the right to vote, the Catholic Church canonized Joan, designating her a saint. Her fascinating story has been portrayed in dozens of books, movies, and plays. Movies about her include a critically acclaimed 1928 French silent production, a 1948 film starring celebrated actress Ingrid Bergman as Joan, a 1962 French movie focusing on Joan's trial, a 1999 film by the renowned French director and producer Luc Besson, and a 2019 French movie directed by Bruno Dumont. Arguably, no other assessment of the Maid of Orleans is as surprising, sympathetic, or sanguine as Twain's.

Twain and the Bible

While extolling Joan, Twain during the 1890s increasingly challenged the authenticity, reliability, and morality of the Bible. In his published works, Twain typically attacked how people used and interpreted the Bible rather than its actual content, but privately he often raged against various doctrines and stories.

From the founding of Plymouth in 1620 to the Civil War, the Bible significantly shaped all aspects of American life. During the Gilded Age, the challenges of Darwinism and critical and literary study of Scripture, trends in graduate education, and increasing industrialization, immigration, urbanization, and poverty combined to produce widespread questioning of the Bible's divine authorship and authority. "Debate over the character of the Bible and how best to study, understand, and interpret the scriptures moved to center stage among all major Christian and Jewish groups." Theological liberals maintained that the Bible should not be interpreted literally but rather on the basis of the continually progressing consciousness of the Christian community.[22] Some liberals denied that the Bible was infallible or inerrant, leading to celebrated heresy trials, most notably those of Presbyterians David Swing, Charles Briggs, Henry Preserved Smith, and Arthur McGiffert. These developments prompted significant numbers of Americans to deny the Bible's divine inspiration and miracles while still affirming its basic moral principles and the exemplary character and ethical teachings of Jesus. For numerous Americans, more technical, skeptical, and allegedly scholarly ways of interpreting the Bible were replacing a more devotional reading of Holy Writ.[23]

Many scientists, skeptics such as Robert Ingersoll, and even some biblical scholars and theologians argued that the Bible was not a divinely revealed text and that people had evolved from animals instead of being directly created by God. However, Christianity, both in its evangelical and liberal forms, continued to strongly influence American life through the revivals of Dwight Moody and other evangelists, the rise of the Social Gospel and the Holiness movements, and the flourishing of foreign missions, especially through the work of the Student Volunteer Movement. Theological conservatives, led by B. B. Warfield and his colleagues at Princeton Seminary, staunchly defended God's authorship of Scripture. At many colleges and universities, Christian principles and values still had a powerful influence. Seminary professors penned impressive works on the Bible, theology, and church history, and countless churches thrived. American society continued to pay homage to Christianity even though some intellectuals had begun to question or reject fundamental biblical doctrines. The Bible remained the great textbook for Western culture and literature; many Gilded Age Americans knew it better than any other book.

The Bible's importance and impact on American culture, as well as his own socialization and interests, led Twain to employ biblical material extensively in his writing. His letters, essays, and fictional works abound with religious imagery and biblical quotations and allusions. Louis Budd points out that Twain's collected works cite the Bible more than any other literary work—about three thousand times overall. Scriptural motifs, ideas, and images inspired and helped shape many of his novels and short stories.[24] Dozens of his stories and sketches are based on biblical characters and episodes.

By his mid-teens, Twain had read the entire Bible. Scripture was deeply ingrained into his mind as a child and significantly affected his thinking, writing, social activism, and ethical views. Throughout his life, he expressed many different views of the Bible, carrying on what William Phipps calls "a lover's quarrel" with it. Twain, Stanley Brodwin adds, experienced great "religious anguish and intellectual conflict with the Bible."[25] Twain was alternately intrigued, inspired, and infuriated by Holy Writ. He frequently praised its prose and stirring stories while often (usually privately) denying its divine inspiration and criticizing its doctrines. The Bible, Twain asserted, was "gemmed with beautiful passages." He parodied, derided, and reviled Scripture (although often through characters in his stories rather than his own voice), but at other times he treated it respectfully. Twain testified that he had been "taught to revere the Scriptures, and that reverence is pretty firmly grounded."[26] Expressing his ambivalence, Twain wrote late in life that the Bible "is full of interest. It has noble poetry; and some clever fables; and some blood-drenched history; and some good morals; and a wealth of obscenity; and upwards of a thousand lies."[27]

Twain admired the Bible's simplicity of language, "felicity of expression," and pathos, along with its authors' ability to sink out of sight and allow their narratives to "stand out alone."[28] He also appreciated the Bible's blunt honesty about the human condition.[29] In 1867, visiting the American Bible Society's Bible House in New York City, Twain effused that the organization printed more than one million Bibles there each year in fifty different languages to further Christian missions around the world. New York, he declared, had "no institution she has more reason to be proud of than this colossal Bible Association."[30]

The three biblical stories Twain cited most often in his published works and letters were the Prodigal Son; Adam, Eve, and the fall; and Noah and the flood. In his early thirties, Twain often saw himself as a prodigal son striving to abandon his sinful ways, return home, and experience the Father's affection. In his letters to Mary Fairbanks, Twain called himself an "improving Prodigal," a "Reformed Prodigal," and a "Returning Prodigal." In his later years, he more often viewed himself "as another Adam exiled from Paradise."[31]

In his published works, Twain discusses Adam more than any other biblical figure, almost twice as often as Jesus (76 to 44 times).[32] He referred to Adam in an ironic and humorous way in such works as "Tomb of Adam," "Extracts from Adam's Diary," and *Captain Stormfield's Visit to Heaven.* Allison Ensor claims that Twain wrote more about Adam, Eden, and the fall than any other major American writer. For Twain, Adam's disobedience brought sin, shame, suffering, sorrow, death, hardship in labor, the loss of innocence and joy, and the beginning of "moral sense" that had "corrupted human nature under the guise of elevating it."[33] Twain challenged the conventional view that Adam and Eve had the freedom to choose right or wrong. Because of his nature and inexperience, Adam could not have refrained from eating the apple.[34] Twain protested that God created a weak Adam instead of a strong one, "then laid a trap for him which He foreknew he would fall into." Then God punished Adam even though "He was solely responsible for Adam's crime."[35] Twain contended in "That Day in Eden" that God's command to Adam and Eve not to eat from the tree of the knowledge of good and evil (Gen. 2:16–17) was foolish; because they could not understand this command, they could not reasonably be expected to obey it. Punishing Adam and Eve for disobedience was unfair, and punishing all humanity for their act was even more unjust.[36] Twain wished that Martin Luther and Joan of Arc had been substituted for Adam and Eve. "By neither sugary persuasions nor by hellfire could Satan have beguiled them to eat the apple."[37]

Some of Twain's stories feature the psychology underlying "the Eden myth." For example, in the memorable episode where Tom Sawyer entices his friends to whitewash a fence, Tom employs "a great law of human action": to make people covet a thing, "it is only necessary to make the thing difficult to attain." Flashing his remarkable wit, Twain decried Adam's foolishness: everything was going his way, and he had gained "the love of the best-looking girl in the neighborhood," but he still ate the "miserable little apple." Why? "Because it was forbidden. It would have been better for us... if the *serpent* had been forbidden."[38]

Twain also argued that if God was the ultimate author of the Bible, he had chosen a very ineffective way to communicate with humanity. God had ensured that the sun and the moon could "be depended upon to do their appointed work every day and every night," and he had no difficulty proving many other things beyond doubt. But when God wanted to prove that people would have an afterlife, he confronted a problem his alleged omnipotence could not solve. This message was infinitely more important than all the world's other messages combined, Twain asserted, but God could not devise a better medium than "a book written in two languages" to convey this truth to humanity. Over the centuries, the Bible's message had changed so much that it had become "wholly unintelligible." It was impossible to ever translate the scriptures "with perfect clearness into any one of the [world's] thousand tongues."[39]

In 1878, Twain told Joseph Twichell, "I don't believe one word of your Bible was inspired by God any more than any other book. I believe it is entirely the work of man from beginning to end." The issues of "eternity and the true conception of God," he added, are bigger than what is "contained in that book."[40] By the 1880s, Twain had privately repudiated the Bible's divine authorship, affirming that men had written both the Old and New testaments; God had not inspired or even approved a single line in Scripture,[41] nor had he sent messages to humanity through any means. Twain later insisted that the Bible "was not even written by remarkably capable *men*" and that it was the most "damnatory biography" in print.[42] Ron Powers contends that Twain agreed with Thomas Paine that "it is impossible to conceive a story more derogatory to the Almighty, more inconsistent with his wisdom, [and] more contradictory to his power" than the Bible.[43] "It ain't those parts of the Bible that I can't understand that bother me," Twain declared, "it is the parts that I do understand."[44] Albert Bigelow Paine argued that in his final decades Twain viewed

Scripture as "a mass of fables and traditions, mere mythology."[45] Moreover, the Bible was not original; it was based on the writings of other ancient books.[46]

Twain denounced both the Bible's harmful influence and its frequent misuse.[47] He deprecated some of its teaching, especially its condoning of slavery and the execution of alleged witches and its endorsement of the slaughter of non-Israelites. Twain also repeatedly complained that people misquoted the Bible or ignored the context of biblical passages. In a 1905 essay, Twain censured Belgium's King Leopold II for using Scripture to justify imperialism in the Belgian Congo. In other essays, he criticized Christians' failure to reject the Bible's teaching on slavery, infant damnation, and hell. Many Christians, he protested, had beaten the slaves' "handful of humane defenders with Bible texts." "Thick-headed" Bible commentators and "stupid preachers and teachers," Twain averred, did "more damage to religion than sensible, cool-brained clergyman" could effectively counter.[48]

Twain also challenged the accuracy of numerous biblical accounts, including that of Noah and the flood. He argued that the ark could have housed only a small fraction of the 146,000 species of birds, beasts, and freshwater creatures and the two million varieties of insects present in the contemporary world.[49] He faulted God for not destroying grasshoppers and locusts in the flood and for allowing pests and cholera germs into the ark. God was either "stupid or malevolent—or else the Bible is wrong."[50] Toward the end of his life, Twain concluded that "Noah's flood never happened, and couldn't have happened." He pointed out that the flood story appears in numerous mythologies including the *Gilgamesh Epic*.[51]

In addition, Twain sometimes censured the Bible as obscene. He resented "the faithful guardians" of his youth who "compelled me to read an unexpurgated Bible through before I was 15 years old." By its depiction of violence, cruelty, and sexuality, the Bible had soiled the mind of every Protestant boy and girl who read it. More than "all the other unclean books in Christendom" combined, Twain claimed, the Bible did "its baleful work" in propagating "vicious and unclean ideas" among children. The young could be easily protected from these other pernicious books, "but they have no protection against the deadly Bible"; it "defiles all Protestant children."[52]

Twain was a literary luminary and an armchair theologian, not a biblical scholar. In 1879, he read Henricus Oort's three-volume *Bible for Learners*, which introduced him to modern German scholars' historical and literary criticism of the Bible. He sent his brother Orion a copy to help him use historical-literary criticism to interpret the Scriptures.[53] Nevertheless, Allison Ensor calls Twain an "inept and amateurish Bible critic" who knew little about "critical biblical scholarship." His attacks on the Bible rested on arguments previously advanced by Thomas Paine, Robert Ingersoll, and other skeptics. Ensor maintains that Twain did not study the Bible systematically, wrongly assumed that many interpretations espoused by "ultra-fundamentalists" were correct, rejected the concept of progressive revelation, and largely ignored the books of Job, Ecclesiastes, and the Old Testament prophets that supported some of his analysis of the meaning of life and his denunciation of various social ills. William Phipps argues that Twain might have curbed his censure of the Bible if he had better understood the higher-critical, liberal Protestant interpretations that made the Bible more palatable to many Americans who shared his intellectual concerns and religious doubts.[54]

The Basis of Knowledge

Twain insisted that evidence and reason, rather than a reputedly inspired text, intuition, or people's socialization and environment, are the best basis for knowledge and belief. A person's worldview should be based on thought, study, and "deliberate conviction."[55] Religion and politics, however, were usually domains of the heart, not the head. When people did reflect on these matters, Twain complained, most of them did so only to reinforce their own positions, not to consider alternatives. They read only arguments that supported their own perspectives, avoiding books that would challenge their entrenched views.[56]

Most Christians, Twain claimed, used the Bible to reinforce their sectarian positions rather than examining it closely. People's religious and political views were almost always derived secondhand from alleged authorities whose opinions "were not worth a brass farthing," rather than from personal examination and rational analysis.[57] "Hardly a man in the world," Twain avowed, "has an opinion upon morals, politics, or religion which he got otherwise than through his associations."[58] In religious and political matters, people's "reasoning powers," Twain complained, "are not above the monkey's."[59] People should instead use the empirical method and reason to determine what is true.

In the laboratory, Twain avowed, there are no pretentious ranks and no counterfeit aristocracies; "the domain of Science is a republic, and all its citizens are brothers and equals." Twain challenged people to consider new information, counterarguments, and contrary evidence, continually reevaluate their beliefs, and adopt a better basis for judgment. A person's worldview, he insisted, should be based on "thought, and study, and deliberate conviction." He agreed with theological liberals that religious truth could be attained only "through a never-ending process of criticism and experiment."[60] In "My First Lie and How I Got Out of It" (1899) and "Corn-Pone Opinions" (1901), Twain strove to expose the misguided ideologies upon which most people based their understanding of truth.

Sadly, Twain argued, most people's religious convictions were based on their socialization and ethnicity. "If you know a man's nationality," he asserted, one could easily guess "the complexion of his religion." People's environment, not their evaluation of evidence, made them Presbyterians, Baptists, Mormons, Catholics, Muslims, or Buddhists. A Presbyterian family, he argued, did not produce Catholics or "other religious brands," but only "its own kind"; it did this not by "intellectual processes" but simply by association. Muslims, Twain argued, practiced Islam "because they are born and reared among that sect, not because they have thought it out and can furnish sound reasons" for their faith.[61] Twain told Howells in 1884 that he had begun writing a story whose "hidden motive will illustrate a but-little considered fact in human nature: that the religious folly you are born in you will *die* in, no matter what apparently reasonabler religious folly may seem to have taken its place meanwhile & abolished & obliterated it." After a person was convinced that he had discovered the truth, Twain asserted, he stopped thinking about other alternatives and instead concentrated on devising arguments to defend his perspective.[62]

Twain claimed that most people's epistemologies led them to approach the Bible as sentimentally and unthinkingly as they viewed allegedly sacred sites in Europe and the Holy Land. Most Christians venerated the Bible without examining it carefully; they relied on what pastors and biblical commentators told them to believe rather than investigating Scripture themselves. They pretended to have the same convictions about the Bible at age fifty they had as children. "I wonder how they can lie so," Twain mused. "It comes of practice, no doubt. They would not say that of [Charles] Dickens's or [Walter] Scott's books."[63] For the average person, religion consisted of a set of things he believed and wished he were certain about.[64] In *Following the Equator* (1896), Twain argued that "Faith is believing something you know ain't true." People were accepted as members of churches based on what they believed—and expelled for what they came to know. The only way people could espouse particular religions, Twain insisted, was by intentionally closing their minds.[65]

Twain on God

Twain's denial of biblical inspiration strongly affected his understanding of God, although determining just what he believed about God is very difficult because he wrote extensively on this subject and his views changed significantly over time. Until about age forty-five, Twain often affirmed orthodox views and sometimes, especially in letters to Livy and friends, expressed warmth toward God, thanking him for his providential care and asking God to bless his letters' recipients.[66] From about 1880 on, however, Twain often sharply criticized God's character and actions and contrasted the Bible's descriptions with what he considered the real or true God. Twain denigrated the biblical God as immoral and cruel, denounced predestination and Christ's invention of hell, and protested that God admitted only a small percentage of people to heaven. He argued that God did not answer prayer and complained that God unfairly punished families or nations because of individuals' sin. His attacks on God, the Bible, and Christianity during the last thirty years of his life were as scathing and substantive as those of Robert Ingersoll, British philosopher Bertrand Russell, or such contemporary critics as Sam Harris, Christopher Hitchens, and Richard Dawkins, although most of it occurred in private letters or works published posthumously.

Twain's perspective on the biblical God was generally positive before 1880, as indicated by various letters and exchanges with Twichell and other ministers and by his church involvement. In an 1872 letter to Livy, Twain declared, "God is good, & constantly raises up people to take care of the shiftless and helpless." Contemplating the marvels of nature—mountains, flowers, and butterflies—inspired religious ecstasy in Twain throughout his life.[67] Some of the passages in *A Tramp Abroad* (1880), a book based on Twain's hikes in the Swiss Alps, praise the grandeur of God's creation. Reflecting on that experience in a letter to Joseph Twichell, Twain declared that people are "puny" and "insignificant" in the presence of the majesty, tranquility, and blessedness of "God's Alps & God's ocean." Twain also praised God as "the perfect artist." Everything God has made "is beautiful; nothing coarse, nothing ugly has ever come from His hand." Contemplating God's creative activity produced an awe similar to observing "the march of the comets through their billion mile orbits."[68]

In his autobiography, however, Twain portrayed the biblical God as "an avenging hit man," "a cruel fiend," and "an immoral monster."[69] God's actions in the Old Testament, Twain argued, demonstrated that he was "vindictive, unjust, ungenerous, pitiless and vengeful." Perhaps embittered by his trials and tribulations during his final decade, Twain complained that God constantly punished "trifling misdeeds" with tremendous severity, innocent children for their parents' transgressions, and unoffending populations for the sins of their rulers. God's biography in the Bible made "Nero an angel of light" by comparison.[70] Twain told of one man who went home swearing after a prayer meeting; the man's wife and seven children were "attacked by a loathsome disease" and all died within a week. Twain objected that God had unfairly punished the man's family for his sins.[71]

"The day we are born," Twain bemoaned, God "begins to persecute us." People's smallness, innocence, and helplessness did not move him to pity or gentleness. Every day "the wanton torture" continued.[72] As illustrations of God's lack of mercy, Twain pointed to the flood, the plagues on Egypt, and the slaughter of the Midianites.[73] Twain was outraged by God's commands to the Israelites to kill the innocent as well as the guilty. "In Biblical times," he protested, "if a man committed a sin," a whole nation was likely to be exterminated. If

God had a motto, it was "Let no innocent person escape." Humans were more moral than God, he insisted, because they did not inflict misery and death on the innocent. In addition, people "are more compassionate" and "generous than God; for men forgive the dead, but God does not." According to the Bible, God is responsible for miners in Pennsylvania "working for a pittance in the dark" and for all "the cruelties, oppressions, injustices everywhere." "I'd rather have Satan any day," Twain insisted, "than that kind of God."[74]

Twain especially deplored God's cruelty. Even the Church, which Twain accused of spilling "more innocent blood" since the time of Constantine than all the world's politically based wars combined, had "observed a limit." However, "when the Lord God of Heaven and Earth, adored Father of Man, goes to war, there is no limit." He displayed no mercy; God "slays, slays, slays."[75]

Twain argued that God, who devised diseases, should learn a lesson from the compassionate Christian medical missionaries who labored in Africa to cure them. God "invented & distributed" awful diseases among "helpless, poor savages, & now" he "enjoys this wanton crime."[76] God instructed people to cure the ills which he had inflicted on humanity and "could extinguish with a word if He chose."[77] Twain accused God of devoting substantial thought "to the great work of making man miserable" and complained that nine-tenths of the diseases God invented afflicted the poor. If scientists exterminated a disease, God received the credit and all the pulpits proclaimed "how good he is!" In other words, God "commits a fearful crime" for 6,000 years and then feels "entitled to praise because he suggests to somebody" to reduce its severity.[78] Twain also repudiated the moral maxim that suffering develops character. Affliction, he argued, harmed people more often than it edified them.[79]

No evidence indicated, Twain alleged, that God was just, kind, or compassionate.[80] Christians brazenly called "God the source of mercy," but they knew that he had never "exercised that virtue." They considered him the source of morals, but God's history and daily conduct revealed that "He is totally destitute" of morals. Christians called God Father, but they "would detest and denounce any earthly father" who inflicted upon "his child a thousandth part of the pains and miseries and cruelties which our God deals out to His children every day."[81] Bringing a child into this sinful world, Twain argued, was similar to "building a village on the slope of a volcano directly in the path of the lava flow." Having children was an even worse offense until ministers finally abolished the concept of hell, which taught a person "had only one chance in a hundred of escaping the eternal fires of damnation." "There is not another temper as bad as mine except God Almighty's," Twain flippantly told Howells.[82]

God could have created good people as easily as bad ones, Twain maintained, but he preferred to make evil ones; he could have made everyone happy, but he made no one happy; he stingily gave people a short lifespan; he gave angels unearned eternal bliss and a pain-free existence but required human beings to work to attain heaven and cursed his earthly "children with biting miseries and maladies of mind and body." Twain was astonished by God's "all-comprehensive malice" in creating "elaborate tortures for the meanest and pitifulest of creatures." God demanded that human beings act uprightly, but he did not do so himself. Writing to Twichell, Twain complained that God has "no morals, yet blandly sets Himself up as Head Sunday School Superintendent of the Universe." God "has no idea of mercy, justice, or honesty, yet obtusely imagines Himself the inventor of these things."[83] In addition, God was staid, serious, and sullen, lacking the one attribute that "keeps the others healthy" and that Twain greatly valued—humor.[84]

Twain also argued that the biblical God was responsible for human sin. If he were indeed all-powerful and all-controlling as Calvinists argued, then God was to blame for human depravity, disobedience, and the fall. God designed human beings so that they could not escape obeying their passions, appetites, and "various unpleasant and undesirable qualities." Moreover, Twain contended, God had so arranged the world that people's lives were beset by unavoidable traps" and compelled them to "commit what are called sins." And then God punished people for doing things he had always intended them to do. God should admit, Twain asserted, that he is "the Author and Inventor of Sin" and take full responsibility for human iniquity. God alone "is responsible for every act and word of a human being's life between cradle and grave." Therefore, people are not culpable for their sins, have no obligations to God, and owe him no "thanks, reverence, and worship."[85]

In addition, Twain criticized God for selecting the Jews as his special people. During Old Testament times, God had chosen a few million Jews to carry out his purposes, Twain maintained; he had coddled them and damned the rest of humanity. God sulked, cursed, raged, and grieved over "this small and obscure people," this "handful of truculent nomads," in "a peculiarly and distractingly human way," but his efforts were futile because "he could not govern them."[86]

Disillusioned with the biblical conception of God, Twain, influenced by his reading of Thomas Paine while working in his late twenties as a riverboat pilot, espoused for a while the deist perspective that God created and sustained the world but did not direct history, converse with people, or answer prayers. In the 1880s, Twain accepted the deist assumptions that God had abandoned the world after creating it, governed the world through his unchanging natural laws, had provided no written revelation to instruct humanity, and expected people to observe nature and use reason to determine religious truth. The universe, Twain avowed, was too well "assembled and regulated" to have emerged by chance. It had been produced by "a great Master Mind, but it cares nothing for our happiness."[87] The God who brought this stupendous universe into being with one "flash of thought and framed its laws with another," he insisted, possessed unlimited power. God foresaw everything that would occur from the moment of creation until the consummation. Twain often portrayed God as omnipotent but not benevolent. God was "utterly indifferent to human prayer or concerns" and thus provided no consolation to people when they experienced suffering and evil.[88] God set "in motion the laws and machinery" that continued to operate without his supervision and thereafter troubled "himself no further about the matter."[89]

Continuing to express a deistic perspective, Twain wrote in his *Notebook* in 1898, "The Being who to me is the real God is the One who created" and ruled this majestic universe. This God "cares nothing for men's flatteries, compliments, praises, [and] prayers." Why would he value the "mouthings of microbes"? God's "real character" is plainly "written in His real Bible, which is Nature and her history; we read it every day, and we could understand and trust in it if we would burn" the spurious Christian Bible. The bible of nature said nothing about a future life. It clearly reveals that "God cares not a rap for us" and "that His laws inflict pain and suffering and sorrow," but the book of nature cannot tell people what their purpose is.[90]

Twain strove to distinguish between the allegedly vengeful God of the Old Testament and the deist God who created the astounding universe and devised its immutable laws. He eventually came, however, to view the deist God as malicious too, since he had constructed a world where misery abounded.[91] Longing for what he deemed a better God than that of Christianity or deism, the celebrated author offered an alternative that he called the real or true God. As early as the 1870s, Twain argued in "God of the Bible vs. God of the Present Day" that the new conception of the universe scientists were providing comported "with the dignity of the modern God," not the biblical God. The universe "consists of countless worlds of so stupendous dimensions that, in comparison, ours is grotesquely insignificant." "The God of the Bible is "an irascible, vindictive, fierce and ever fickle and changeful master," whereas the true God is a being "whose beneficent, exact, and changeless ordering of the machinery of His colossal universe is proof that He is at least steadfast to His purposes." His unwritten laws, "being equal and impartial, show that he is just and fair." These considerations indicated that if God did "ordain us to live hereafter, he will be steadfast, just and fair toward us."[92]

Unable to accept the Psalmist's conception of God as good, trustworthy, righteous, "gracious and compassionate, slow to anger and rich in love" (Ps. 145:8), Twain contrasted the true God—the "Incomparable One that created the universe and flung abroad upon its horizonless ocean of space its unaccountable hosts of giant suns"— with the "little God whom we manufactured out of waste human material; whose portrait we accurately painted in a Bible and charged its authorship upon Him; the God who created a universe of such nursery dimensions that there would not be room in it for the orbit of Mars." This God "put our little globe" in its center, making people incorrectly think Earth was the only important thing in the universe.[93] "The real God," the "sublime and supreme God, the authentic Creator," had made an incredibly vast universe. Compared with this real God, the gods produced by "the feeble imaginations of men are as a swarm of gnats scattered and lost in the infinitudes of the empty sky."[94]

In his later years, Twain increasingly argued that his real God was vastly superior to the biblical God. He told Livy in 1889 that the real God "is as good & just as Man is." The true God made goodness greater than injustice and evil. Moreover, this God "must have admired" goodness "because he discovered it to be his own principal feature." As a result, Twain concluded, "I am plenty safe enough in *his* hands. I am not in any danger from that kind of Deity." As for the false caricature of God taught in the Bible, Twain insisted, "I have met his superior a hundred times—in fact I amount to that myself."[95]

If he were to construct a God, Twain declared, he would have numerous qualities and characteristics the imaginary biblical God lacked. Twain complained that the biblical God was a glory hog who "sits purring & comfortable" during Sunday sermons while people offered "praises & distinctions" to him.[96] Even Asian rulers who loved flattery, Twain wrote, could not stand "the rank quality of it which our God endures with complacency and satisfaction from our pulpits every Sunday."[97] In addition, Twain declared in 1896, the true God "would not sell, or offer to sell, temporary benefits of the joys of eternity for the product called worship." The real God, Twain avowed, was not jealous and would forgive all people's sins if they repented. This God did not boast, praise himself, or enact vengeance. The only hell is the one people lived in on earth "from the cradle to the grave." The true God would spend eons "trying to forgive Himself for making man unhappy when he could have made him happy."[98] In short, Twain envisioned a God who had "a dignity and sublimity proportioned to the majesty of His office and the magnitude of His empire."[99]

Twain lamented that most people failed to recognize the real God and instead clung to Christianity, whose God was the worst one humanity's "insane imagination" had invented. Even worse, he feared that Christianity would eventually be replaced by another God and "a stupider religion."[100]

Conclusion

The despair caused by Susy's death, his financial problems, Livy's precarious health, and his own deteriorating body contributed to Twain's disillusionment with the biblical God and his yearning for a better God. His quest to design and defend the "real God" displays Twain's continued interest in metaphysical and spiritual issues and his deep desire to find or invent a God whom he could believe in, admire, and trust and who could provide a moral foundation for his passionate attack on the injustices of his era, which would intensify during the final decade of his life.

Notes

1. Karen Lystra, *Dangerous Intimacy: The Untold Story of Mark Twain's Final Years* (Berkeley: University of California Press, 2004), 1.
2. MTN, February 20, 1891, 212.
3. MFMT, 179.
4. *San Francisco Examiner*, August 1895, as quoted in "At Home around the World," https://twain.lib.virginia.edu/onstage/world.html.
5. "At Home."
6. Harold K. Bush Jr., "Broken Idols: Mark Twain's Elegies for Susy and a Critique of Freudian Grief Theory," *Nineteenth-Century Literature* 57 (September 2002), 238; LMT, 140; MF, 176.
7. "In My Bitterness," MTFM, 131–2; SLC to Francis Skrine, September 18, 1897, MTP; quotation from MTR, 318.
8. MF, 179; Mark Twain, "Broken Idols," in Bush, "Broken Idols," 263–4.
9. MTSC, 239; Harold K. Bush, Jr., *Continuing Bonds with the Dead: Parental Grief and Nineteenth-Century American Authors* (Tuscaloosa: University of Alabama Press, 2016), 155 (quotation), 156, 161.
10. SLC to WDH, May 12–13, 1899, MTL, 2:680; Mark Twain, "At the Shrine of St. Wagner," August 2, 1891, in *What Is Man? and Other Essays* (New York: Harper and Brothers, 1917), 226.
11. MTB, 1034. See also SLC to Helene Picard, February 22, 1902, MTL, 2:719.
12. SLC to Henry Rogers, January 29, 1895, MTL, 2: 623–4 (first two quotations); SLC to MMF, January 18, 1893, MTMF, 269 (third quotation).
13. Daniel Crown, "The Riddle of Mark Twain's Passion for Joan of Arc," April 3, 2012, https://www.theawl.com/2012/04/the-riddle-of-mark-twains-passion-for-joan-of-arc/; Harris as quoted in Crown, "Riddle." See also Bertram Mott, Jr., "Twain's Joan: A Divine Anomaly," *Etudes Anglaises* 23 (1970), 245–55; Aurele Durocher, "Mark Twain and the Roman Catholic Church," *Journal of the Central Mississippi Valley American Studies Association* 1 (Fall 1960), 32–43.

14. MTB, 81–2; SLC to OL, January 22, 1869, LTR, 3:63; Mark Twain, "Speech at the Scottish Banquet in London," https://americanliterature.com/author/mark-twain/short-story/speech-at-the-scottish-banquet-in-london.

15. SLC to Rogers, January 29, 1895, MTL, 2:624.

16. MTSC, 269 (quotation); Albert Stone, Jr., "Mark Twain's Joan of Arc: The Child as Goddess," in *On Mark Twain: The Best from American Literature*, ed. Louis J. Budd and Edwin Harrison Cady (Durham, NC: Duke University Press, 1987), 74–5. This contrasts strikingly with Twain's statement: "I do not believe He [God] has ever sent a message to man by anybody, or delivered one to him by word of mouth" ("Three Statements of the Eighties," WM, 56).

17. RV, 189 (first quotation); Stone, "Joan of Arc," 75 (second quotation).

18. Susan K. Harris, as cited in Crown, "Riddle."

19. Michael Kenny, review of *Personal Recollections of Joan of Arc*, *America*, April 17, 1909, 18; Daniel Hudson, review of *A Connecticut Yankee in King Arthur's Court*, *Ave Maria* 30 (1890): 116; Hudson, review of *Personal Recollections of Joan of Arc*, *Ave Maria* 75 (1912), 729.

20. Mark Twain, "Saint Joan of Arc," *Harper's Magazine* 110 (December 1904), 10–11; first two quotations from 10, third from 11.

21. Twain, "Joan of Arc," 11–12; quotation from 12.

22. Mark Noll, "Nineteenth-Century American Biblical Interpretation," in *The Oxford Handbook of the Bible in America*, ed. Paul Gutjahr (New York: Oxford University Press, 2017), 126 (quotation), 124.

23. BA, 184; MTSC, 122.

24. Louis Budd, *Critical Essays on Mark Twain, 1910–1980* (Boston: Hall, 1980), 3; Earl Allen Reimer, "Mark Twain and the Bible: An Inductive Study," PhD dissertation, Michigan State University, 1971, concordance.

25. MTR, 262; Brodwin, "Theology of Mark Twain," 173.

26. IA, 492.

27. Mark Twain, "Letters from the Earth," WM, 412.

28. IA, 492.

29. SLC to George Fitzgibbon, November 28, 1873, LTR 5:193.

30. Letter Twain sent to a San Francisco newspaper, in Franklin Walker and G. Ezra Dane, eds., *Mark Twain's Travels with Mr. Brown* (New York: Knopf, 1940), 209.

31. SLC to MMF, MTMF, 6 (December 2, 1867), 24 (March 18, 1868), 32 (June 17, 1868). See also Mark Twain, "The Scriptural Panoramist," Writings 19:392–3; MTATB, 31.

32. Twain made 34 references to Noah, 28 to the Prodigal Son, 27 to Eve, 27 to Solomon, and 22 to Moses. He cites Genesis 295 times, Matthew 133

times, and Luke 78 times. Isaiah was his favorite prophetic book. MTATB, 110; MTR, 239; Alan Gribben, *Mark Twain's Library: A Reconstruction* (Boston: G. K. Hall, 1980), 63.

33. MTSC, 217; MTATB, 44; MTAP, 379. See also "Mark Twain Aggrieved," *New York Times*, December 4, 1883; Writings, 19:30.

34. Writings, 14:19.

35. Mark Twain, "What Is Man? Fragments," WM, 491.

36. Mark Twain, "That Day in Eden (Passage from Satan's Diary)," E&E, 341–5.

37. Mark Twain, "The Turning Point of My Life," WM, 464.

38. TS, 32 (first quotation): MTB, 156 (second quotation); Twain, "Morals Lecture," July 15, 1895, MTS, 284 (third quotation); MTN, February 1, 1896, 275 (fourth quotation).

39. AMT, June 25, 1906, 2:141.

40. MTB, 632.

41. MTB, 1583.

42. Twain, "Three Statements," 58; MTB, 1354; quotations in that order.

43. Thomas Paine, *The Age of Reason* (London: D. Cousins, 1870), 10; Ron Powers, *Mark Twain: A Life* (New York: Free Press, 2005), 81.

44. Alex Ayre, *Wit and Wisdom of Mark Twain* (New York: HarperCollins, 2005), 24.

45. MTB, 411.

46. MTATB, 82.

47. MTATB, 95.

48. AMT, January 23, 1906, 1:314; Twain, *Innocents Abroad*, 440; quotations in that order.

49. Twain, "Letters from the Earth," 421.

50. MTATB, 67.

51. AMT, June 20, 1906, 2:130.

52. SLC to Asa Don Dickson, November 21, 1905, AMT, 2:30 (first quotation); June 22, 1906, AMT, 2:135 (remainder of quotations).

53. Samuel Webster, *Mark Twain, Business Man* (Boston: Little, Brown, 1946), 131.

54. MTATB, 82 (quotation), 86, 99–100; MTR, passim.

55. Mark Twain, letter to San Francisco *Alta California*, November 15, 1868.

56. MTN, October 24, 1896, 307.

57. AMT, July 10, 1908, 3:253.

58. Mark Twain, "Corn-Pone Opinions," E&E, 403.

59. AMT, September 12, 1907, 3:133.

60. Mark Twain, "Three Thousand Years among the Microbes" (1905), in *The Devil's Race-Track: Mark Twain's "Great Dark" Writings*, ed. John Tuckey

(Berkeley: University of California Press, 1980), 174; "Letter from Mark Twain," San Francisco *Alta California*, November 15, 1868; William McGuire King, "Liberalism," in *Encyclopedia of the American Religious Experience: Studies of Traditions and Movements*, 3 vols., ed. Charles Lippy and Peter Williams (New York: Charles Scribner's Sons, 1988), 2:1129; quotations in that order.

61. WM, 162; CS, 65; Twain, "Corn-Pone Opinions," 402–3; quotations in that order.

62. SLC to WDH, January 7, 1884, MTHL, 2:460. Twain never finished this story.

63. SLC to WDH, August 2, 1887, MTHL, 2:595–6.

64. NB&J, 1879, 305.

65. FE, 132; see also MTN, 237.

66. Several dozen examples could be provided, including SLC to Edward Hingston, January 15, 1867, LTR 1:8; SLC to Charles Stoddard, April 23, 1867, LTR, 1:30; SLC to Francis Bret Harte, May 1, 1867, LTR, 1:39. Even during his final decade, Twain continued to occasionally use this language. See, for example, SLC to Henry Huttleston Rogers, July 28, 1902, *Mark Twain's Correspondence with Henry Huttleston Rogers, 1893–1909*, ed. Lewis Leary (Berkeley: University of California Press, 1969), 493.

67. SLC to OLC, September 15, 1872, *Mark Twain's 1872 English Journals*, https://www.marktwainproject.org/xtf/view?docId=letters/MTDP00358. xml; e.g., Mark Twain, *A Tramp Abroad* (New York: Harper and Brothers, 1907), 2:41–2; Twain, "The Cradle of Liberty," CT, 2:49.

68. SLC to JHT, 1879, January 26, 1879, https://www.marktwainproject. org/xtf/view?docId=letters/UCCL01577.xml;query=twichell%20god; searchAll=;sectionType1=;sectionType2=;sectionType3=;sectionType4=; sectionType5=;style=letter;brand=mtp#1; MTN, May 27, 1898, 361.

69. Powers, *Mark Twain*, 31 (first quotation); James Townsend, "Grace in the Arts: Mark Twain: A Bitter Battle with God," *Journal of the Grace Evangelical Society* 17 (Autumn 2004), 62 (second and third quotations).

70. AMT, June 19, 1906, 2:128.

71. AMT, June 13, 1906, 2:117.

72. Twain, "What Is Man? Fragments," WM, 478.

73. Twain, "Letters from the Earth," 450–2; MTB, 1355–6.

74. AMT, June 13, 1906, 2:113; Twain, "Letters from the Earth," 448; N&J 2:416; William McCrackan, "My Interviews with Mark Twain," as quoted in Stephen Gottschalk, *Rolling Away the Stone: Mary Baker Eddy's Challenge to Materialism* (Bloomington: Indiana University Press, 2006), 57; quotations in that order.

75. Twain, "Letters from the Earth," 450.

76. MTB, 1420.

77. AMT, June 19, 1906, 2:130.

78. Twain, "Letters from the Earth," 433–4.

79. Gary Sloan, "Mark Twain's Secret Vendetta with the Almighty," May 2001, https://ffrf.org/faq/feeds/item/17327-mark-twains-secret-vendetta-with-the-almighty.

80. AMT, June 23, 1906, 2:137.

81. AMT, June 19, 1906, 2:128–9.

82. MTMW, 201; MTB, 1508; SLC to WDH, October 19, 1899, MTHL 2:710; quotations in that order.

83. MTMS, 405; June 23, 1906, AMT, 2:138; quotations in that order; SLC to JHT, July 28, 1904, Joseph Twichell Papers, Beinecke Rare Book and Manuscript Library, Yale University.

84. Notebook #35, transcription number, 39–40, MTP.

85. AMT, June 25, 1906, 2:142 (first and second quotations); MTN, June 16, 1896, 301 (third quotation); AMT, June 25, 1906, 2:143 (fourth and fifth quotations).

86. Mark Twain, "God of the Bible vs. God of the Present Day," in *The Bible According to Mark Twain*, ed. Howard Baetzhold and Joseph McCullough (New York: Touchstone, 1995), 315 (quotations).

87. MTB, 1353.

88. Stanley Brodwin, "Mark Twain's Theology: The Gods of a Brevet Presbyterian," in *The Cambridge Companion to Mark Twain*, ed. Forrest Robinson (New York: Cambridge University Press, 1995), 228.

89. Twain, "Fragments," 486. On Twain's deistic views, see Jude Nixon, "God," in *The Mark Twain Encyclopedia*, ed. J. R. LeMaster and Jim Wilson (New York: Garland, 1993), 323–8; and MTAS, 21–3. Twain's perspective on God was influenced by the Freemasons whom he joined in the early 1860s. See Alexander Jones, "Mark Twain and Freemasonry," *American Literature* 26 (November 1954), 363–73.

90. MTN, May 27, 1898, 360–1 (first quotation), 361–2 (third quotation), 362 (fourth and fifth quotations).

91. MTC, 161.

92. "God of the Bible," 317. Cummings argues that this essay, Twain's "Three Statements of the Eighties," and some of his later writings were strongly influenced by Thomas Paine's *Age of Reason*, which provided Twain with "an enlightened theology and cosmology based on Newtonian science" (MTAS, 21–2; quotation from 21).

93. AMT, June 18, 1906, 2:127.

94. AMT, June 23, 1906, 2:136. See Charles Neider, ed., "Concerning the Character of the Real God," *Hudson Review* 16 (Autumn 1936), 343–9.

95. SLC to OLC, July 17, 1889, LLMT, 253–4.
96. SLC to WDH, May 7, 1903, MTHL, 2:770.
97. AMT, June 19, 1906, 2:128.
98. MTN, June 18, 1896, 301–2.
99. Mark Twain, "Aix, Paradise of Rheumatics" (1891), E&E, 97.
100. AMT, June 22, 1906, 2:135.

7

The 1900s

Trying to Make Sense of Life

Mark Twain helped arrange an American lecture tour for Winston Churchill in 1900–1901. Twain introduced the twenty-six-year-old newly elected Member of Parliament at the Waldorf Astoria in New York City on December 12, 1900 as "the hero of five wars, the author of six books, and the future Prime Minister of Great Britain."[1] Twain also took the opportunity to criticize the bellicosity of both Britain and the United States. "I think that England sinned in getting into a war in South Africa which she could have avoided without loss of credit or dignity," he asserted, "just as I think we have sinned in crowding ourselves into a war in the Philippines on the same terms." The two nations were "fellow thieves and robbers"; they were "*kith* and *kin* in *war* and *sin.*"

Churchill wrote later that he was thrilled to spend time with the famous author. When they argued about the Boer War, Churchill had retreated to the position of "My country right or wrong." When a "country is fighting for its life, I agree," Twain replied, but such was not the case in South Africa. Churchill concluded, however, that he had not displeased Twain because the author inscribed "every one of thirty volumes of his works for my benefit."[2] In his twilight years, Twain energetically opposed imperialism and war. In contrast, Churchill would often defend the British Empire's actions as he participated in World War I, helped save the West from Germany's onslaught in World War II, and challenged the Soviet Union during the Cold War.

On the other hand, these two towering figures of their respective eras had much in common. Both were born on November 30; both were deeply affected by losing an infant child; both had a strong sense of adventure and varied life experiences; both smoked many cigars every day and liked to write while in bed. Both wrote articles and books and gave lectures to earn income; both struggled with debt several times in their lives. Both married in their mid-thirties and had wives they cherished as confidantes and on whom they depended greatly.

In addition, Twain and Churchill both cared deeply about their public persona and sought to shape how posterity would view them. Churchill did so by writing the history of major events in which he participated, from the Boer War to the Cold War. Twain planned to keep his name before the public for many decades by writing manuscripts that would be published after his death. Twain's distinctive appearance and extraordinary wit made him the archetypal American for many British; four decades later, Churchill's heroism made him the archetypal Englishman for many Americans. Both had complex, enigmatic religious views that changed over time. Strikingly, Churchill won a Nobel Prize in literature, but Twain did not.[3]

During the final decade of his life, Twain received several devastating blows—the death of his beloved Livy in 1904, the death of his daughter Jean on Christmas Eve 1909, and his own declining health. In addition, he fought to protect his copyrights and dealt with the duplicity of two trusted employees. These problems have led some scholars, relying on Twain's autobiography and Albert Bigelow Paine's 1912 biography, to portray him as a bitter, cynical, disillusioned old man who was hamstrung by his misfortunes and angry as his creative powers diminished and his health deteriorated. This, they say, led him to repudiate Christianity, adopt a deterministic worldview, and savagely rant and rail against an implacable, depraved God, a hypocritical, heartless Christianity, and the damned human race. Twain's writings during his final decade allegedly displayed his relentless despair as he embraced social and spiritual nihilism.[4]

After 1900, Twain continued to disparage God and censure Christianity in numerous writings, although usually through words spoken by characters in his fiction or in works not to be published until after his death. Livy's objections had persuaded him to withhold many of his most vehement attacks on religious orthodoxy, and even after her death in 1904, his concerns about his public reputation and the opinions of his friends prevented him from revealing his strongest reproaches of God and Christianity. Twain's fiercest assault on religion was in his June 1906 autobiographical dictations. During his twilight years, Twain engaged in a "Job-like struggle with the Deity to make sense of human suffering."[5] At the same time, his criticisms of various groups including missionaries, villains (especially Russian Czar Nicholas II and Belgian King Leopold II), and several ideologies—militarism, imperialism, and anti-Semitism—became increasingly caustic.

On the other hand, Twain experienced considerable pleasure during his final years. As Michael Shelden argues, the renowned author's letters reveal that he frequently rose above the limitations and tragedies of his last decade and found "pleasures to offset its pains." Highlighting only Twain's dark side is misleading; his unparalleled sense of humor and keen interest in public affairs continued, and he enjoyed affectionate relationships with many youth. During these years, the literary lion also loudly denounced human moral failings and declared publicly some of the things he had been writing or saying privately about religion for a long time to friends including William Dean Howells and Joe Twichell. During his final four years, Twain built and moved into a mansion in Redding, Connecticut; befriended some of Broadway's most beautiful young actresses including Ethel Barrymore and Billie Burke; helped a group of inner-city youth open a theater; stayed out all night partying with show girls; taught young girls how to play billiards (his relationships with these women and girls were platonic); explored Bermuda; pretended to be lost at sea; conversed with British King Edward VII and his wife at Windsor Castle; and published books on many subjects including Shakespeare, Christian Science, heaven, and Satan.[6]

Despite his private rantings about God, Twain was still influenced by his Presbyterian upbringing. In 1907, for example, he made a 400-mile round trip from his home in New York City to Annapolis, Maryland, to speak at a fundraising event for a Presbyterian congregation. In accepting the invitation from Emma Warfield, the wife of the state's governor, Twain told his secretary, Isabel Lyons, that the offer was "right in my line for I'm nothing if I'm not a Presbyterian."[7]

"Wheresoever She Was, There Was Eden"

Livy's health had been fragile since her teenage years. Twain adored his wife and strove constantly to please her. He explained to a correspondent in 1902 that for thirty years he had refrained from publishing work to which Livy objected "to keep from breaking my wife's heart, whose contentment I value above the salvation of the human race." Livy's physical ailments caused the Clemenses to investigate various types of remedies. During her final years, she received osteopathic treatments to help with an alleged nervous breakdown and was a bedridden invalid who endured substantial pain. As various therapies failed to restore her health or alleviate her suffering, Twain was wracked by guilt. He believed that his criticism of Livy's faith had made her illness worse. Shortly before she died, he wrote her a note declaring, "It so grieves me to remember that I" caused your suffering. "I drove you to sorrow and heart-break." He added, "If ever I do it again, I hope the punishment will fall upon me the guilty, not upon you the innocent."[8]

What Livy believed about religious matters during their marriage is difficult to decipher. She was raised in a devout Christian home and participated faithfully in a Congregational church in Elmira. For several years as a teenager she attended Elmira College, which emphasized study of the Bible and Christian piety, and she displayed a very strong faith and substantial understanding of Scripture during her courtship with Twain. Yet despite the spiritual support the Clemenses received through their involvement in Asylum Hill Church and from their neighbors in Nook Farm, Livy, like Twain, apparently began to experience doubts about her faith and to feel distant from God soon after they moved to Hartford. When Twain was on a lecture tour in the late fall of 1871, Livy, still upset by the death of her father, wrote, "Do you pray for me Youth [her pet name for her husband]? Oh we must be a prayerful family—pray for me as you used to do." She confessed, "I am not as prayerful as of old but I believe my heart prays."[9]

Attending Asylum Hill that fall increased her spiritual anguish. Livy was deeply moved when Twichell "prayed particularly for those who had fallen away and were coming back to God." She told her husband that "I am ashamed to go back, because I have fallen away so many times and gone back feeling that if I should ever fall, grow cold again, it would be useless trying" to regain her faith. A tormented Livy added that she had confided to a friend, "If I felt toward God as I did toward my husband I should never be in the least troubled." She felt, however, "almost perfectly cold . . . toward God."[10]

She told Twain in another letter that when she arrived at Asylum Hill in January 1872 and saw that communion was being offered, "my heart sank because I do feel so unfit to go to the table," but she could not "bear to go away from it." In response to Twichell's "earnest invitation to all those who were feeling cold and far away from God" to receive communion so as to gain comfort, she did participate and prayed for her husband and son. Fathers and mothers, she wrote, had "much to pray for, so very much that they need guidance in." She loved to hear Twichell, a good and godly man, preach and pray.[11]

Despite her wavering faith, during the 1870s Livy ensured that their family said grace before meals, read a chapter of the Bible together every morning, and prayed together regularly. One friend who visited the Clemenses early in their marriage was shocked to see Twain ask a blessing before a meal and participate in family worship. How long these practices continued is unknown. Albert Bigelow Paine contends that Twain asked to be excused at some point because his involvement was hypocritical, but that at that time he still believed, like Livy, that the Bible was the word of God.[12] By 1879, Paine claims, Livy, like her husband, had stopped believing in the God of the Bible who person- ally supervised all earthly life. Visiting other nations, talking with her husband, and being exposed to various philosophies had changed her worldview. Like Twain, she came to view God as a great mind and "the Supreme Good" that directed the universe through immutable laws. This "larger faith," however, could not supply the comfort she craved as they dealt with suffering and death.[13]

Resa Willis argues similarly that by the mid-1890s Livy's childhood and early adult faith "had long ago been undermined by life's harsh realities." Twain's tirades against God continued to weaken what had earlier been the foundation of her life.[14] When Twain told her that he was certain he would go to hell, Livy replied, "Why, Youth, who, then, can be saved?"[15] Desperate for proof that an afterlife existed and that she would see Susy again, she and Twain attended several seances, but they had no contact with their beloved daughter.[16] As they grappled with their bereavement, Twain declared, "Livy, if it comforts you to lean on the Christian faith do so." She replied, "I can't Youth. I haven't any." His guilt about destroying her faith without providing any "compensating solace," Paine contends, haunted Twain for the rest of his life.[17] The paper trail, however, is very meager, and other evidence hints that Livy's Christian faith continued to some extent; for example, she and Twain were "very fond" of a Catholic priest during her last months of life in Italy, and she left behind a well-worn Bible.[18]

The Clemenses moved to Florence, Italy in November 1903, hoping that its climate would help Livy feel better. As her health instead continued to deteriorate, Twain penned the conclusion to his gloomy *Mysterious Stranger*. Perhaps expressing Twain's personal feelings, Its protagonist "Number Forty-four" proclaims, "There is no God, no universe, no human race, no earthly life, no heaven, nor hell." Everything is "a grotesque and foolish dream." Furthermore, perhaps echoing Twain's emotional state, the novel declares that earthly life is weary, groveling, and nasty. People's ambitions are paltry and the things they value are empty.[19]

As Livy lay dying, however, Twain told a friend that he was praying for her, although his prayers were "unutterable from any pulpit!"[20] Also, probably to comfort her, Twain played the piano and sang "Swing Low, Sweet Chariot," which promises "a band of angels coming after me; coming for to carry me home," and "My Lord He Calls Me," which proclaims, "Steal away, steal away, steal away to Jesus! Steal away, steal away home, I hain't got long to stay here."[21]

When Livy died on June 5, 1904 aged fifty-eight, Twain was both brokenhearted and guilt-ridden. He had lost his cherished wife, closest companion, and best editor (Livy often edited his manuscripts for grammar, accuracy, tact, and taste). "This evening, she that was the life of my life, passed to the relief and heavenly peace of death after 22 months of unjust and unearned suffering," he wrote. "I am full of remorse for things done and said in these thirty-four years of married life that hurt Livy's heart."[22]

Twichell, who had officiated at their wedding ceremony, presided at Livy's funeral service. Twain noted that he "committed her departed spirit to God," and mourners sang "Nearer, My God, to Thee." Twichell apparently said nothing about Livy's faith in his eulogy or his encomium in the *Hartford Courant*, in which he described

her as "one of the loveliest and best of women," revered for her
kindness and good will, "a perfect wife and mother," and an "intellectual companion and helpmate" to her husband.[23] Twain had
her headstone inscribed with "God be gracious, Oh, my Bliss!" in
German.[24] In "Eve's Diary" a distraught Adam, standing at her grave
and speaking for Twain, declares, "Wheresoever she was, *there* was
Eden."[25]

"How Poor I Am"

Twain's middle daughter Jean had struggled with epilepsy since age
fifteen. After seeking a cure for her in the United States and Europe,
he sent her to a sanitarium in Katonah, New York, where she resided
from fall 1906 to spring 1909. Jean was frustrated by her neurological
disorder and waning marital prospects. Like many other Americans
including her family members, she viewed epilepsy as a personal
defect; its victims lived with the stigma that they were irrational and
potentially violent. Jean's seizures had prompted Twain to cry out in
anguish several years earlier, "I cannot think why God, in a moment
of idle and unintelligent fooling, invented this bastard human race."[26]
Meanwhile, Twain's youngest daughter Clara was having an affair
with a married man, causing him further distress.

Jean's death on December 24, 1909 of an apparent heart attack,
caused by a seizure in the bathtub at the family estate in Redding,
Connecticut, was Twain's last torment. At the graveside service for
Livy, Twain had expressed hope that "I would never again look into
the grave of anyone dear to me," but now he was staring death in the
face again. Reflecting on the death of Jean, Susy, Livy, Henry Rogers,
and other friends, Twain wrote movingly, "How poor I am, who was
once so rich . . . . I sit here—writing, busying myself, to keep my heart
from breaking." With Clara gone to Europe, Twain had hoped that
he and Jean "would be close comrades and happy," but now she was
gone. "Telegrams of sympathy are flowing in, from far and wide,"
Twain reported, just as had occurred in Italy five years earlier when
Livy "laid down her blameless life. They cannot heal the hurt, but they
take away some of the pain." He was grateful that Jean had not died in
the sanitarium "in the hands of strangers, but in the loving shelter of
her own home." Lying on her bed, her face displayed "the dignity of

death and the peace of God." "God rest her sweet spirit!" Twain declared.[27]

Despite his agony, when the San Francisco *Call* sent Twain a telegram inquiring how he was doing, he replied humorously, "I hear that the newspapers say I am dying. I would not do such a thing at my time of life. I am behaving myself as well as I can. Merry Christmas to everybody." Twain's "The Death of Jean," the final chapter of his autobiography, Harold Bush, Jr. contends, features two elements that were central to his response to the spiritual crisis of his own life and his era: the search for home and the pain people experienced when they could not find one. To Bush, these were "sentiments at the heart of the biblical mythos," dating back to the Garden of Eden. Although Twain had enjoyed a happy marriage with Livy, in some ways the comforting home and hearth he craved, especially spiritually, remained elusive.[28] Four months later, Twain would be dead.

"The Greatest Figure in English Literature"

As he entered his seventies, literary giants showered Twain with praise. He was hailed as "the greatest figure in English literature" and "the greatest of living humorists and the uncrowned king of American letters."[29] The 170 luminaries, including female and African-American authors, who gathered in New York City in 1905 to celebrate Twain's seventieth birthday acknowledged him as their literary master. At this party, the humorist declared, "Threescore years and ten! It is the Scriptural statute of limitations. After that, you owe no active duties; for you the strenuous life is over. You are a time-expired man, to use [Rudyard] Kipling's military phrase: You have served your term, well or less well, and you are mustered out."[30] Nevertheless, works still flowed from Twain's pen, and tributes to his literary achievements continued unabated. Twain, William Lyon Phelps avowed, "is a true genius, whose books glow with the divine fire," and most of his contemporaries view him "not as their peer, but as their Chief." Twain's "humor is boisterous, uproarious, colossal, overwhelming." To understand the American spirit characterized by common sense, enterprise, energy, and good humor, Lyons avowed, foreigners should read Mark Twain.[31]

Despite relishing this effusive praise and having many friends, Twain often felt utterly alone and despondent after Livy died. "When I am not away from home I live in bed, to beat the lonesomeness," he wrote in 1906 to Mary Rogers, the daughter-in-law of his business advisor. Other letters to her during his last years are filled with his insuppressible humor, dejection, and "rage against brutal Nature."[32] In addition, the often compassionate and generous author sometimes held grudges for a long time and viciously denounced people who offended him.

Throughout his life, but especially in his final years, Twain was haunted by tragedies: the early death of two young siblings and his father; two deaths for which Twain felt personally responsible—his brother Henry at age twenty due to a steamboat explosion, and his son Langdon at nineteen months—and the later loss of his two daughters, his wife, and numerous close friends.

"Our Strained Relations"

During his final years, Twain often professed skepticism and doubts about Christianity. He raged against the pitiless, immoral Christian God, featured Satan in his tales, and wrote texts to convey his apostasy posthumously. Nevertheless, Ron Powers argues, his relationship with God was more like that of "a jilted lover" than a "coldhearted nonbeliever." Like Job, his suffering led him to reject "the comforts of orthodox faith." But unlike Job, who eventually stopped questioning God and reaffirmed his faith, Twain sought to find or devise a new religious system to satisfy his deepest longings. When a woman effused to Twain around 1906, "How God must love you!" he replied, "I hope so." After she left, he sadly told Albert Bigelow Paine, "I guess she hasn't heard of our strained relations."[33]

In his June 1906 autobiographical entries, Twain fumed against God, Jesus, the Bible, the virgin birth, predestination, providence, prayer, and Christianity. After finishing this diatribe, Twain wrote to Howells, "I have been dictating some fearful things for 4 successive mornings—for no eye but yours to see until I have been dead a century—if then. But I got them out of my system, where they had been festering for years—& that was the main thing. I feel better now." Disagreeing that Twain embraced atheism during his twilight years, Bush maintains that, although Twain was often emotionally distraught during this period, his grief prompted occasional "traces of a purely religious fervor." Twain sometimes repudiated the dire implications of determinism and instead preached a gospel of social amelioration.[34]

Anti-imperialism

Highlighting some of the international developments he deplored, Twain wondered in a 1905 essay how God felt as Americans prepared to celebrate Thanksgiving. Every Thanksgiving, he noted, Americans accentuated the blessings God had conferred upon them and citizens of other nations during the past year. This was good, Twain insisted, but no one considered how little God "had to be thankful for during the same period." The pens of many distinguished citizens expressed the nation's unstinted thankfulness, but was God grateful for human actions? Was God happy with the Russian government's butchering of 50,000 Jewish men and women "with knife and bayonet" or setting them on fire and drenching their children with boiling water? God was probably happy, Twain declared sarcastically, that King Leopold of Belgium had not killed as many innocent Congolese as last year; undoubtedly, God was "thankful that matters in the Congo are not as irretrievably bad as they might be, and that some natives still are left alive." God was upset, Twain added seriously, that the United States and other world powers were not stopping this slaughter. God's Thanksgiving Day, Twain concluded, "is not as rosy as ours."[35]

Twain's attacks on imperialist activity in South Africa, China, the Philippines, the Congo, and other locales in articles, pamphlets, newspaper interviews, and speeches made him a leading adversary of European and American empire building. Jim Zwick calls Twain the nation's "most prominent and outspoken opponent of imperialism" during the first decade of the twentieth century, and a Republican newspaper labeled him President William McKinley's "most dreaded critic."[36] Twain belonged to the American Friends of Russian Freedom, the Anti-Imperialist League, and the American Congo Reform Association, a branch of the first major international human rights organization.

In several of the anti-imperialist movement's most widely distributed and influential publications, Twain deplored the activities of
missionaries, European and US governments, Russian Czar Nicholas II, and Belgian King Leopold II. He denounced the Boer War in
South Africa, the suppression of the Boxer Rebellion in China, US
control of the Philippines, and the Russian seizure of Port Arthur
and Manchuria. Two of Twain's anti-imperialist essays (discussed
later in the chapter), written in 1901 and 1905 respectively, created
"a national sensation." Twain criticized the United States for
extending the doctrine of manifest destiny to Hawaii, Puerto Rico,
and the Philippines while allowing racial injustices at home. "I bring
you the matron named Christendom" (i.e., European and American
imperialists), Twain wrote as the nineteenth century ended,
"returning bedraggled, besmirched, and dishonored, from pirate
raids in Kiao-Chou [an area of China controlled by Germany],
Manchuria, South Africa, and the Philippines, with her soul full of
meanness, her pocket full of boodle, and her mouth full of pious
hypocrisies."[37] The New England Anti-Imperialist League printed
this statement on cards and disseminated it throughout the United
States.

Twain's denunciation of imperialism began much earlier. In 1873,
he argued satirically in an article in the New York *Tribune* that by
annexing Hawaii the United States could "afflict them with our wise
and beneficent government." The United States "can give them
railway corporations who will buy their Legislatures" and "some Jay
Goulds who will do away with their old-time notions that stealing is
not respectable." Americans could bequeath to the islands "the moral
splendor of our high and holy civilization."[38] During his 1895–1896
speaking tour, Twain visited India, Sri Lanka, New Zealand, Australia, and South Africa, where he observed the effects European nations
had on indigenous groups. In *Following the Equator* (1896), Twain
lamented that Europeans had usurped the land of native peoples in
many countries, forced them into slavery, destroyed their sense of
dignity, and overworked them until they dropped dead. "Land-
robbery," he protested, was becoming "a European governmental
frenzy."[39]

Twain insisted that imperialism had some benefits: as all "the
savage lands in the world" were controlled by "the Christian

governments of Europe," longstanding "bloodshed and disorder and oppression will give place to peace and order and the reign of law." The British prohibition of female infanticide and suttee (women throwing themselves on the funeral pyres of their husbands) would save thousands of lives. The Indian multitudes, he argued, were better off under British rule than that of Hindus or Muslims because the British governed "through tact, training, and distinguished administrative ability, reinforced by just and liberal laws."[40]

Nevertheless, in 1901 Twain scathingly depicted Western imperialists as "a majestic matron in flowing robes drenched in blood" and wearing "a golden crown of thorns"; impaled on her spine were "the bleeding heads of patriots who died for their country—Boers, Boxers, Filipinos; in the one hand a slingshot; in the other a Bible, open at the text 'Do unto others'" and "a banner with [the] motto—'Love your Neighbor's Goods as Yourself.'" The United States, Twain lamented, had instructed Europeans how to use widows and orphans to make profits.[41] William McKinley, Teddy Roosevelt, and "the multimillionaire disciples of Jay Gould," Twain argued, had incited Americans to abandon their "high and respectable ideals" and convert their Christianity into "a shell, a sham, [and] a hypocrisy." Americans had forgotten their "sympathies for oppressed peoples struggling for life and liberty." When Twichell counseled Twain not to deprecate imperialism publicly, the author responded that if the pastor instructed his parishioners "to hide their opinions when they believe the flag is being abused and dishonored" because doing so might bring them censure, "how do you answer for it to your conscience?" In disparaging imperialism, Clara Clemens argued, her father had the support of Livy and Howells, which enabled him "to stand like the Statue of Liberty," unweakened by his critics' "waters of condemnation."[42] In addition, by 1900 Twain was no longer financially dependent on the sales of his books for income and was willing to take unpopular stands.

Twain condemned British actions in South Africa and American policies in the Philippines, worked to end two of the greatest tragedies of the first decade of the twentieth century—czarist Russia's persecution and murder of thousands of Jews and Leopold's slaughter and torture of millions of Congolese—and strove to prevent war.

The Boer War

Twain accused mining magnate Cecil Rhodes, who used blacks as slave labor to procure South Africa's enormous wealth in diamonds, and his fellow British capitalists of causing the Boer War (1899–1902). He lambasted Rhodes as a Cain and a Judas and indicted British entrepreneurs for robbing and slaying countless South Africans.[43] Did anyone else notice, Twain asked, "that God is on both sides in this war"? The British and the Dutch think "He is playing the game" only on their side. By sending 300,000 soldiers and spending 800 million dollars, Twain's Mysterious Stranger sarcastically declares, Britain had made the Boers "better and purer and happier than they could ever have become by their own devices," although "there were only eleven Boers left now."[44]

The Philippines

The Anti-Imperialist League was formed on November 19, 1898 in response to US actions in the Philippines. Its members argued that Filipinos had simply exchanged masters—the United States for Spain—and were still being deprived of their rights. Seizing control of the archipelago without the free consent of its people, anti-imperialists warned, violated constitutional principles, wasted American resources, endangered the republic, and was "fraught with moral and physical evils." The league's platform stated that "all men, of whatever race or color, are entitled to life, liberty, and the pursuit of happiness."[45] League members failed to stop the Senate from narrowly approving the Treaty of Paris in February 1899, which gave Cuba, Guam, Puerto Rico, and the Philippines to the United States. Thereafter, they focused on defeating Republican William McKinley in the 1900 presidential election, because his party platform argued that America was obliged "to confer the blessings of liberty and civilization upon all rescued people." Some of the nation's most prominent citizens joined the league, including former president Grover Cleveland, social reformers Jane Addams and Josephine Shaw Lowell, American Federation of Labor president Samuel Gompers, philosophers John Dewey and William James, Rabbi David Philipson, and Society for Ethical Culture founder Felix Adler; by

February 1899, it had more than 25,000 members. Twain served as vice president of its New York branch, and several of his friends were also league officers, including Henry Van Dyke, Andrew Carnegie, William Dean Howells, and journalist Carl Schurz. After McKinley was reelected and assassinated in September 1901, Theodore Roosevelt became president, and Emilio Aguinaldo led a Filipino revolt against American rule, the league continued protesting American policies.[46]

While living in Austria, Twain supported the US declaration of war against Spain in 1898, which he believed was intended only to free Cuba from Spain's oppressive control. He refuted European claims that the United States was fighting to achieve imperialist objectives. Twain rejoiced that the US military's actions had placed Cuba "among the galaxy of free nations of the world." "This is the worthiest" war a nation has ever fought, he told Twichell in June 1898. Fighting for one's own freedom was commendable, Twain declared; fighting for other people's freedom was even more praiseworthy. "I think this is the first time it has been done." In demanding that Spain stop its atrocities in Cuba, the United States had adopted "the highest moral position ever taken by a nation since the Almighty made the earth."[47] The liberation of Cuba was consistent with America's great traditions. By not forcibly annexing Cuba, which would have been "criminal aggression," the United States had "fired another 'shot heard round the world.'"[48]

Twain's attitude toward imperialism and the results of the Spanish-American War soon changed, however. Returning from Europe in October 1900, Twain announced, "I am an anti-imperialist." When he had left Vancouver in 1895 to begin his world lecture tour, Twain explained, he was "a red-hot imperialist. I wanted the American eagle to go screaming into the Pacific" and "spread its wings over the Philippines." The Filipinos had suffered under Spanish rule for three centuries, and the United States could "make them as free as ourselves," give them their own government, and create a new republic. Twain concluded, however, that the United States intended to subjugate rather than liberate the Filipino people. "We have gone there to conquer, not to redeem," he protested.[49]

Opposing the United States' control of the Philippines became one of Twain's principal activities during the final decade of his life.[50] In addition to serving as an officer of the Anti-Imperialist League, Twain used his powerful pen to denounce US policies in the archipelago and supported political initiatives to change these policies. After criticizing American actions in a newspaper interview, Twain wrote to Twichell, "I'm not expecting anything but kicks for scoffing at McKinley, that conscienceless thief & traitor, & am expecting a diminution of my bread & butter by it, but if Livy will let me I will have my say. This nation is like all the others"; it is ready to support "any cause that will tickle its vanity or fill its pocket."[51]

Livy apparently had no objection, because Twain did not stop his vehement attacks. He deplored the Treaty of Paris, especially the idea of the United States paying $20 million for the Philippines. He labeled this "the stupendous joke of the century" because the United States already controlled the islands at the time of the sale. This payment, he protested, was "an entrance fee" into the European imperialist "Society of Sceptred Thieves." "We are now on par with the rest of them."[52]

Twain further censured US policies in "To the Person Sitting in Darkness," published in February 1901. The "Philippine temptation," he argued, had been too strong to resist. If the United States had obeyed its traditional rules, Admiral George Dewey would have sailed away after destroying the Spanish fleet in Manila Bay on May 1, 1898. Americans could have allowed Filipino citizens to set up whatever form of government they preferred and to deal with Spanish friars according to their own "ideas of fairness and justice," which were equal to any in Europe or America. Instead, however, the United States had played the European game and lost its chance to add "another honorable deed to our good record." "The Person Sitting in Darkness," Twain insisted, would surely conclude that "there must be two Americas: one that sets the captive free, and one that takes a once-captive's new freedom away from him," picks "a quarrel with him," and "then kills him to get his land." Adopting the European strategy, the United States sent an army to the Philippines, "ostensibly to help the native patriots" finish "their long and plucky struggle for independence," but actually to steal their land. Americans "lied to them—officially proclaiming that our land and naval forces came to give them their freedom and displace the bad Spanish Government." Americans tricked the Filipinos and used them until they were no longer needed, while offering assurance that "the ways of Providence are best." Americans supposedly lied for "a good cause." They acted treacherously so that "good might come out of apparent evil." "We have turned against the weak and the friendless who trusted us," Twain protested; "we have stamped out a just and intelligent and well-ordered republic; we have stabbed an ally in the back" and "robbed a trusting friend of his land and his liberty."[53] The United States controlled the Philippines, Twain avowed, "as if it were our property"; Americans had destroyed Filipinos' crops, burned their villages, made countless widows and orphans homeless, and subjugated millions to achieve their commercial purposes. When the United States "snatched the Philippines," Twain asserted, "she stained the flag."[54]

Twain denounced American policies in the Philippines in other publications too. One of his poems portrays a dying McKinley beseeching God to forgive him for making the United States a "Conqueror of helpless tribes, [and an] Extinguisher of struggling liberties!" In an accompanying illustration, an American flag signifies the nation's sins: a "Skull & Bones" replaces the stars, the red bars are soaked with blood, and the white bars have become black. In 1901, *Harper's Magazine* editor John Kendrick Bangs and Twain debated the question, "Is the Philippine Policy of the administration just?" In reviewing a book about Aguinaldo that year, Twain compared him with Joan of Arc, his greatest hero.[55]

In February 1902, Twain signed a petition authored by Republican Senator George Hoar of Massachusetts, asking the Senate to hold discussions with Filipino leaders to end the hostilities in the islands. Other prominent signers included William Dean Howells, Carl Schurz, historian Charles Francis Adams, Jr., Presbyterian pastor Charles Parkhurst, Episcopal Bishop Frederic Dan Huntington, and social activist William Lloyd Garrison, Jr. When the war finally ended in July 1902, 4,234 US soldiers had died, the American military had killed an estimated 20,000 Filipino soldiers, and violence, famine, and disease had murdered as many as 200,000 Filipino civilians.[56]

Russia

In numerous articles and speeches, Twain censured Russian Czar Nicholas II, who ruled from 1894 to 1917, for ruthlessly attacking other nations, callously mistreating his countrymen, and brutally persecuting his nation's Jewish inhabitants. His great concern for the plight of the Russian people prompted Twain to work to end their oppression. Twain was an original member of the American Friends of Russian Freedom, founded in 1891 to "aid by all moral and legal means the Russian patriots in their efforts to obtain" self-government. The organization's leaders included William Lloyd Garrison, Jr., Unitarian minister Thomas Wentworth Higginson, and Frederic Dan Huntington.[57]

Twain complained in 1901 that Russia had stolen Port Arthur from Japan while spilling much Chinese blood and had seized Manchuria, raiding its villages and choking its major river "with the swollen corpses of countless massacred peasants." Russia was another allegedly "Civilized Power that held its "banner of the Prince of Peace in one hand and its loot-basket and its butcher-knife in the other."[58]

In Twain's satirical article, "The Czar's Soliloquy," published in *North American Review* in March 1905, Nicholas II provides a woeful, self-incriminating justification for his rule. Because of his clothes and title, Nicholas proclaims, an emperor could get his people to worship him as a deity and could hunt, harry, exile, and destroy them, just as people treated rats. For centuries, Nicholas declares, the Russian masses had "meekly allowed our Family to rob them, insult them, [and] trample them under foot"; they lived, suffered, and died with no purpose except to make the royal family comfortable. Nicholas insists that Russian czars are above the law; they had done as they "pleased for centuries. Our common trade," Nicholas admits, "has been crime, our common pastime murder, our common beverage blood—the blood of the nation. Upon our heads lie millions of murders." His ancestors, Nicholas states, used murder, treachery, torture, banishment, and imprisonment to establish and maintain their rule, and "by these same arts I hold it to-day."[59]

Twain's essay included a July 1904 *The Times* of London article on residents of a city in western Russia who pressed against the czar's "carriage in order to carry away an indelible memory of the hallowed features of the Lord's Anointed. Many old people had spent the night" praying and fasting "to be worthy to gaze at his countenance." "With one hand I flogged unoffending women to death and tortured prisoners to unconsciousness," Nicholas boasts in Twain's parody, "and with the other I held up the fetish toward my fellow deity in heaven and called down His blessing upon my adoring animals whom, and whose forbears, with His holy approval, I and mine have been instructing in the pains of hell" for four centuries.[60]

As "cruel and pitiful as life was throughout Christendom in the Middle Ages," Twain wrote, it was not as vicious and miserable as contemporary life in Russia. For three centuries, Russia's vast population had been "ground under the heels" for "the sole and sordid advantage of . . . crowned assassins and robbers" who "all deserved the gallows." Speaking at a meeting in New York City to honor Russian author Maxim Gorky in 1906, Twain praised efforts to make Russia free.[61] However, as long as Nicholas commanded the army, navy, and treasury, he declared, Russia had no hope. All the concessions the czar had recently made would amount to nothing unless the Russian people gained control of these three entities.[62]

Twain especially deplored the persecution and pogroms the Jews suffered in Russia. In the 1860s, Twain insisted that God's choice of the Jews as his special people was a stunning mystery. By the 1890s, however, Twain often praised the Jews for their intelligence, business acumen, and work ethic and denounced their mistreatment. In 1890, Twain praised Jewish charity and family loyalty and denounced "anti-Semitism as an irrational manifestation of inherited prejudice."[63] Twain attacked anti-Semitism in two versions of the same story, probably written in 1896—"Newhouse's Jew Story" and "Randall's Jew Story."

Living in Vienna from September 1897 to May 1899 gave Twain more contact with and greater appreciation of Jews. He concluded that they were more intelligent than other ethnic groups and were persecuted for economic more than religious reasons. Her father, Clara Clemens insisted, had long greatly admired Jews, and residing in Vienna enabled him "to test and prove the soundness of his good opinion." While there, Twain often participated in arguments about the virtues and flaws of Jews and ardently defended them.[64] Twain deprecated malicious Austrian attacks on Jews in both "Stirring Times in Austria" (1898) and "Chronicle of Young Satan," written between 1897 and 1900.

Although not all Jews had been geniuses, Twain argued, their level of intelligence was far above average, which was one reason non-Jews sought to "drive them out" of the higher echelons of business and the professions. Jews, Twain added, were "the world's intellectual aristocracy." The Jews, he told Twichell, were "the most marvelous" ethnic group in the world. "I have no prejudices against Jews," Twain wrote in his autobiography.[65] Twain supported Clara's marriage to Ossip Gabrilowitsch, a Jewish refugee from Russia, in 1909.[66]

Such convictions prompted Twain to deplore the unjust treatment of Jews in Russia. He called Alexander III, who ruled from 1881 to 1894, "his Satanic Majesty of Russia" partly because he mistreated religious minorities, especially the Jews.[67] Twain repeatedly censured Nicholas II for massacring thousands of Jews.[68] Twain and French actress Sarah Bernhardt were the principal speakers at a December 1905 benefit matinee, which raised $3,000 to assist Russian Jews. "All of us that deserve it," Twain declared, would hopefully someday enjoy "a heaven of rest & peace," whereas others would be "permitted to retire into the clutches of Satan, or the emperor of Russia, according to [their] preference."[69]

The Congo

Twain was also deeply moved by the plight of the Congolese and strove to end their suffering. King Leopold II, who ruled Belgium from 1865 to 1909, had persuaded the United States and Western European nations to recognize a large part of Central Africa as his personal property. Twain's advocacy helped end the genocide caused by famine, disease, and Leopold's horrific policies and to transfer control of the Congo in 1908 from the king to the Belgian parliament, which adopted a much more humane policy.

The atrocities occurring in the Congo led E. D. Morel to found the English Congo Reform Association in March 1904. Meanwhile, William Morrison, a Presbyterian missionary to the Congo, organized a protest movement in the United States. In April a group of missionary societies petitioned the Senate to help the Congo gain independence from Belgium. The Senate's refusal to act contributed to the creation of an American branch of the Congo Reform Association (CRA) in September.

In *King Leopold's Soliloquy* (1905), as in "The Czar's Soliloquy," a villain provides an appallingly inadequate defense of his actions. Twain portrays Leopold as a pious hypocrite who uses Christianity to justify his abominable policies. Leopold argues that European powers had agreed to "place the vast and rich populous Congo Free state in trust in my hands as their agent, so that I might root out slavery," lift twenty-five million "gentle and harmless blacks out of darkness" into "the light of our blessed Redeemer," and help "them comprehend that they were no longer outcasts and forsaken, but our very brothers in Christ." Leopold maintains that he had carefully guarded the persons, liberties, and properties of the natives against hurt and harm; prohibited whisky and gun traffic; provided courts of justice; allowed merchants of all nations to trade; and welcomed and safeguarded "missionaries of all creeds and denominations."[70]

Despite these achievements, Leopold protests, meddlesome American missionaries, outspoken British consuls, and "blabbingblabbing Belgian-born traitor officials" claimed that for twenty years he had ruled as an "irresponsible, above all law" sovereign and had trampled the Congo charter devised by the Berlin Congress of 1884–1885 under foot. These groups argued that Leopold had treated millions of people as serfs and slaves. Like Nicholas II, Leopold contends that a king is "a sacred personage and immune from reproach" because God had appointed him. Criticizing his acts was blasphemy, since God had not "hampered nor interrupted them in any way."[71]

Nevertheless, critics continue their broadside in the soliloquy. They accuse Leopold of placing "incredibly burdensome taxes upon the natives." These taxes could be paid only by gathering rubber under increasingly "harder conditions, and by raising and furnishing food supplies gratis." And when they failed to complete their tasks because of "hunger, sickness, despair, and ceaseless and exhausting labor" and fled to the woods "to escape punishment," Leopold's soldiers, recruited from non-Congolese tribes, hunted them down, butchered them, and burned their villages. Critics claim that "if the innocent blood shed in the Congo State by King Leopold were put in buckets and the buckets placed side by side, the line would stretch 2,000 miles; if the skeletons of his ten millions starved and butchered dead could rise up and march in single file," it would take more than seven months for them to pass.[72]

Further underscoring the claimed connection between Christianity and imperialism, the cover of *King Leopold's Soliloquy* shows a crucifix superimposed over a machete, accompanied by the inscription, "By this sign we prosper." Twain donated all profits from the pamphlet to the CRA and paid for copies to be sent to 100 influential Protestant ministers, to help convince them to support the CRA's work.

Twain's soliloquy, the *Boston Daily Globe* asserted, poured vials of "wrath and sarcasm" on Leopold's head. In an interview, Twain denounced a report made by a committee the king appointed to investigate conditions in the Congo as "a farce and a lie," trusting instead the accounts of missionaries who contradicted the committee's conclusions and presenting several photographs of mutilated Congolese. "I have seen [other] photographs of the natives with their hands cut off," he added, "because they did not bring in the requited amount of rubber. If Leopold had only killed them outright it would not be so bad," Twain sarcastically commented; "but to cut off their hands and leave them helpless to die in misery—that is not forgivable."[73]

After the work's publication, Twain strove vigorously to stop the carnage in the Congo.[74] In November 1905, he became the first vice-president of the CRA. G. Stanley Hall, a prominent psychologist and president of Clark University, served as president; the other vice-presidents included Congregational minister and editor Lyman Abbott, Stanford University's president David Starr Jordan, Henry Van Dyke, and Booker T. Washington.

Later that month, Twain penned another essay, "A Thanksgiving Sentiment," which censured the United States as the "official godfather of the Congo Graveyard" because it was the first nation to recognize Leopold's pirate flag and refused to condemn "the prodigious depredations & multitudinous murders" of "helpless natives" committed by Leopold's agents.[75] Twain denounced Leopold in an interview in the *New York World Sunday Magazine* on November 26, 1905 as a "wholesale murderer," a "greedy, grasping, avaricious, cynical, bloodthirsty old goat!" The king sat "in luxury and debauchery, placidly ordering [that] thousands of innocent human creatures" be "tortured, crippled, [or] massacred" to increase his wealth. "If only we could bring home that picture" to the American people, Twain asserted, they would "destroy that aged, brutal trafficker in human flesh!"[76]

In a third essay, which was not published, Twain again argued that the US government, by its many years of silence, shared responsibility with other Christian powers for "the most prodigious crime in all human history."[77] From November 1905 to January 1906, Twain made at least three trips to Washington to discuss the tragic conditions in the Congo with State Department officials and President Theodore Roosevelt.

In his autobiography, Twain protested that the Belgian king, a professed Christian, had "stolen an entire kingdom in Africa" and in fourteen years had reduced the Congolese population from thirty to fifteen million "by murder, mutilation, overwork, robbery, rapine— confiscating the helpless native's very labor, and giving him nothing in return but salvation and a home in heaven, furnished at the last moment by the Christian priest." Leopold could carry out this slaughter and theft because none of "the Christian powers except England" lifted "a hand or voice to stop these atrocities," even though they had signed a treaty pledging to protect and uplift the Congolese.[78]

Neither in his soliloquy nor anywhere else did Twain propose a solution to Leopold's horrendous rule. Meanwhile, the CRA simply called for an independent international body to investigate conditions in the Congo. The solution it eventually recommended was not independence but a transfer of governing authority from Leopold to the Belgian parliament, which took place in 1908.[79]

Twain and Missionaries

While lambasting Leopold's actions in the Congo, Twain also accused missionaries serving with the American Board of Commissioners for Foreign Missions (ABCFM, responsible for about four thousand foreign workers in 1900) of serving as agents of imperialism. His evaluation of the missionary enterprise throughout his life, however, was mixed. Illustrating this ambivalence, Twain satirized missionaries in *Roughing It* (1872) but published a disclaimer in the *New York Tribune*, declaring that although missionary work was "slow and discouraging" and did not yield immediately results, it was not "hopeless or useless." The seeds missionaries sowed, he predicted, "will produce wholesome fruit in the third generation, & certainly that result is worth striving for."[80] Twain gave generously to missionary causes and spoke at numerous mission fundraisers, helping to attract larger audiences and gifts. He contributed substantially to Twichell's American Chinese Educational Mission, which enabled Chinese youth to study in the United States, culminating in attending Yale University. This program introduced these students to both American education and the gospel. Twain also helped convince the Chinese government to not shut down the program.[81]

Twain sometimes praised missionaries for their character, sacrifice, and efforts to improve people's living conditions, political circumstances, education, health, and morality. He described the Protestant missionaries he met on an 1866 trip to the Hawaiian islands as "pious; hard-working, hard-praying; self-sacrificing; hospitable," and committed to the indigenous people's well-being. Twain similarly lauded Catholic missionaries as "honest, straightforward, frank," industrious, and "devoted to their religion and their work." He rejoiced that Protestants and Roman Catholics were "striding along, hand in hand, under the banner of the Cross!"[82] Since arriving in Hawaii in 1820, Twain argued, missionaries had broken the power of chiefs, set people free, and taught many people to read and write.[83] They had also provided religious freedom, a written language, and the Bible. Missionaries had "made honest men out of a nation of thieves," instituted marriage, improved family life, increased the rights and privileges of women, abolished infanticide and intemperance, helped the islands' inhabitants pass laws to improve moral practices, largely eliminated idolatry, and made many converts.[84] Before missionaries arrived, Hawaiians had been "thundering barbarians," offering human sacrifices to appease hideous idols as late as the eighteenth century, but now they were "the kindest-hearted, the most unselfish creatures that bear the image of the Maker." The benefits of the missionaries' work were evident in how much conditions in Hawaii had improved by the mid-1860s, compared to what English captain James Cook observed in 1778. "Well done, good and faithful servants!" Twain declared.[85]

In 1870, Twain praised the ABCFM for "supplying the kindly and refining influences of the gospel" to people living in Asia and islands in the Pacific, but he urged missionaries to stay home because there were "no meaner, mangier, filthier savages" in the world than in places like Cohocton, a small town in north central New York.[86] In the 1890s,

Twain commended Western missionaries who brought Christianity to indigenous populations in Australia, as well as the Salvation Army and Trappist monks in South Africa for alleviating poverty and educating natives.[87] Almost all missionaries serving throughout the world, Twain asserted in 1901, were "kind hearted, earnest, devoted to their work." Missionaries would not make "such large sacrifices" unless they had loving hearts. They displayed great faith, zeal, courage, and passion by leaving their homes and friends, patiently enduring "discomforts, privations, [and] discouragements," and willingly facing death by serving God.[88]

On the other hand, Twain disapproved of some of the missionaries' teachings and accused many of them of forcing Western norms and customs on converts, compelling children to worship unfamiliar gods, and promoting Americanism. Missionaries, Twain argued, had made many Hawaiian islanders "miserable by telling them how beautiful and blissful a place heaven is, and how nearly impossible it is to get in" and, conversely, how dreary perdition is and how likely it is that they would go there. Sadly, Twain wrote sarcastically, multitudes had died in these beautiful islands without knowing "there was a hell!" Missionaries also taught Hawaiians how delightful it was to work all day for Americans to earn money to buy food, instead of fishing as a pastime, lounging in the shade, and eating the bounty that nature provided.[89]

In the final decade of his life, Twain's criticism of missionaries intensified. In an essay submitted to *The Times* of London in 1900, Twain declared that missionaries from Turkey, China, or Polynesia had not intruded on Westerners "to break our hearts" by destroying "our children's faith & winning them to the worship of alien gods." Westerners did not know how indigenous parents felt when their children derided and blasphemed the religion of their ancestors. Westerners had not experienced a foreign missionary "lauding his own saints & gods & saying harsh things about ours." Christian missionaries did not wish to offend their potential converts, but their message was insulting nevertheless, regardless of how it was presented. Christian missionaries with children, Twain asserted, should feel deep compassion for parents whose hearts they broke by enticing their children to leave the family religion for a new faith that the parents considered "treachery and apostasy."[90]

In 1909, Twain complained to Twichell that missionaries preyed on children because they could not convert adults. Missionaries beguiled little children to abandon their parents' religion, causing them immeasurable grief. "Would you be willing to have a Mohammedan missionary do that with your children or grandchildren?" Twain asked, or would you support a government that allowed Muslim missionaries to ply their trade? Since Twichell would not want these things to occur, Twain argued, the pastor must not support Christian missionaries imposing their message upon foreign peoples who did not want to hear it, for such behavior did not comply with Christ's admonition to "do unto others." "The Christian missionary," Twain wrote, was the planet's greatest criminal and worst malefactor. In fact, Twain urged Twichell to bring his dear, sweet daughter home from mission work in Turkey and be thankful that she had not been killed.[91]

Missionaries, Twain contended, converted few people because there were 210 varieties of Christians, all of whom believed that their version of the faith was the truest. Indigenous groups did not want to give up the certainty of their religions "for an uncertainty." Many followers of other religions had no doubts about their own faith and were reluctant to lose their way among the plethora of Christian groups. "Since the beginning of the world," Twain claimed, 225,000,000,000 "savages" had been "born and damned, and [only] 28,000 saved by missionary effort!"[92]

Twain derided missionaries for assisting US imperialism.[93] Although they had brought many benefits to Hawaii, they also advanced the interest of American merchants and promoted businessmen's political aspirations. The work of Christian missionaries in Africa and Asia, Twain argued, was even more exploitative than in Hawaii, and the image of Jesus had become a "sign of racial oppression."[94] Missionaries had been laboring in China for eighty years "with the best intentions," Twain asserted in 1896. Nevertheless, through their work, nearly 100,000 Chinese had unfortunately acquired American civilization. "By the compassion of God," thankfully four hundred million Chinese had escaped America's corrupting effects. In a satirical essay, written in 1901 but not published until 1923, Twain urged American missionaries to return from China to help end lynching in the South. These 1,500 missionaries, he claimed, were currently converting 3,000 "pagans" per year while 12 million Chinese were born every year. Since they were not making any significant progress, why not undertake a better assignment at home? Moreover, the Chinese, Twain asserted, "are universally conceded to be excellent people, honest, honorable, industrious, trustworthy, [and] kind-hearted." Therefore, missionaries should leave them alone, and "besides, almost every convert runs a risk of catching" harmful aspects of American civilization.[95] The missionary enterprise, Twain argued, was doomed to fail. Throughout history, nations had occasionally changed religion because of compulsion but never because of persuasion.[96]

In 1901, Twain's satirical essay "To the Person Sitting in Darkness," published in the *North American Review*, garnered national attention and produced a heated debate between the celebrated author and missionary leaders. Twain complained that William Ament, head of the ABCFM, had imposed excessive financial penalties on the Chinese for the murders of Chinese Christians and the property damage that occurred during the Boxer Rebellion in 1900. Perhaps worse, Twain contended, Americans expected their missionaries not only to represent their religion but also to promote "the American spirit" and advance US interests.[97] The essay's title alluded to Matthew 4:16, which missionaries often used to designate the "pagan," "uncivilized" residents of areas controlled by European powers.

Twain's essay vilified those he considered the principal proponents of imperialism—William McKinley, Kaiser Wilhelm of Germany, and Joseph Chamberlain, the British secretary for the colonies. Referring to the description of major business enterprises as "trusts," Twain complained that missionaries helped advance "the Blessings-of-Civilization Trust" promoted by wealthy businessmen. The real goal was to give Western nations more territory, trade, and money in exchange for bequeathing their allegedly superior moral values and cultural practices to "lesser developed" nations. The people who sit in darkness, however, had "become suspicious of the Blessings of Civilization." Numerous events had revealed the negative effects of Western civilization including the Boer War, conflicts between European nations, and the extreme reparations Germany had demanded from the Chinese to pay for their losses during riots in Shantung in 1899. Observing Christians fighting Christians to gain filthy lucre prompted the people sitting in darkness to ask, "Is this a case of magnanimity, forbearance, love, gentleness, mercy, protection of the weak?" They were also left wondering if there were "two kinds of Civilization—one for home consumption and one for the heathen market." These experiences left them understandably skeptical about the merits of Western civilization.[98]

American missionary leaders denounced Twain's "sensational and ugly bombardment" of Ament. They pointed out that a cable error had led the author to believe that the Chinese were asked to pay indemnities of thirteen times the cost of the damages inflicted, whereas the actual amount was only one and one third times. When missionary leaders demanded an apology, Twain instead responded with a second article in the *North American Review*, containing further attacks. He protested that Ament had not taken his claim to Chinese courts for redress; instead, the missionary leader threatened to use foreign soldiers to collect the indemnity and then falsely claimed that the Chinese were happy to pay it. Twain denounced the extra one-third the board extracted from impoverished Chinese peasants in damages as "theft and extortion."[99] The board responded that it was customary in China to hold the residents of a village responsible for crimes its members committed and to collect a third more than the damage incurred, which the board had used to support the widows and orphans of slain converts.[100] Several prominent diplomats also defended Ament's actions: New York lawyer and future Secretary of State Henry Stimson; Charles Harvey Denby, former US Minister to China; Edwin Conger, the current Minister to China; and Colonel Claude MacDonald, the principal British diplomat in Beijing during the Boxer Rebellion. On the other hand, Livy reported to a friend that the hundreds of letters sent to her husband from around the world were running ten to one in favor of his position.[101]

Twain's extensive travels reinforced his natural inclination to value a wide variety of religions and his distaste for efforts to convert people who espoused other faiths. In a lecture frequently delivered in the late 1860s titled "The American Vandal Abroad," Twain argued that international travel enlarged people's charity and benevolence, broadened their understanding of humanity, deepened their generosity, and increased their sensitivity to the shortcomings of others.

Experiences abroad taught people that "God put something good and loveable" into everyone he created.[102]

Twain insisted that Christians should be unconcerned about other people's religious convictions. "So much blood has been shed by the Church," Twain lamented, "because of an omission from the Gospel: 'Ye shall be indifferent'" about "'your neighbor's religion.'" Unfortunately, many people lived by the motto, "If a man doesn't believe as we do, we say he is a crank, and that settles it." Twain greatly admired the "healthy" religious environment he observed in southern Australia, which enabled all groups living there—agnostics, atheists, freethinkers, infidels, pagans, Mormons, various Protestant denominations, Roman Catholics, and Eastern Orthodox—to spread and prosper.[103]

Clara Clemens argued that her father was especially moved by his experiences with Hindus in India. Despite "father's inability to adhere to any religious belief himself," she declared, "he loved to see evidences of that higher life in others." Many Indians spent hours kneeling in worship on the banks of the Ganges, Twain noted, while Americans were "robbing and murdering." At times her father "seemed almost awed" by "the gentleness of the Indian people," as if "it were an undeniable gift from God."[104]

In 1902, Twain started a club and named it after the Hindu god Juggernaut, whom he considered the best god he knew. Juggernaut had no preferences, partialities, prejudices, or resentments and placed no person higher than others.[105] All his actions "are kind, gentle, merciful, beautiful, lovable." When people visited his temple, all ranks and economic statuses vanished; the street sweeper, prince, outcast, mendicant, and millionaire all stood on the same level. Other gods, Twain proposed, could improve by studying Juggernaut.[106]

Opposition to War

Twain's close relationship with Twichell, some Civil War veterans, and Ulysses S. Grant helps explain his reluctance to criticize war before 1900. Twain deeply admired Grant and some other Union leaders, had great sympathy for Grant's financial woes after a business partner cheated him out of most of his assets, and published Grant's *Personal Memoirs*. In various writings and speeches, most notably *Life on the Mississippi* (1883), "The Private History of a Campaign that Failed"

(1885), and "On Lincoln's Birthday" (1901), Twain emphasized the two principal objectives of Northern discourse after the war: endorsing Northern civil religion, which lauded the Union for cleansing the nation from slavery and promoting equal rights for all, and rejecting Southern civil religion, especially the myth of the Lost Cause.[107]

During his final decade, however, Twain, in addition to censuring imperialism and some missionary activities, became a staunch and outspoken critic of war. He denounced the US effort to end the insurgency in the Philippines and the increase in armaments and bellicosity among Western nations that eventually led to World War I. Twain condemned the folly and horrors of war in his autobiography, *The Mysterious Stranger, What Is Man?*, and the "Chronicle of Young Satan." "Man is the only animal," Twain declared, that participates in the "atrocity of atrocities, War." Man alone goes "forth in cold blood and calm pulse to exterminate" his own species and slaughter strangers "who have done him no harm and with whom he has no quarrel."[108] Statesmen, Twain protested, invented "cheap lies" to convince themselves that war is just and thanked God for the better sleep they enjoyed "after this process of grotesque self-deception."[109]

In *The Mysterious Stranger*, Satan warns that the implements of war are becoming increasingly destructive: Cain committed "his murder with a club; the Hebrews did their murders with javelins and swords; and the Greeks and Romans added protective armor" and military organization. Ignoring the Chinese contribution, Twain asserted that Christians invented guns and gunpowder. In the future, Satan asserts, "the pagan world will go to school to the Christian; not to acquire his religion, but his guns."[110]

Protesting American efforts to suppress the Philippine revolt against US control of their archipelago as the twentieth century began, Twain lamented, "Against our traditions we are now entering upon an unjust...war against a helpless people, and for a base object—robbery." Many Americans, he objected, had accepted the empty, silly slogan, "Our Country, right or wrong!" Every newspaper and pulpit shouted this phrase, and every school in the nation displayed it. To be considered patriotic, people had to repeat this slogan and support this unjust war. Even if a war were wrong, Twain argued, Americans falsely believed they could not "retire from it without dishonor." Withdrawing from "this sordid raid" and granting independence to Filipinos upon their terms, he insisted, would not dishonor Americans.[111] Those who abided by the principle of "Our country, right or wrong!" threw away their "most valuable asset"—the right "to oppose both flag and country" when they believed their nation's actions were wrong.[112]

Twain also repudiated Brooklyn Congregational pastor Newell Dwight Hillis's claim that the 1904–1905 Russo-Japanese War was God's "way of destroying tyranny." The villainies, slaughter, and despotism that had "so suddenly dawned on the Deity and excited" Hillis had been going on for three hundred years. If abolishing these tyrannies was good now, Twain avowed, it would have been infinitely better for God "to do it three centuries ago." Hillis should be lamenting that "the deep miseries of the hungry and oppressed Russian millions" had not ended much earlier. People should not praise someone, Twain declared, if he arrived three centuries late to fight a fire with his hook and ladder company.[113]

Twain also denounced the unending competition of France, Britain, Russia, and the United States to build battleships. Someday, he warned, all men would be at sea manning fleets and only women would remain on land. This silly, costly, ruinous game was called statesmanship, but it differed from "assmanship" only in spelling. "Anybody but a statesman," Twain reasoned, "could invent some way to reduce these vast armaments to rational and sensible and safe" levels so that "all Christians could sleep in their beds unafraid, and even the Savior could come down and walk on the seas, foreigner as He is, without dread of being chased by Christian battleships." The only peaceful nations, Twain asserted, are the "unhappy ones" that had "not been invaded by the Gospel of Peace. All Christendom is a soldier-camp." During the last two decades, he protested, "the Christian poor have been taxed almost to starvation-point to support the giant armaments," which European Christian governments had produced to protect themselves "from the rest of the brotherhood" and to snatch any real estate left exposed by poorer nations. England alone had already stolen millions of acres from "helpless and godless pagans."[114]

Twain's "War Prayer" may be his strongest denunciation of militarism. A women's magazine declined to publish it in 1905, and it was not made public until 1923. In Twain's story, a town holds a church service to support its young men as they head off to war. A stranger enters the service and warns the patriotic worshippers that by asking God to give them victory, they will also be praying for their enemies to be destroyed. Fulfilling his admonition, the congregation prays, "O Lord our God, help us tear their soldiers to bloody shreds with our shells; help us to cover their smiling fields with the pale forms of their patriot dead; help us to drown the thunder of the guns with the shrieks of their wounded, writhing in pain; help us to lay waste their humble homes with a hurricane of fire; help us to wring the hearts of their unoffending widows with unavailing grief; help us to turn them out roofless with their little children to wander unfriended the wastes of their desolated land in rags and hunger and thirst." Unable to accept the stranger's reasoning, the worshippers conclude that he is "a lunatic."[115] The "War Prayer" was very popular with Vietnam War protesters in the 1960s and was circulated widely on the internet after the US invasion of Iraq in 2003.

Determinism and *The Mysterious Stranger*

Influenced by William Lecky, Thomas Hobbes, David Hume, and others, Twain, during his final fifteen years, frequently professed belief in determinism. He defended this philosophical perspective in two of his last books—*What Is Man?* and *The Mysterious Stranger*—as well as in his autobiography and several essays including his last published one, "The Turning Point in My Life." These works also contain some of his most caustic attacks on Christianity.

Twain privately published *What Is Man?*, which he called his Bible, in 1906 and shared it with friends. Through a dialogue between an old man (the enlightened Twain who conveys the truth) and a young man (his youthful self, full of illusions), the celebrated author sought to systematically explain his mechanistic worldview. Twain argued that people's training and temperament, coupled with their circumstances, account for everything they think, say, or do—their preferences, aversions, politics, morals, and religion. People naively think they adopt such views themselves because they have never carefully examined the matter. Moreover, people are driven by an overarching motive—the drive for self-approval—that determines every decision they make.[116]

Not published until after Twain died, *The Mysterious Stranger* offers a more engaging explication of Twain's deterministic philosophy. It lampoons providence, the nature of hell, and other theological concepts; numerous aspects of church history, especially the persecution of alleged witches and the torture of people accused of heresy; and Catholicism's attempt to restrict people's knowledge and its teaching on last rites and purgatory. The stranger, Philip Traum, befriends Theodor, the young narrator of the story, and his friends Nikolaus and Seppl in an Austrian village during the late sixteenth century. Claiming to be Satan, the handsome stranger dazzles the boys with stunning miracles and intervenes in the lives of numerous villagers. He unfairly reprimands people for doing acts that fate required them to perform. As a supernatural being, Traum can transcend the deterministic universe in which all humans are enmeshed, and, unlike them, express views based on rational analysis rather than on social conditioning.[117]

Traum explains that people have no control over their destiny, because everything that happens is part of a linked chain of cause and effect. Twain's essay traces his becoming a writer back to Julius Caesar crossing the Rubicon and ultimately to Adam's decision to eat the forbidden fruit. As with a row of bricks placed closely together, if the first brick is knocked over, the rest will soon fall. Nothing in people's lives can change "because each act unfailingly" causes another act, and "that act begets another, and so on to the end." People, Theodor deduces, are thus prisoners who can never become free.

Traum alters small links in the life-chains of several villagers that dramatically change the course of their lives. For example, he intervenes in the lives of Nikolaus and a small girl named Lisa Brandt with striking results. The original chain of events would have enabled Nikolaus to save Lisa from drowning. By changing one apparently trivial incident in Nikolaus's life, Traum causes him to arrive too late to save her, and his attempt to rescue Lisa causes both to drown. Traum explains to Theodor that if Nikolaus had saved Lisa, he would have contracted scarlet fever and spent the remainder of his life as "a paralytic log, deaf, dumb, blind, and praying night and day for the blessed relief of death." If Lisa had survived, she would have become a criminal and been executed.

Twain's story ends in nihilism, even solipsism. The only way to escape the heartbreak and horror of earthly existence is to die or become insane like Father Peter, the kindhearted village priest. "Nothing exists; all is a dream," Traum declares. "God—man—the world—the sun, the moon, the wilderness of stars"—are "all a dream; they have no existence. Nothing exists save empty space—and you!" Traum then lambasts God for creating bad children instead of good ones, choosing to make people sad instead of joyful, giving them short lives, cursing people with "biting miseries and maladies of mind and body," trumpeting justice, mercy, and forgiveness but inventing hell, requiring individuals to earn eternal happiness in heaven, denying people free choice but blaming them for their actions, and obtusely inviting these poor, abused slaves to worship him.

Further parodying the biblical God, Twain's mysterious stranger insists that people are as important "to me as the red spider is to the elephant." The elephant does not care whether the spider is happy, wealthy or destitute, "his sweetheart returns his love or not," he is admired, his enemies "smite him or his friends desert him," or he dies "in the bosom of his family or neglected and despised in a foreign land."

The Mysterious Stranger also burlesques various religious teachings and practices. The boys in the village are "trained to be good Christians" and to revere the Virgin Mary, the church, and the saints, but are allowed to know little else. Knowledge could make the common people "discontented with the lot which God had appointed for them, and God would not endure discontentment with His plans." Mocking Catholic teaching, Twain has the boys insist that a cruel man who died would have gone to heaven if a priest had administered last rites, but because the priest arrived an hour too late, the man now had "gone down into the awful fires, to burn forever." As a spoof of Twain's caricature of Calvinism, which he interpreted as teaching that God cruelly limited the number of the redeemed, Father Peter is condemned by the town's authorities for saying that "God was all goodness and would find a way to save all his poor human children." Twain also derided the traditional view of hell as a place of torment. Traum had seen the damned, including babies, "writhing in the red waves of hell," "shrieking and supplicating in anguish," and was "as bland about it as if it had been so many imitation rats in an artificial fire."

Despite his own hardheartedness, Traum continually censures people's lack of morality and callousness and pokes fun at the concept of conscience or "moral sense." People are the only animals afflicted "with the disease called the Moral Sense." Undoubtedly castigating the "robber barons" of his era, Twain ridicules rich, "very holy" proprietors who force their employees to work up to sixteen hours per day and pay "only enough to keep them from dropping dead with hunger."

Twain explicitly explained his deterministic philosophy in other works. The holy trinity of training, temperament, and circumstances, he insisted, prescribed people's actions and the course of their lives. Twain viewed the human being as an "automatic machine" composed of thousands of parts over which he or she has no authority or control. Conscience is simply a "creature of *training*"; it is whatever an individual's mother, the Bible, comrades, laws, system of government, habitat, and heredity have made it.[118] A person's temperament, he insisted, is "an iron law" that must be obeyed. People should no more be blamed for their evil acts than spiders, tigers, foxes, or goats, which (commanded by their temperaments), killed, stole, or had sexual relations with numerous fellow animals. People, Twain argued in his autobiography, did not invent their traits; they inherited them at birth. As hard as they may try, people could not change their attributes. Some people are born murderers and scoundrels and commit crimes because they obey the law of their nature.[119]

In a November 1904 letter to Twichell, Twain said he wished he could stop blaming humanity for its acts. People were merely machines, "moved wholly by outside influences." God alone was responsible for people's actions. Twain admitted that he should not castigate Theodore Roosevelt for his words or deeds, since Roosevelt was "merely a helpless and irresponsible coffee-mill ground by the hand of God." On a personal level, Twain told Jean in a June 1907 letter, "God Almighty alone is responsible for your temperament, your malady and all your troubles and sorrow. I cannot blame you for them."[120] Nevertheless, he did condemn Roosevelt, Leopold II, Nicholas II, and many other leaders. In fact, his attack on many social ills and frequent advocacy of moral positions shows that Twain did not

consistently espouse determinism. Like many contemporary proponents of moral relativism, he denounced particular acts as evil and
worked to change social conditions.

In "The Turning Point in My Life," Twain accentuated the role
that circumstances—links in the inexorable sequence of incidents in
each person's life—played, in conjunction with temperament, in
determining people's lives. He compared human beings with a
watch, which does not wind or regulate itself; "these things are done
exteriorly." Likewise, outside influences or circumstances program
and regulate people. The first circumstance in world history, Twain
contended, produced all subsequent ones. God appointed that first
incident and never ordered another one.[121] Twain could not conceive
of an accident—"an event without a cause. Each event has its own
place in the eternal chain of circumstances" and, whether it is big or
little, would "infallibly cause the *next* event."[122] Reading Jonathan
Edwards's *Freedom of the Will*, Twain complained in 1902, was like
spending "a three days' tear with a drunken lunatic." To Twain,
Edwards correctly recognized that people were moved to act by
impulses beyond their control but illogically held people responsible
for their thoughts, words, and acts rather than the exterior forces that
dictated their thinking, speaking, and behavior.[123]

On the other hand, Twain inconsistently argued that some
individuals—Joan of Arc, Martin Luther, Napoleon, and Jim in
Huckleberry Finn—had escaped from this "web of cosmic determinism"
and performed heroic deeds.[124] Twain was often troubled by the
implications of his deterministic philosophy; he frequently encouraged
people to act ethically, constantly reproached himself for contemptible
conduct, and struggled mightily with personal guilt. For example,
after Susy's death, Twain wrote to Livy, "I pitied you in this awful
trouble that my mistakes have brought upon you. You forgive me,
I know, but I shall never forgive myself."[125] If he were a mere
machine, however, he was not responsible for his actions and would
not need forgiveness.[126] Many of Twain's other writings assume that
people can make genuine choices and work to improve their communities and the world. And if people are mere machines, why are their
lives important?

The Afterlife

Whether Twain believed in an afterlife is an intriguing question. As William Phipps puts it, throughout his life Twain wavered "between hopefulness and despair" on the subject of life after death. Expressing his ambivalence, Twain declared, "As to a hereafter, we have not the slightest evidence that there is any—*no* evidence that appeals to logic and reason. I have never seen what to me seemed an atom of proof that there is a future life." Nevertheless, "I am strongly inclined to expect one." "I am wholly indifferent," he stated on another occasion, about the possibility of a hereafter.[127]

He was not, however, indifferent. Throughout his life Twain often found the "notion that he would live beyond earthly death" attractive,[128] and sometimes he expressed belief in life after death. After his friend Franklin Rising died in a boating accident in 1868, Twain proclaimed, "The glories of heaven are about him." Twain told his wife in 1893 that for three thousand years the wise in many countries had believed in immortality; "let us accept their verdict." He promised her, "I will try never to doubt it again." Twain assured Livy on several other occasions that he believed in an afterlife, and after her death in 1904, he professed a desire to be reunited with her and his deceased children. After much examining, searching, and analyzing, Twain concluded, "I more believe in immortality of the soul than disbelieve in it. Is this inborn, instinctive, and ineradicable, indestructible? Perhaps so."[129] "When my physical body dies," he declared, "my dream body will doubtless continue its excursions and activities without change, forever." Twain told Helen Keller that "there was nothing like" their "affectionate friendship" in heaven and probably would not be "until we get there and show off." After Jean died, Twain informed his housekeeper Katy Leary that she was "in heaven with her mother." Leary testified, "I am sure he believed in the hereafter." "Sometimes he believed death ended everything," his daughter Clara wrote, "but most of the time he felt sure of a life beyond."[130] Twain's childhood friend Laura Hawkins Frazer (the model for Becky Thatcher in *Tom Sawyer*) declared that near the end of his life, he told her, "We will meet in Heaven." Twain's final words, spoken to Clara, expressed his hope that they might meet again.[131]

At other times, however, Twain insisted that people had no compelling reasons to believe in an afterlife. Nature, Twain asserted, told people nothing "about any future life . . . . It does not promise a future life; it does not even vaguely indicate one." "One of the proofs" put forth for "the immortality of the soul," Twain averred, "is that myriads have believed it. They also believed the world was flat."[132] In his private musings, Twain sometimes asserted that ceasing to exist after death is the best option.[133] "I have long ago lost my belief in immortality . . . . Annihilation has no terrors for me, because I have already tried it before I was born." Howells claimed that Twain "denied himself the hope of life hereafter" until his very last hour, when, entreated by those dearest to him, he acknowledged the possibility.[134]

Despite this mixed evidence, numerous Twain scholars confidently assert that he did not believe in the hereafter and that his affirmations of an afterlife were white lies told to please Livy. Justin Kaplan, for example, argues that Twain strongly doubted that life after death existed, although "heaven and hell appealed to him as imaginative constructs." Twain was much more noncommittal. "My life is fading to its close," he wrote in 1901, "and someday I shall know" if heaven exists.[135]

Heaven and Hell

Twain commented on the nature of heaven and hell in many stories and articles. In an 1877 article, Twain declared that if heaven was populated with people like Captain Charles Duncan, a cheerless, insufferable man who led their prayer meetings aboard the *Quaker City*, he was in no hurry to get there. This jibe is related to Twain's famous assertion: go to "heaven for climate but hell for company." "Many of the people I once knew in Hannibal are now in heaven," he added. "Some, I trust, are in the other place." He jokingly told Mary Fairbanks that he wanted to stay in this world when he died because many people who have gone to the other world "know about me & will talk, of course."[136]

Twain described heaven in substantial detail in *Captain Stormfield's Visit*. Apparently written between 1867 and 1871 but not published until 1907, this story is a response to "the romanticized view of the afterlife" that dominated postbellum women's fiction, especially Elizabeth Stuart Phelps's *The Gates Ajar* (1868).[137] Phelps, Twain protested, portrayed heaven as "about the size of Rhode Island." It could accommodate only "about a tenth of 1 per cent of the Christian billions who had died in the past nineteen centuries. I raised the limit; I built a properly and rationally stupendous heaven, and augmented its Christian population to 10 per cent of the contents of the modern cemeteries" and also let in "a tenth of 1 percent of the pagans who had died during the preceding eons."[138] New arrivals such as Stormfield learn that heaven is not a democracy, that the great figures of the Bible are not accessible to ordinary folk, and that T. DeWitt Talmage, Dwight Moody, and other Gilded Age religious luminaries had deceived them about the afterlife. In both *Captain Stormfield's Visit* and *Letters from Earth*, Twain depicts heaven as populated by all races and ethnic groups, who get along splendidly despite their prejudices and animosities toward each other on earth. In addition, Twain portrays people espousing varied religious perspectives as all being welcome in heaven. Belief in Jesus as the divine savior is not required to enter heaven's splendor.

If heaven did exist, Twain suggested, it might be very different from what most Christians expected, characterized by work, growth, and pain. People would need two eternities to learn everything possible about their own world and the thousands of nations in world history. Mathematics alone could occupy a person for "eight million years."[139] Standing in heaven's "enchanted surroundings" and listening to William Shakespeare, John Milton, and John Bunyan read from their classic works would be wonderful. Twain hoped to able to read some of his stories to these illustrious authors, but he was sure they would not know him and would claim they had a previous engagement. When the archbishop of Orleans promised Twain that he would be welcomed into heaven because he wrote so beautifully about Joan of Arc, Twain replied that he would be happy to go if he were assigned a place near Joan and far away from the Catholic authorities who put her to death.[140] He would be satisfied just to be in heaven, Twain asserted, walking around, looking, and listening without saying anything.[141] If God's goodness, justice, and mercy were manifested toward people on earth, Twain reasoned, these divine attributes would also be prevalent in a future life, if one existed.[142]

On the other hand, Twain sometimes depicted heaven negatively, as a place where everyone thought alike and there was no humor.[143] In the Presbyterian conception of heaven, he protested, there was nothing to do. In the "wildcat" version of some religious sects, heaven's occupants would think they were in hell because they would have to study all the time, "and if this isn't hell I don't know what is."[144] Twain also insisted that heaven might be hellish because so many hypocrites resided there.[145]

Like the nation's leading postbellum pulpiteer, Henry Ward Beecher, Twain was repulsed by the concept of eternal punishment in hell. Beecher denounced the idea that for thousands of years God had swept people "like dead flies—nay, like living ones—into hell" as abhorrent. It made God much worse than any medieval conception of the devil. Beecher repudiated this portrait of hell and accentuated God's love. Twain also deplored the conventional depiction of hell. As bad as contemporary "bloody, merciless, money-grabbing, and predatory" Christianity was, he asserted, it was "a hundred times better than the Christianity of the Bible with its prodigious crime—the invention of Hell." "Nothing in all history," Twain declared, "remotely approaches in atrocity" the idea of hell. And nothing was worse than billions of people who had never even heard of Christ or the terms of salvation being "burned throughout all eternity." Twain rejoiced that many people were renouncing the concept of hell. "No enemy of perdition [people who rejected the concept of hell] was more pleased" by this development, Howells contended.[146]

His baptism in a Presbyterian church, Twain argued tongue-in-cheek, entitled him "to be punished as a Presbyterian" in the hereafter—that is, to be consigned to "fire and brimstone instead of the heterodox hell of remorse of conscience" envisioned by the "blamed wildcat religions." Twain contemplated writing a story in which "the halls of heaven are warmed by radiators connected with hell," which added "a new pang to the sinner's suffering to know that the very fire which tortures him is the means of making the righteous comfortable."[147]

Continuing his lampooning of hell, Twain declared that he was comforted by the knowledge that if he wound "up in the fiery pit hereafter," his sister-in-law Susie Crane would "flutter down there every day, in defiance of law & the customs" of heaven and "bring ice & fans & all sorts of contraband things" to cheer "me up, & then go back home not caring two cents that her scorched feathers, & dilapidated appearance & brimstone smell are going to get her into trouble & cause her to be shunned by all proper angels as an eccentric and disreputable saint. I can believe a good deal of the bible," Twain added, "but I never will believe" in a heaven that would keep Crane from spending "most of her time in Hell trying to comfort the poor devils down there." She would not enjoy heaven if others were suffering in hell.[148]

Conclusion

The *Chicago Daily Tribune* reported on December 21, 1909 that Twain had returned home ill from Bermuda. He had begun to decline physically after the death of his longtime companion Henry Rogers the previous May. His attempt to regain his strength and vitality had not succeeded. "My work is over in this life and this world," Twain declared. A few weeks later, he wrote, "There is not another orphan who is so wrecked, so ruined, so forsaken, as I am. Just a battered old derelict washing about the wastes of the great seas, with nobody on the bridge."[149]

Twain went back to Bermuda on January 5, 1910, and on April 14, 1910, he returned to Manhattan. Altogether, Twain made eight trips to the island and spent 187 days there. He once quipped, "You can go to heaven if you want. I'd rather stay right here in Bermuda."[150] Twain was carried off the ship in Manhattan seated on a deck chair as reporters waited at the dock, hoping to interview the famous author one last time. A year before his death, Twain, referring to Halley's Comet and himself, proclaimed: "The Almighty has said, no doubt, 'Now here go those two unaccountable freaks; they came in together, they must go out together.'"[151] His prophecy was fulfilled as he died of angina pectoris on April 21, one day after the comet's perihelion.

Notes

1. John Pearson, *Private Lives of Winston Churchill* (New York: Simon & Schuster, 1991), 105.
2. Mark Twain, "Introducing Winston S. Churchill," December 12, 1900, MTS, 368; Winston Churchill, *My Early Life* (London: Thornton Butterworth, 1930), 376.

3. Lewis Lehrman, "Great Contemporaries: Winston Churchill and Mark Twain," March 15, 2018, The Churchill Project, https://winstonchurchill.hillsdale.edu/mark-twain-winston-churchill/#_ftn. See also Gary Scott Smith, *Duty and Destiny: The Life and Faith of Winston Churchill* (Grand Rapids, MI: Eerdmans, 2021).

4. Tracy Fessenden, *Culture and Redemption: Religion, the Secular, and American Literature* (Princeton, NJ: Princeton University Press, 2013), 141; REV, 155.

5. Dwayne Eutsey, "Mark Twain's Attitudes toward Religion: Sympathy for the Devil or Radical Christianity?" *Religion & Literature* 31 (Summer 1999), 45.

6. MIW, xxxii (quotation), xxv–xxvi.

7. Isabel Lyon journals, March 9, 1907, MTP.

8. SLC to Carl Thalbitzer, November 26, 1902, *Mark Twain, Day by Day*, 3:83, https://daybyday.marktwainstudies.com/category/volume-3/page/83/(first quotation) MF, 251 (second and third quotations).

9. OLC to SLC, November 28, 1871, MTP.

10. OLC to SLC, December 2, 1871, LTR, 4:510.

11. OLC to SLC, January 7, 1872, LTR, 5:17.

12. MTB, 411.

13. MTB, 650–1; quotations from 651.

14. Resa Willis, *Mark and Livy: The Love Story of Mark Twain and the Woman Who Almost Tamed Him* (New York: Athenaeum, 1992), 243.

15. Grace King, *Memories of a Southern Woman of Letters* (New York: Macmillan, 1932), 172–3.

16. Willis, *Mark and Livy*, 245.

17. MTB, 651.

18. SLC to JHT, May 11, 1904, MTL 2:753; SLC to WDH, June 6, 1904, MTL, 2:757.

19. MTMS, 405 (quotations), 369.

20. SLC to Richard Watson Gilder, May 12, 1904, MTL 2:755.

21. MTB, 1217–18.

22. Willis, *Mark and Livy*, 243; MTN, June 5, 1904, 387; MF, 253.

23. *Hartford Courant*, June 12, 1904, MTP.

24. AMT, July 14, 1904.

25. MTB, 1225.

26. SLC to Pamela Moffett, April 25, 1899, in Hamlin Hill, *Mark Twain: God's Fool* (New York: Harper & Row, 1975), 9.

27. AMT, December 24, 1909, 3:312 (first and second quotations), 3:316 (fourth quotation), 3:317 (fifth quotation); December 25, 1909, 3:318 (sixth quotation); December 26, 1909, 3:319 (third and eighth quotations).

28. "Last Journey of Mark Twain to God's Acre," San Francisco *Call* 107 (April 24, 1910), 1; MTSC, 273 (quotation), 274.

29. Brander Matthews, quoted in "Twain the Greatest," *New York Times*, February 21, 1906, http://www.twainquotes.com/19060221.html; "Celebrate Mark Twain's Seventieth Birthday," *New York Times*, December 6, 1905, https://twain.lib.virginia.edu/onstage/70bday2.html.

30. "Mark Twain's Seventieth Birthday"; "Mark Twain's 70th Birthday Speech," https://twain.lib.virginia.edu/onstage/70bday.html.

31. William Lyon Phelps, "Mark Twain," *North American Review* 185 (July 5, 1907), 541 (second quotation), 542 (first and third quotations), 548.

32. "New Letters Show Twain's Loneliness in His Last 4 Years," *New York Times*, April 26, 1961, 41.

33. Ron Powers, *Mark Twain: A Life* (New York: Free Press, 2006), 31; MTB, 1292.

34. SLC to WDH, June 25, 1906, MTHL, 2:815; MTSC, 271.

35. "America's Greatest Humorist and His Thanksgiving Message: Less Cause for Thanks Than Man Has His God," *Washington Times*, November 27, 1905, 1.

36. Jim Zwick, "Mark Twain and Imperialism," in *A Historical Guide to Mark Twain*, ed. Shelley Fisher Fishkin (New York: Oxford University Press, 2002), 241; *Springfield* (Massachusetts) *Republican*, February 3, 1901, 8.

37. MTAP, 205; Mark Twain, "A Salutation from the 19th to the 20th Century," *New York Herald*, December 31, 1900, in *A Pen Warmed Up in Hell*, ed. Frederick Anderson (New York: Harper & Row), 13.

38. Quoted in Janet Smith, *Mark Twain on the Damned Human Race* (New York: Hill & Wang, 1994), 70.

39. FE, 212–13, 624 (quotation).

40. FE, 625–6 (first quotation), 397, 462, 518 (second quotation).

41. Mark Twain, "A Stupendous Procession," MTFM, 405; AMT, September 7, 1906, 2:227.

42. AMT, March 30, 1906, 1:462; quoted in CAR, 155; SLC to JHT, January 29, 1901, MTL, 1:391; MF, 220; quotations in that order.

43. FE, 691.

44. SLC to WDH, January 26, 1895, MTL, 2:694; Twain, "The Dervish and the Offensive Stranger," E&E, 313.

45. Anti-Imperial League, "Address to the People of the United States," November 19, 1898; "Platform of the American Anti-Imperialist League," in Carl Schutz, *The Policy of Imperialism*, Liberty Tract No. 4 (Chicago: American Anti-Imperialist League, 1899), inside front cover.

46. E. Berkeley Tompkins, *Anti-Imperialism in the United States* (Philadelphia: University of Pennsylvania Press, 1970), 132.

47. Mark Twain, "Dinner Speech," November 10, 1900, MTS, 350; SLC to JHT, June 17, 1898 (letter and last quotation from MTB, 1064).

48. Mark Twain, "To the Person Sitting in Darkness," *North American Review* 172 (February 1901), 169.

49. Mark Twain, interview with *New York Herald*, October 15, 1900, *Friends Intelligencer*, November 3, 1900, 815.

50. See Jim Zwick, "'Prodigally Endowed with Sympathy for the Cause': Mark Twain's Involvement with the Anti-Imperialist League," *Mark Twain Journal* 32 (Spring 1994), 3–25.

51. SLC to JHT, January 29, 1901, MTL, 2:705.

52. Mark Twain, "The Stupendous Joke of the Century," in *Mark Twain's Weapons of Satire: Anti-Imperialist Writings on the Philippine-American War*, ed. Jim Zwick (Syracuse, NY: Syracuse University Press, 1992), 185, as reported by the *Baltimore American*, May 9, 1907.

53. Twain, "Person Sitting in Darkness," 169 (first quotation), 170 (second through fourth quotations), 171 (fifth quotation), 172 (sixth quotation), 174 (remaining quotations).

54. MTB, 1164, 1064.

55. Arthur Lincoln Scott, *On the Poetry of Mark Twain* (Urbana: University of Illinois Press, 1966), 35; Twain, "Review of Edwin Wildman's Biography of Aguinaldo," in *Weapons of Satire*, ed. Zwick, 92, 100.

56. "Petition to Stop War; Senator Hoar Presents One Signed by Well-Known Men," *New York Times*, February 5, 1902, 3; "The Philippine-American War, 1899–1902," US State Department, Office of the Historian, https://history.state.gov/milestones/1899–1913/war.

57. Zwick, "Mark Twain and Imperialism," 235.

58. Twain, "Person Sitting in Darkness," 169.

59. Mark Twain, "The Czar's Soliloquy," *North American Review* 180 (March 1905), 322, 323 (first quotation), 324 (remaining quotations).

60. Twain, "Czar's Soliloquy," 325, 326; quotations in that order.

61. AMT, December 5, 1906, 2:307; Twain, "Dinner Speech," April 11, 1906, MTS, 513.

62. Gary Scharnhorst, *Mark Twain: The Complete Interviews* (Tuscaloosa: University of Alabama Press, 2006), 500.

63. Twain's response to a questionnaire sent by the New York *American Hebrew*, April 4, 1890, SMT, 560; Kaplan's words.

64. Mark Twain, "Concerning the Jews," *Harper's Magazine*, September 1899, 527–35; MF, 203 (quotation), 204.

65. Clara Clemens, *My Husband Gabrilowitsch* (New York: Da Capo Press, 1979), 16; MTB, 644; SLC to JHT, October 23, 1897, in *The Letters of Mark Twain and Joseph Hopkins Twichell*, ed. Harold Bush, Jr., Steve Courtney, and Peter Messent (Athens: University of Georgia Press, 2017), 201; AMT, May 31, 1906, 2:69; quotations in that order.

66. On Twain's view of the Jews, see Philip Foner, *Mark Twain, Social Critic* (New York: International Publishers, 1958), 288–307; and Shelley Fisher Fishkin, "Mark Twain and the Jews," *Arizona Quarterly* 61 (Spring 2005), 137–66.

67. Mark Twain, "Aix, Paradise of Rheumatics," E&E, 95.

68. E.g. "America's Greatest Humorist," 1.

69. MTB, 1229.

70. Mark Twain, *King Leopold's Soliloquy: A Defence of His Congo Rule* (London: Unwin, 1907), 30.

71. Twain, *King Leopold's Soliloquy*, 32–3.

72. Twain, *King Leopold's Soliloquy*, 33–6; first three quotations from 33, fourth quotation from 36.

73. "In Genial Mood, Mark Twain Talks to Newspaper Men," *Boston Daily Globe*, November 6, 1905, 9.

74. Hunt Hawkins, "Mark Twain's Involvement with the Congo Reform Movement: 'A Fury of Generous Indignation,'" *New England Quarterly* 51 (June 1978), 161.

75. Quoted in Foner, *Mark Twain*, 297.

76. "What I Am Thankful For," interview with Mark Twain by W. O. Inglis, *New York World Sunday Magazine*, November 26, 1905, https://brook lyntheborough.com/2009/11/26/undusted-mark-twains-the-strangest-thanksgiving-sentiment-ever-penned/.

77. DV370-370A, MTP, as cited in Hawkins, "Congo Reform Movement," 162.

78. AMT, June 22, 1906, 2:134; AMT, December 5, 1906, 2:307; quotations in that order.

79. Hawkins, "Congo Reform Movement," 159.

80. SLC to Whitelaw Reid, January 14, 1873, LTR, 5:272.

81. MTSC, 136–7.

82. Mark Twain, *Letters from the Sandwich Islands* (New York: Haskell House, 1972), 101, 121; quotations in that order.

83. Mark Twain, "Sandwich Islands Lecture," given intermittently from October 2, 1866 to December 8, 1873, in MTS, 7.

84. MTN, July 30, 1866, 21, 28 (quotation); Mark Twain, "The Sandwich Islands," *Mark Twain's Speeches*, ed. Albert Bigelow Paine (New York: Harper and Brothers, 1923), 34; Twain, *Sandwich Islands*, 117–18.

85. Twain, *Sandwich Islands*, 17 (first quotation); SLC to Whitelaw Reid, January 3, 1873, LTR, 5:560–1 (second quotation); *Mark Twain's Speeches*, ed. Paine, 18 (third quotation).

86. Mark Twain, "Domestic Missionaries Wanted," CT, 1:432.

87. FE, 626, 183, 318ff.; Notebook #30, transcription number 39, MTP.

88. Mark Twain, "To My Missionary Critics," *North American Review* 172 (April 1901), 532 (first quotation), 534 (remaining quotations).

89. RI, 186.

90. MTN, March 28, 1896, 285.

91. Mark Twain, "The Missionary in World-Politics," in Robert Hirst, *Who Is Mark Twain?* (New York: HarperStudio, 2009), 103–9 (the *Times* did not publish his editorial); SLC to JHT, April 19, 1909, *Letters of Twain and Twichell*, ed. Bush, Courtney, and Messent, 408–9. Twichell's half-sister Olive was a missionary in Turkey, not his daughter.

92. MTN, March 28, 1896, 290–1 (first quotation from 290); MTN, October 4, 1895, 252 (second quotation).

93. See Richard Gamble, *The War for Righteousness: Progressive Christianity, the Great War, and the Rise of the Messianic Nation* (Wilmington, DC: ISI Books, 2003), chapter 3.

94. MTAP, 115.

95. Twain, "The Dervish and the Offensive Stranger," 314 (first quotation); Twain, "The United States of Lyncherdom," E&E, 247.

96. MTN, February 15, 1896, 278.

97. Twain, "Person Sitting in Darkness," 163.

98. Twain, "Person Sitting in Darkness," 165–7: first two quotations from 165, third from 166, fourth from 167.

99. Twain, "Missionary Critics," 520, 527; quotations in that order.

100. MTB, 1132.

101. OLC to Grace King, February 2, 1901, Grace King Papers as cited in Willis, *Mark and Livy*, 260.

102. *Mark Twain's Speeches*, ed. Paine, 29–30.

103. MTB, 1537 (first quotation); FE, 2:171–3 (173, second quotation).

104. MF, 159.

105. Mark Twain, "Constitution and Laws of the Juggernaut Club," April 10, 1902, in Barbara Schmidt, "Mark Twain's Juggernaut Club Correspondence," http://www.twainquotes.com/picard.html.

106. AMT, April 9, 1906, 2:28–9.

107. MTSC, 168, 176, 179, 196–7. See also Neil Schmitz, "Mark Twain's Civil War: Humor's Reconstructive Writing," in *The Cambridge Companion to Mark Twain*, ed. Forrest Robinson (Cambridge: Cambridge University Press, 1995), 74–92.

108. Mark Twain, "Man's Place in the Animal World," WM, 84.

109. MTMS, 156.

110. MTMS, 137.

111. Mark Twain, "Glances at History," in *The Bible According to Mark Twain*, ed. Howard Baetzhold and Joseph McCullough (New York: Touchstone, 1995), 87–8.

112. MTN, October 13, 1904, 395.

113. "God Behind This War. It Is His Way of Destroying Tyranny, Dr. Hillis Says," *New York Times*, June 12, 1905, 9; AMT, 2:369.

114. AMT, June 22, 1906, 2:134.

115. Mark Twain, "The War Prayer." https://warprayer.org/.

116. See Alexander Jones, "Mark Twain and the Determinism of *What Is Man?*" *American Literature* 29 (March 1957), 1–17.

117. MTC, 156.

118. Mark Twain, "Letters from the Earth," WM, 427; MTN, January 7, 1897, 348–9; quotations in that order.

119. February 4, 1907, AMT, 2:428 (quotation), 429.

120. SLC to JHT, November 4, 1904, MTL, 2:763–4; quotations from 764; SLC to Jean Clemens, early October 1907, MTP.

121. Mark Twain, "The Turning Point in My Life," WM, 463.

122. AMT, October 2, 1906, 2:236.

123. SLC to JHT, February 1902, MTB, 1156–7; quotation from 1157.

124. RV, 185 (quotation); MTA, 1:263.

125. SLC to OLC, August 16, 1896, LLMT, 323.

126. MTSC, 259.

127. MTR, 299; MTB, 1431 (first and second quotations); Twain, "Three Statements," 57 (third and fourth quotations).

128. Harold Bush, Jr., "Broken Idols: Mark Twain's Elegies for Susy and a Critique of Freudian Grief Theory," *Nineteenth-Century Literature* 57 (September 2002), 255.

129. SLC to OL, December 19 and 20, 1868, LTR, 2:334; SLC to OLC, May 8, 1893, quoted in MF, 177; SLC to OLC, September 30, 1903, LLMT, 344.

130. MTN, 350; SLC to Helen Keller, March 17, 1903, MTL 1:405; LMT, 212; MF, 280.

131. January 23, 1923 letter in Joseph Twichell Papers, MF, 291.

132. MTN, May 27, 1898, 362, December 30, 1902, 379; quotations in that order.

133. See Benjamin Griffin, "Mark Twain's Apocrypha: Infant Jesus and Young Satan," *The Mark Twain Annual* 14 (2016), 15; Gregg Camfield, *The Oxford Companion to Mark Twain* (New York: Oxford University Press, 2003), 157.

134. AMT, May 31, 1906, 2:69; William Dean Howell, "Editor's Easy Chair," *Harper's Magazine* 136 (March 1918), 603.

135. Kaplan, *Mark Twain*, 370. See also Camfield, *Oxford Companion*, 22, 156; Powers, *Mark Twain*, 615; Mark Twain, About Cities in the Sun, 19 of the original manuscript, MTP, as quoted by Bush, "Broken Idols," 255.

136. *New York World*, February 18, 1877 (this may also be the original source of Twain's famous statement, "heaven for climate but hell for company"); N&J, May 13, 1882, 2:478 (second quotation); SLC to MMF, January 18, 1893, MTMF, 269 (third quotation).

137. MTSC, 123.

138. AMT, August 29, 1906, 2:194.

139. Notes 1883, MTN, 170.

140. Quotation from Ray Browne, ed., *Mark Twain's Quarrel with Heaven* (New Haven, CT: College and University Press, 170), 37; James Walsh, "To the Editor," *Commonweal*, August 23, 1935, 408.

141. Twain, Cities in the Sun.

142. Twain, "Three Statements," 56–7.

143. FE, 119.

144. Mark Twain, "Reflections on the Sabbath," March 18, 1866, http://www.twainquotes.com/Era/18660318.html.

145. See, for example, SLC to JHT, January 29, 1901, MTL, 2:705.

146. Henry Ward Beecher, "The Background of Mystery," in *The Complete Preacher*, ed. I. K. Funk (New York: Funk and Wagnalls, 1895), 213; AMT, June 22, 1906, 132; AMT, June 19, 1906, 2:130; 2:129; MMT, 1.

147. Twain, "Reflections on the Sabbath"; AMT, July 30, 1907, 3:86; MTN, Notes 1883, 168–9; quotations in that order.

148. SLC to MMF, November 6, December 10, 1872, LTR, 5, https://www.marktwainproject.org/.

149. "Mark Twain Comes Home Ill," *Chicago Daily Tribune*, December 21, 1909, 5; "Mark Twain," *Collier's*, 45, April 30, 1910, https://twain.lib.virginia.edu/sc_as_mt/mtobit3.html.

150. Quoted in Lynn Cullen, *Twain's End* (New York: Gallery Books, 2015). See also Donald Hoffman, *Mark Twain in Paradise: His Voyages to Bermuda* (Columbia: University of Missouri Press, 2006).

151. MTB, 1511.

8

Conclusion

Assessing what Mark Twain believed about religious matters is complicated by his desire not to hurt Livy, her censorship of some of his writings, his desire to avoid the fate of Thomas Paine (who was attacked in pulpits across America for his skeptical positions), and his wish not to tarnish his reputation or hinder the sale of his books. Van Wyck Brooks argues that Twain withheld views he thought his Nook Farm neighbors would consider "shocking, heretical and blasphemous." Concealing his actual opinions, he "spoke of himself in public to the end of his life as a Presbyterian." Like a chameleon, he publicly took on the religious color of his community, just as he adopted its social and financial hues.[1] Keeping this interpretive challenge in mind, in this final chapter I examine what Twain's family, friends, and acquaintances said about his religious convictions, discuss his funeral and obituaries, and evaluate the conflicting views of scholars.

The Conflicting Testimony of His Contemporaries

Biographer Albert Bigelow Paine contends that every Christian publication "was filled with lavish tribute" for Twain and "pulpits forgot his heresies and paid him honor."[2] Reality is more complicated; those who knew Twain offered differing perspectives on his religious commitments. Some stated that Twain's actions and character demonstrated that he was a Christian. Twain dealt justly, loved mercy, and walked humbly with God, Henry Van Dyke asserted, even though the author could not define the deity. Twain's honesty, fidelity, and loving kindness "were fruits of faith" and Christian loyalty. He was keenly aware of "the perversions and literal misinterpretations" of Christianity and sometimes his ridicule was excessive, Van Dyke acknowledged, but he always spoke lovingly and reverently about "genuine, simple Christian faith." The assertion that Twain was an atheist grossly misrepresented his spiritual qualities and moral conduct. Denying God's existence, Van Dyke opined, "would have seemed to him the height of impudent folly." Undoubtedly speaking for many of his friends, Hamilton W. Mabie, an editor of the *Outlook*, praised Twain's Christian character in 1905.[3]

Katy Leary, a devout Christian, worked for Twain and his family from 1880 until 1910 as their seamstress, nursemaid, nanny, and housekeeper. "I know you do believe the way I do," she told Twain; "you believe there is a God, no matter what you say! I know it." Leary pointed to Twain's avowal that his daughter Susy was "in heaven with her mother" as proof. Twain "was really a good Christian man," she declared, "but people really never understood that." He "was one of the purest men that I ever knew." Albert Bigelow Paine maintained that Twain's religion was "too wide for doctrines"; his benevolence transcended creeds, and both his life and his work expressed his religion. At the final judgment, William Dean Howells contended, "the Searcher of Hearts" would not disgrace Twain because his character was noble and he had readily confessed his mistakes.[4]

Others emphasized that Twain attacked the pretense and hypocrisy of Christians but not Christianity itself. Southern Presbyterian editor Alexander McKelway, for example, declared that Twain was a Christian but hated sham so much that he sometimes shocked "the religious sense of others," or rather their "religious non-sense."[5]

Both Leary and Twain's daughter Clara highlighted his love of Christian songs. Leary emphasized that Twain liked to sing Negro spirituals. One time, while singing "Nobody Knows the Trouble I Got, Nobody Knows but Jesus," Twain shouted, just as blacks did, "Glory, Glory Halleluiah!" When her father sang "Rise and Shine and Give God the Glory, Glory," Clara maintained, his "fervor of spirit" was unforgettable. Twain frequently sang spirituals including "Swing Low, Sweet Chariot" and "Were You There When They Crucified My Lord," while accompanying himself on the piano. Echoing the assessment of Leary and Clara Clemens, Shelley Fisher Fishkin contends that Twain's passion for spirituals expressed "the core of his being; they spoke uniquely to a part of himself that no other art could touch."[6]

Clara Clemens and William Dean Howells claimed, however, that Twain rejected Christianity. Clara declared that her "father had no faith in any orthodox religion." When he became an adult, Twain abandoned "the faith he had been taught in his childhood," Howells argued, but it "remained in his affection long after it had ceased in his conviction," and eventually "his church-going became a meaningless form."[7] When he was "in the first fine flush of his agnosticism" in the mid-1880s, Howells avowed, Twain rejoiced that he had broken the "shackles of belief" that had ensnared him for so long. Twain greatly admired agnostic Robert Ingersoll and regarded him as an evangelist of "the gospel of free thought."[8] Howells insisted that Twain never returned to his earlier faith in Christianity.[9]

Some of Twain's obituaries similarly described him as a religious skeptic. The *Truth Seeker* alleged that Twain's religious views were essentially the same as those of prominent agnostic Robert Ingersoll. Yale English professor William Lyon Phelps contended that Twain professed no belief in God; Twain "never thanked Him for his amazing successes, nor rebelled against Him for his sufferings." Stuart Sherman, another literary critic, called Twain "an agnostic over whom had fallen the shadow of Robert Ingersoll." Reared in the Sunday school, Twain "stumbled over the book of Genesis" but was emancipated. "The loss of faith," which to many "is a terrible bereavement," was to him "a blessed relief." Twain, another commentator added, courageously renounced "any hope of living again" or "seeing those he had lost."[10]

Twain's Funeral

Mark Twain's funeral was held on April 23, 1910 at the Brick Presbyterian Church (pastored by Henry Van Dyke) in New York City, with Van Dyke and Joseph Twichell officiating. Fifteen hundred mourners, including Howells, Andrew Carnegie, and former Missouri governor Joseph Folk, crowded into the church to say goodbye to their beloved friend.[11] Van Dyke claimed that Twain would have sympathized with the funeral service's efforts to help people have "better, truer, kinder thoughts in the presence of life's mysteries," act more courageously and cheerfully in the midst of life's sorrows, and peaceably accept "the will and wisdom of the unseen Ruler of life's events."

Van Dyke praised Twain's tender affections, honesty, efforts to pay off his debts, and "irrepressible humor." The things at which Twain poked fun were humorous to God. His higher humor, Van Dyke argued, did "not laugh at the weak, the helpless, the innocent," but "only at the false, the pretentious, the vain, the hypocritical." Twain "laughed many of the world's false claimants out of court, and entangled many of the world's false witnesses in a net of ridicule." Van Dyke insisted that Twain "loved much and faithfully" and bravely faced many adversities and misfortunes. Twain's "tender love and friendship," Twichell added, had helped countless people.[12]

Neither Van Dyke nor Twichell claimed that Twain was a Christian, but they both asserted that he had gone to heaven. Van Dyke declared that the revered author had been "carried to rest in God's Acre" beside his loved ones. Twain, Twichell avowed, had "been translated to the glories of the hereafter."[13] Twichell usually explicitly mentioned people's Christian faith in his eulogies, but neither at his funeral nor in his published remarks about Twain after his death did Twichell make such a statement; he instead stressed Twain's character and made only indirect comments about his faith.[14] The next day, Samuel Eastman, pastor of Park (Congregational) Church in Elmira, New York, where Twain had been married and frequently worshipped during the summers, conducted a brief service before the writer was buried in Woodland Cemetery beside Livy.

Assessing Twain's Religious Convictions

Scholars sharply disagree about Twain's worldview. Most have labeled him an atheist, agnostic, unbeliever, a skeptic, heretic, or "critic of God."[15] Max Eastman calls Twain "the great infidel" (a title usually ascribed to Ingersoll), while Nelson Burr brands the celebrated author an "inconsistent naturalist." John Q. Hays contends that Twain created an alternative belief system to Christian orthodoxy. Maxwell Geismar describes Twain as "an eloquent and outraged atheist" who powerfully indicted organized religion. Fred Kaplan maintains that Twain viewed God merely "as a convenient rhetorical locution."[16] "Twain was as close to being an agnostic," S. T. Joshi asserts, as someone can be "without actually stating any definite doubt of God's existence"; he was one of the "pre-eminent religious skeptics of his time."[17]

In contrast, others accept Albert Bigelow Paine's contention that the aging Twain continued to believe in a creator God, but one very different from the God he had learned about in Hannibal. Many insist that Twain had a contentious relationship with God, although some view it as "a lover's quarrel," whereas others see it as leading to a divorce based on irreconcilable differences. In his "twilight years," Gary Sloan asserts, Twain became a "bilious adversary of the Almighty" who "poured forth ceaseless vitriol against his Maker."[18]

Some characterize Twain's philosophical outlook as prefiguring the bleak naturalistic poems, short stories, and novels of such "grim prophets of disaster and meaninglessness" as Stephen Crane, Theodore Dreiser, and Jack London, who portray humans as having little worth and values as nonexistent. Crane, for example viewed people as lice clinging to "a whirling, icelocked, disease-stricken, space-lost bulb."[19]

On the other hand, several scholars insist that Twain primarily attacked perversions and misrepresentations of Christianity and that many of his views accorded with conventional Christian faith. The negative attitudes toward religion that dominate academia, Harold Bush, Jr. maintains, have produced "a caricature of Mark Twain as an acidic, cynical and finally even blasphemous observer of American religious life." Ample evidence demonstrates, Bush asserts, that Twain had "strong religious proclivities throughout his life." The humorist doubted numerous Christian tenets and publicly questioned or attacked some doctrines, but he persisted in various Christian "habits of the heart" throughout his life. For Bush, Twain's statement that every American, no matter what his creed, was "indisputably a Christian to this degree—that his moral constitution is Christian" applied to the author himself.[20] Twain repudiated biblical passages he regarded as either intellectually absurd or morally repulsive, but to William Phipps he was still "a feisty Christian." Although Twain struggled mightily with the problem of evil, Edward Wagenknecht contends, he had "a religious temperament" and the moral commitments of a Christian. Many passages in *Innocents Abroad* are written from the standpoint of a Christian. Joe Fulton contends that for six decades Twain supported conventional Christian beliefs in both form and content, even in seemingly skeptical works such as *What Is Man?* and *The Mysterious Stranger*.[21] For these scholars, being a Christian appears to be based much more on espousing and trying to live by a biblical moral code than on affirming traditional Christian beliefs.

A third group of scholars presents a mixed assessment of Twain's religious convictions. Twain's attitude toward "religion was complex and often contradictory," asserts Peter Messent.[22] Henry Lindborg suggests that Twain could neither believe nor be happy in unbelief.[23] With Twain, Daniel Pawley contends, "blasphemy and belief" sat "uneasily side by side" and squabbled. The humorist "camped in the no man's land between faith and doubt."[24] Twain "threw out the Bible," Edward Lee Masters declared, "but it seemed to be attached to a rubber band" and frequently bounced back to him.[25] As a "Protestant evangelist, freethinker, and literary comedian," writes Stanley Brodwin, "Twain embodied contradictions that gave his best work a comic complexity and depth."[26] The great variety in Twain's writings, insists Tracy Fessenden, makes it harder to assess his religious perspective as simply agnostic or atheist. She criticizes scholars for framing his religious convictions in terms of a binary choice between belief and unbelief and concluding that he abandoned his Calvinist upbringing and adopted a secular worldview. Scholars often describe Twain's alleged religious transformation as liberating, Fessenden asserts, but he remained dogged by his "Presbyterian conscience," which, despite arduous efforts, he could not exorcise.[27]

Offering a similar perspective, James Wilson argues that despite Twain's persistent attack on the flaws of the churches of his era and his "contempt for the moral and theological perversions of institutional religion," his writings celebrate authentic religious faith and display "a latent yearning for the transcendent vision" he thought such faith could alone supply. Wilson calls for rejecting "the prevalent conception of Mark Twain as agnostic or skeptic" and "an inveterate enemy not only of the church but of the principles upon which it is based." Although Twain expressed hostility toward the Christian God, he sometimes offered "sincere confessions of religious faith" and believed that "properly directed religious faith" could generate salutary spiritual power. Twain strove to create morally and spiritually themed literature that pleased his wife, Mary Fairbanks, and ministers he respected. In numerous ways, Wilson avers, Twain's religious perspective was that of a mature Tom Sawyer: he denounced "the pious hypocrisies of Sunday-school Christianity," parodied biblical stories, and ridiculed human weaknesses and superstitions.[28]

Paul Boller agrees that Twain's religious views are complex. Twain began rebelling against Christian orthodoxy in his early twenties, Boller maintains, but he could not emancipate himself emotionally from the Calvinism in which he was steeped as a boy. Twain complained that Puritan morality had been drilled into him as a youth and that he had inherited "an ineradicable sense of guilt." Although he strove diligently to act uprightly, Twain lamented that he often failed and became increasingly bitter and cynical when he could not square his life experience with his religious socialization. Moreover, he was troubled by three problems: extensive human suffering, which clashed with the idea of a benevolent God; the massive, implacable universe revealed by modern science, which undermined the view that people were God's principal delight; and the callousness, complacency, and hypocrisy of church members both throughout history and in his own experience, which contradicted the widely held belief that Christianity improved human conduct.[29]

Brodwin argues that Twain briefly accepted the Christian worldview but soon chafed against the traditional Christian understanding of the character of God, the proper interpretation of the Bible, and the problem of evil. Despite the efforts of Twichell and others to counter Twain objections, Christianity ultimately failed to provide Twain with the spiritual sustenance he craved.[30] As his written works demonstrate, Twain became increasingly disillusioned, Brodwin contends, because a treacherous God did not reward moral goodness with wealth, health, and inner peace. Twain eventually viewed himself as a banished Adam, prohibited from returning "to an Eden imagined or real"—the Hannibal of his boyhood, the Far West, or the Holy Land—and "his anger at God and the unfairness of the fall" grew fiercer throughout his life.[31]

Dwayne Eutsey praises Phipps, Bush, and Fulton for providing a "counterbalance to the prevailing" assessment of Twain "as a mocking skeptic or embittered atheist." Twain's darker views are similar to some biblical themes in Ecclesiastes or the book of Revelation, but those who view Twain as espousing generally orthodox Christian beliefs must also ignore or "accommodate in some way the apparent nihilism permeating his later, more theologically challenging works."[32] Eutsey contends that Twain's religious thought and writing were influenced most deeply by three nineteenth-century liberal religious movements—Unitarianism, Universalism, and Transcendentalism.[33]

As noted earlier, I think the best explanation of the complexity of Twain's religious views is that he affirmed orthodox Christianity for a time but then departed from it. The argument by some scholars that Twain never accepted Christianity as a system of belief clashes with statements he made prior to 1875 cited in Chapter 3. While courting Livy and trying to provide an emotionally secure and satisfying environment for his new family, Twain very likely espoused conventional Christian views of God, Jesus, providence, prayer, and redemption. In his last twenty-five years, however, as clearly articulated as early as his "Three Statements from the 1880s," Twain rejected orthodox doctrines of God, his direction of history and oversight of people's lives, Christ's virgin birth, divinity, and atonement for sin, the divine inspiration and authority of the Bible, salvation through faith, the efficacy of prayer, and the existence of hell. Moreover, many of his published works—especially those that Twain deemed too provocative to print while he was alive—as well as his autobiography scathingly condemn not only "the repeated failings of Christians to live up to the best features of their faith" but also "the metaphysical and the ethical foundations" of Christianity.[34]

In *Evangelical Disenchantment: Nine Portraits of Faith and Doubt*, David Hempton examines the faith journeys of nine English, American, and Dutch creative artists, social reformers, and public intellectuals, including novelist George Eliot, professor Francis Newman, abolitionist Theodore Dwight Weld, and feminist leaders Sarah Grimke and Elizabeth Cady Stanton, all of whom repudiated the evangelical tradition with which they had been associated.[35] Other prominent authors and social critics also rejected the evangelicalism of their youth as did several leaders of the American free thought movement.[36] The pattern of children raised in devout Christian homes abandoning their parents' faith is a common one.[37] Although many scholars have accentuated the problems evangelicals faced in reconciling faith and science, Hempton argues, the difficulty of reconciling "artistic creativity with Christian orthodoxy" has been a "much bigger stumbling block" for evangelicals, in part because of the tradition's long-standing "distrust of the evils of fiction, theater, and the visual arts" and more generally of "strictly imaginative pursuits that emphasize passion over piety."[38]

In their earlier lives, Hempton's subjects found aspects of the evangelical tradition appealing, especially the character of Jesus and his emphasis on love, forgiveness, and sacrifice. Most of them embraced evangelicalism through the influence of a friend or mentor—often a teacher, minister, or author—who prized Jesus and the Bible and displayed admirable personal qualities. Most nineteenth-century conversions to evangelicalism occurred during people's teenage or early adult years, usually in connection with a personal crisis.[39] Twain never claimed to have had a definitive conversion experience, but he did declare while courting Livy that he had become a Christian. Although ministers he had known earlier, especially Franklin Rising, and family members, especially his sister Pamela, planted seeds, Livy, Mary Fairbanks, and Joseph Twichell, all of whom he greatly respected, played the primary role in eliciting Twain's profession of faith. During his scrutiny of Christianity under the tutelage of these three mentors, Twain was attracted to the person, actions, and teaching of Christ. Twain continued to admire Christ in many ways throughout his life, but he could not forgive "the savior," as he often called him, for "inventing" hell.[40]

Hempton explains that his subjects' disenchantment often resulted, like Twain's, from becoming disillusioned with evangelical doctrines and dogma and disgusted with evangelicals' moral lapses. These nine individuals and many others during the second half of the nineteenth century experienced cognitive dissonance when they read the Bible carefully and concluded that it focused on violence, divine judgment, and eternal punishment as much as on love and mercy. For many who abandoned evangelicalism during this period, an aversion to biblical ethics played a greater role than did the difficulties presented by biblical criticism and Darwinian evolution. Many of those who embraced evangelicalism because of its emphasis on love, forgiveness, moral earnestness, and commitment to assisting the disadvantaged and outcasts, Hempton asserts, later repudiated it because of its stress on dogma and the letter, not the spirit, of the law.[41] All this was true for Twain. Although he was somewhat troubled by the issues higher criticism and evolution raised, he was appalled by aspects of biblical morality, especially God's commands to the Israelites to exterminate their enemies and the conception of everlasting physical torment in hell.

Hempton argues that creative personalities were more likely than other Gilded Age people to reject doctrines they viewed as implausible, including the Trinity, biblical inerrancy, and miracles. Many of these artistic individuals also denounced predestination, limited atonement (the concept that Christ's death on the cross atoned for only the elect not all humanity), and eternal punishment as unjust. They often saw evangelicalism as too narrow, dogmatic, sectarian, and exclusive. The disillusioned frequently protested that evangelicals (and Christians more generally) supported the status quo, opposed constructive reforms, served as obstacles to eradicating social evils, and pursued money and fame more than God. Their disappointment with evangelical actions and negative experiences with fellow evangelicals all sowed seeds of disenchantment.[42] Twain similarly complained that many Christians opposed racial and gender equality, supported imperialism and unjust wars, promoted materialism and greed, and even used the Bible to justify their positions. On the other hand, evangelicals had a long history of social activism, and Twain recognized that, inspired by their desire to emulate Christ and care for the least of these, many Christians, especially proponents of the Social Gospel, shared his commitments.[43]

As Hempton argues, orthodox Christians confronted formidable challenges in the Gilded Age. The higher criticism of the Bible and new developments in philosophy and theology threatened the credibility of Scripture and its supernatural presuppositions. Scientific studies, especially ones providing evidence for the earth's lengthy history and evolution of the species through natural selection, raised major questions about the traditional interpretation of Genesis, the uniqueness of human beings, and "the Fall as an explanation for death and imperfections in the natural order." Meanwhile, growing information about the world's cultures and religions cast doubt on the uniqueness of Christianity by emphasizing its similarities with the creation stories, rituals, and cultic practices of other religions. The West's increasing encounter with other religious traditions also raised thorny questions about whether Christianity was the only path to a relationship with God and salvation.

In addition to these developments, Hempton maintains, Christians faced "the more insidious secularizing dynamics of new traditions of realist literature and new experiments in artistic representation." Because evangelicalism was strongly based on the divine authorship of Scripture and the paramount importance of such supernatural events as the virgin birth and bodily resurrection of Christ, it was "especially vulnerable to the new climate of thought." Evangelicals tended to give dogmatic answers to threatening scientific and theological questions, further undermining their belief system's appeal to well-educated and thoughtful individuals.[44] Twain grappled with all these issues. He questioned fundamental Christian doctrines and was especially affected by living many years in Europe and by his world lecture tour, which exposed him to a wide variety of cultures and religious beliefs and practices.

Hempton concludes that disenchantment with one's religious tradition was often "a painful and lonely experience." Some individuals, such as George Eliot and Vincent van Gogh, experienced "a sense of release" by eluding "the constraints of dogmatism," but this plunged others into philosophical confusion, uncertainty, and even despair.[45] That was the case for Twain. Although a few close friends (such as William Dean Howells) shared his doubts about Christianity and others (notably Joseph Twichell) sympathized with his earnest quest for truth, Twain's faith journey was a lonely and often tortuous one. His public notoriety, his desire to preserve his reputation, and his wife's concerns led him to withhold many of his true religious views until after his death. The guilt he experienced for doing this and for, as he feared, destroying Livy's faith weighed heavily upon him.

In addition, Twain's situation was more complicated than that of most of Hempton's subjects in that he rebelled not only against the evangelicalism of Hannibal and the Langdons but against the more liberal Christianity of Twichell, many other clergy friends, and numerous advocates of the Social Gospel. He eventually also became disenchanted with deism and strove to create his own God and belief system. Nevertheless, he never completely escaped the sway of his religious upbringing, his Presbyterian conscience, and the Bible's teaching. Despite his diatribes against God and Christianity, religious orthodoxy influenced him in many ways until his death.

Samuel Clemens Is Dead, but Mark Twain Lives

During the last twenty years of his life, Twain "was an international celebrity and an American institution" feted for both his wit and wisdom. For two decades he was "toasted by royalty, wooed by moguls, and embraced by the intelligentsia," as indicated by the honorary doctorates awarded to him by Johns Hopkins in 1888, Yale in 1901, and Oxford in 1907.[46]

After Twain died on April 21, 1910, obituaries in American and European newspapers and magazines praised his literary accomplishments, character, exposure of artifice and hypocrisy, and prophetic attacks on America's ills. Many editors and pundits lauded Twain as among his era's greatest philosophers, defenders of democracy, and social critics. Some obituaries commented on his religious views and critique of Christianity. Speaking for many, the *Detroit Free Press* proclaimed that "Clemens Is Dead but Mark Twain Lives." Twain's works would forever brighten the lives of millions, declared the *Hartford Courant*. "Through all his tears," the *Presbyterian Banner* asserted, Twain smiled and "led others to smile with him."[47]

The *New York Times* noted that Twain arguably had been the world's supreme living humorist and satirist as well as "the greatest American writer of fiction."[48] *Harper's Magazine* extolled him as "the greatest American writer of his generation."[49] American poet Wilbur Nesbit argued that Twain was Miguel de Cervantes, Thomas Carlyle, Victor Hugo, and Charles Dickens rolled into one.[50] Encomiums compared Twain's stature as a writer to that of Aristophanes, Geoffrey Chaucer, François Rabelais, Jonathan Swift, Washington Irving, William Makepeace Thackeray, and Leo Tolstoy.[51] Others lauded Twain's skill as a lecturer. Only Robert Ingersoll, Hamlin Garland asserted, was as powerful an orator as Twain.[52]

Numerous obituaries spotlighted Twain's prophetic role. The *New York Times* labeled Twain a "Philosopher of Democracy" who loved liberty, hated deception, and advocated every reform that expanded human rights. If Twain situated his critiques of American actions in humorous settings, few people objected. However, when he "dropped the comic mask" and savagely denounced US policy in the Philippines or the actions of missionaries in China, many derided Twain for taking polemical political positions. Twain, the *Dial* declared, attacked "monstrous wickedness" including American political corruption and "the infamy of the royal libertine [Leopold II of Belgium] who distilled a fortune from the blood of the miserable natives of the Congo." Providence had appointed Twain, Stuart Sherman argued, to help preserve the American republic. The *Chautauquan* called him "a staunch and courageous defender" of political morality, freedom, human equality, and democracy who promoted numerous social and industrial reforms, social settlements, and other enterprises to assist immigrants and the poor.[53]

Other obituaries lauded Twain's keen insights into human nature; his critiques of social ills had great "weight and import."[54] He was more of a philosopher than a humorist, the San Francisco *Call* asserted.[55] Twain was a creative artist "in the deeper sense" who accurately assessed the human condition, and a sage to whom Americans looked for counsel as much as amusement.[56] Twain, the *Washington Post* opined, "poked the false gods in the ribs" and "emancipated human beings from their foolish prejudices." He banished sham by making it look ridiculous. To understand the thoughts, temper, and dominant psychology of late nineteenth-century America, the *San Francisco Examiner* maintained, people needed only to read *Innocents Abroad, Tom Sawyer*, and *Huckleberry Finn*.[57]

Other contemporaries commended Twain's character, life, and philosophy. Andrew Carnegie praised Twain's passionate sense of justice. Some lauded his deep affection for his wife and children, integrity, sympathy, efforts to help the needy, and love of truth, justice, and honor.[58] Twain, Edith Wyatt argued in 1917, "was a penetrating and imaginative critic not only of the failures of democracy" around the globe, but also of "the failures of our prevailing theology." For him, she contended, Christianity's explanation of the universe "is too small." In the last ten years, Phelps wrote in 1920, Twain's "fame has grown steadily brighter, his personality more salient and imposing, his masterpieces more mountainous."[59]

A Final Assessment

No American author has attracted as much scholarly or popular attention as Mark Twain. Hundreds of books, articles, and films tell the story of his life, writings, and influence. Two academic journals are dedicated exclusively to publishing material about the literary giant.

During his life, Twain played an incredibly diverse set of roles. He was a preacher, philosopher, moralist, satirist, poet, riverboat pilot, traveler, lecturer, and "sham-smasher."[60] Six weeks before his death, Twain wrote, "if I were to start over again I would be a Reformer."[61] Through his many books, short stories, essays, and novels, Twain preached, prophesied, philosophized, and promoted numerous political and social reforms, impacting countless readers and policymakers in many ways.

Twain was a master of mirth, a teller of tremendous tales, and the sage of satire, but on a deeper level, he was a preacher, prophet, and social philosopher. Like Elijah, whom King Ahab derided as the "troubler of Israel," Twain disturbed America by denouncing complacency, corruption, and callousness. Twain was an instigator, an agitator, and a maverick who challenged the United States to achieve its promise and potential. Although he often delivered his barbs wrapped in humor, Twain insisted that only the cold, hard, unvarnished truth could compel people to understand and work to remedy social ills. Twain would have agreed with celebrated Russian author Aleksandr Solzhenitsyn's statement that "the line separating good and evil cuts through every human heart."[62] For Twain, the battle between good and evil was ferocious, but he saw no way to alleviate it. He judged himself, others, Christian practice, and American culture by very high standards and was acutely afflicted by his own moral failure.[63] Twain, Dwayne Eutsey argues, had an "extraordinary talent to intuit a deeper, universal level of human experience and express it in a uniquely American voice."[64]

One of Twain's last stories depicts a man who tries to prove that he is worthy of entering heaven's gates. After nervously watching a Quaker, a Muslim, an English bishop, a Chinese Buddhist, a Catholic priest, a Freewill Baptist, a Persian fire eater, and a Scottish Presbyterian gain admission, Captain Simon Wheeler, whose religious views were based on his own thought, is questioned by the Beautiful Personage. Wheeler confesses that he "didn't know the right way" and "went a-blundering along and loving everyone" the same—Indians, blacks, Presbyterians, and the Irish. Fearing that he would be rejected because he did not belong to a particular religious group, he begs the examiner to "have pity on a poor ignorant foolish man." To his amazement, his inquisitor tells him that "the gates of heaven stand wide to welcome you!" Whereas all the others who had been admitted must spend eternity with their own groups in specific areas, Wheeler can travel as freely throughout heaven as the angels. As a brother of "all nations and peoples," the whole expanse of the blessed is his home.[65] This story, as much as anything Twain wrote, summarizes his religious convictions, at least on his brighter days.

Louis Budd contends that Twain was burdened by his belief that people were sinful because God created them shabbily with innate defects; humans were thereby "unreformable and incorrigible" and divine grace could not save them. His belief that people were damned and had no hope of redemption produced Twain's pessimism in later life.[66] Edward Wagenknecht maintains that Twain's despondency stemmed from his inability "to believe in a God of Heal, not Hurt, who did not make cancer and yellow fever, but who operated to conquer them." Twain strove to find a secular solution for life's problems and was "profoundly unhappy because he could not."[67] He apparently could not believe that the Bible affirmed rather than despised human frailty and that God could liberate individuals from the shackles of sin and their futile quest for personal righteousness. Twain rejected the view that Christianity brought forgiveness to individuals and promoted goodness, reconciliation, and healing.[68] Stanley Brodwin argues that through his theological protests Twain was seeking release from the damaging impact of the fall and "from the very weight of the Bible itself with its call to repentance and the acceptance of God's creation."[69] Like Huck Finn, Twain believed that he could not attain "the heavenly glory and psychological peace" reserved for God's chosen people.[70]

In the 1870s, Twain befriended another trenchant critic of American Christianity—black abolitionist and civil rights activist Frederick Douglass. Like Douglass, Twain lamented that many Christians used the Bible to justify slavery and treated their slaves inhumanely. Like Douglass, Twain denounced America's systemic racism that endangered African Americans' lives and prevented them from reaching their potential. Twain, however, viewed Jesus very differently from Douglass. "I love the religion of our blessed Savior," Douglass declared, that "is based upon the glorious principle, of love to God and love to man; which makes its followers do unto others as they themselves would be done by." "The Christianity of Christ," Douglass insisted, supplied a powerful foundation for freedom and equality. The Christ who "poured out his blood on Calvary cared for me equally with any white master."[71] Twain viewed Jesus as an exemplary role model and an incredibly empathic individual and praised many of Christ's teachings. But he repudiated Christ's deity, rejected the doctrine that Christ's death on the cross atoned for human sin, and denounced Jesus's "invention" of hell.

What Twain wrote to Livy in December 1868 seems to summarize his entire life: he had gone through another season when "religion seems far away and well-nigh unattainable, and when one feels grimly like jesting with holy things and giving up in despair. Why is it that godliness flies [from] me? Why is it that prayer seems so unavailing and all my searching and seeking a mockery?"[72] Despite his Presbyterian upbringing, substantial knowledge of the Bible, frequent worship at Congregational churches as an adult, friendships with many ministers, and occasional references to himself as a prodigal son, Twain seemed unable to believe the central Christian message that one of his characters in *Pudd'nhead Wilson* clearly articulates: God loves people unconditionally and offers them his grace, and salvation depends on people's response to Christ, not their good deeds.[73] Numerous individuals including his sister Pamela, Franklin Rising, Mary Fairbanks, Livy, Joseph Twichell, and Susan Crane sought to win Twain to Christ. Given the inconsistencies of Twain's pronouncements on religion, some scholars accord him more clarity of theological vision than the facts warrant. In any case, there can be no dispute that despite his statement that "I would not interfere with any one's religion, either to strengthen it or weaken it," Twain quite forcefully challenged people's religious views by raising questions about Christianity, expressing doubts about the Christian God, Jesus, and the Bible, and offering an alternative conception of God.[74]

Laughter, wrote editor and professor Norman Cousins, "is the best medicine."[75] Substantial evidence indicates that laughter reduces stress, lowers blood pressure, improves resilience, and increases happiness.[76] Despite his many personal trials and troubles, Twain, arguably America's greatest physician of humor, dispensed dozens of doses of mirth for five decades. For the last century and a half, millions of readers have benefited from his wit and insights. "You ought to believe in God's goodness," Howells wrote Twain, "since he has bestowed upon the world such a delightful genius as yours to lighten its troubles."[77]

Twain, however, was more than a humorist. As a preacher, prophet, and social philosopher, Twain, like a good doctor, identified human maladies and deficiencies and proposed remedies for ills. His search for truth never brought him philosophical certainty or personal peace, but the questions he posed and the falsehoods and shams he exposed help us think about the most important issues of life—the existence and nature of God, the divinity of Christ, the mission and practice of the Christian church, the disposition of human beings, the veracity of the Bible, and the meaning of life. Harold Bush, Jr. argues that despite all his grief, suffering, doubts, and anger toward God, Twain still expressed hope that shalom—peace, wholeness, tranquility, harmony, and prosperity—would prevail. People throughout the world "still look to Twain for hope, comfort, and courage in times of trouble," thereby affirming his spiritual legacy.[78]

Ironically, a man so wracked with guilt, so tormented by loss, so preoccupied with human foibles, so pessimistic about human nature, and so angry with God wrote some of the world's wittiest prose and evoked laughter in countless people. Strikingly, a man who loved his family and friends so deeply did not, during his final decades, feel the love of God. Sadly, a person who produced such acclaimed literature continually flagellated himself for his personal failures.

Although he also questioned the veracity of some biblical stories, much of Twain's religious skepticism revolved around the common objection that a loving and all-powerful God cannot coexist with the evil and suffering present in this world. Christian apologists generally respond to this objection by arguing that God gave us free will, but we rejected God and brought evil into the world; God could not eliminate evil without overriding free will; God still loves people (and shows his solidarity with our plight through Christ's suffering), and God will make everything right at some future time. If this argument was ever cogently presented to Twain, however, there is no extant evidence of how he evaluated it.

One of America's greatest prophetic voices, neo-Orthodox theologian Reinhold Niebuhr, argued that humor, which recognizes the incongruities of life, "is more profound than any philosophy which seeks" to use reason to "devour incongruity." Nevertheless, Niebuhr insisted, humor deals only "with immediate issues" and "the obvious surface irrationalities. It must move toward faith or sink into despair" when confronting the ultimate issues of life. "Faith is the only possible response to the ultimate incongruities of existence, which threaten the very meaning of our life."[79] "True religion," Niebuhr added, produces "a profound uneasiness about our highest social values."[80] Twain has brought immeasurable laughter to millions and was a staunch critic of the West's principal social values, but he did not ultimately place his faith in God, the Bible, Christianity, or any set of religious principles. Despite his exhaustive searching, he never found a religion that satisfied him as being true or certain.

Notes

1. Van Wyck Brooks, *The Ordeal of Mark Twain* (New York: Dutton, 1920), 127.
2. MTB, 1579.
3. Van Dyke quoted in Cyril Clemens, "Mark Twain's Religion," *Commonweal*, December 28, 1934, 254–5; Mabie, in "MT 70th Birthday Supplement," *Harper's Weekly Magazine* (December 23, 1905), 49.
4. LMT, 69–70, 211; MTB, 1584; MMT, 100.
5. Alexander McKelway, *Presbyterian Standard*, November 14, 1900, 3.
6. LMT, 213; MF, 188; Shelley Fisher Fishkin, *Was Huck Black? Mark Twain and African-American Voices* (New York: Oxford University Press, 1993), 7.
7. MF, 26; William Dean Howell, "Editor's Easy Chair," *Harper's Magazine* 136 (March 1918), 603.
8. MMT, 31. See Thomas Schwartz, "Mark Twain and Robert Ingersoll: The Freethought Connection," *American Literature* 48 (May 1976), 183–93. Twain told Ingersoll's niece that his reverence for Ingersoll "was deep and genuine" (SLC to Eva Farrell, summer, 1899, MTL, 2:682).
9. William Dean Howells, "My Memoirs of Mark Twain," *Harper's Monthly* 121 (July 1910), 178.
10. "What Was Mark Twain's Religion?," *Truth Seeker*, May 7, 1910, 292; William Lyon Phelps, "Mark Twain, Artist," *The American Review of Reviews*, June 1910, https://twain.lib.virginia.edu/sc_as_mt/mtobitm9.html; Stuart Sherman, "Mark Twain," *Nation* 90 (May 12, 1910), https://twain.lib.virginia.edu/sc_as_mt/mtobit6.html; Simeon Stransky,

"Serious Humorists," *Nation* 90 (June 30, 1910), https://twain.lib.vir ginia.edu/sc_as_mt/mtobit6.html.

11. "Last Glimpse of Mark Twain," *New York Times*, April 24, 1910, http://www.twainquotes.com/19100424a.html.

12. "Dr. Van Dyke Conducts the Service," *The Christian Work and the Evangelist* 88 (April 30, 1910), 573, 575–6.

13. "Dr. Van Dyke Conducts the Service," 573, 575–6; Twichell, as quoted in an Associated Press story, April 24, 1910, https://twain.lib.virginia.edu/sc_as_mt/obitap3.html.

14. MTSC, 279.

15. The last phrase is from Lawrence Berkove and Joseph Csicsila, *Heretical Fictions: Religion in the Literature of Mark Twain* (Iowa City: University of Iowa Press, 2010), xv.

16. Max Eastman, *Harper's Magazine*, May 5, 1938, 621; Nelson Burr, "New Eden and New Babylon: Religious Thoughts of American Authors: A Bibliography," *Historical Magazine of the Protestant Episcopal Church* 55 (June 1986), 147; John Q. Hays, *Mark Twain and Religion: A Mirror of American Eclecticism* (New York: Peter Lang, 1989), 12; MTAP, 384; SMT, 170. For similar appraisals, see J. Harold Smith, *Mark Twain: Rebel Pilgrim* (New York: Heath Cote, 1973), 13; Caroline Harnsberger, *Mark Twain's Religion* (Evanston, IL: Schori Press, 1961), 17; and Wesley Britton, "Mark Twain: 'Cradle Skeptic,'" September 1997, http://www.twainweb.net/filelist/skeptic.html.

17. S. T. Joshi, ed., *Mark Twain. What Is Man? and Other Irreverent Essays* (Amherst, NY: Prometheus Books, 2009), 15 (first quotation); second quotation in John Bird, "Swinging the Pendulum: Mark Twain and Religion," *Papers on Language & Literature* 46 (Summer 2010), 342. Cf. Greg Camfield, *The Oxford Companion to Mark Twain* (New York: Oxford University Press, 2003), 156.

18. MTB, 1582; Gary Sloan, "A Connecticut Yankee in God's Court: Mark Twain's Covert War with Religion," *Skeptic* 8:4 (2001), 86.

19. John Timmerman, "Five Travellers," *Reformed Journal*, 6 (May 1956), 9; Stephen Crane, *The Blue Hotel* (1898), https://public.wsu.edu/~campbelld/crane/blue.htm.

20. MTSC, 5, 13, 17, 160; quotations in that order. Bush is quoting Twain's 1906 Tuskegee Institute speech, MTS, 479.

21. William Phipps, "Mark Twain, the Calvinist," *Theology Today* (October 1994), 416; MTMW, 175, 180 (quotation); RMT, 29.

22. Peter Messent, *Mark Twain and Male Friendship: The Twichell, Howells, and Rogers Friendships* (New York: Oxford University Press, 2009), 64.

23. Henry Lindborg, "A Cosmic Tramp: Samuel Clemens' Three Thousand Years Among the Microbes," *American Literature* 44 (January 1973), 656–7.

24. Daniel Pawley, "The Hound of Hannibal," *Christianity Today*, November 8, 1985, https://www.christianitytoday.com/ct/1985/november-8/books.html.

25. Edward Lee Masters, *Mark Twain: A Portrait* (New York: Charles Scribner's Sons, 1938), 15.

26. MTT, 242.

27. CAR, 142–3.

28. RV, 181, 183, 184, 187; quotations in that order.

29. MTC, 162.

30. BA, 178, 169. See NF, 25–77.

31. Brodwin, "Theology of Mark Twain," 170, 187 (first quotation), 188 (second quotation).

32. Dwayne Eutsey, "Waking from This Dream of Separateness: Hinduism and the Ending of *No. 44, The Mysterious Stranger,*" *Mark Twain Annual* 7 (2009), 66.

33. Dwayne Eutsey, "God's 'Real' Message: 'No. 44, The Mysterious Stranger' and the Influence of Liberal Religion on Mark Twain," *Mark Twain Annual* 3 (2005), 55–7; ILR.

34. Bird, "Swinging the Pendulum," 343.

35. Timothy Larsen, conversely, analyzes how seven prominent Victorian secularists reconverted to orthodox Christianity. See *Crisis of Doubt: Honest Faith in Nineteenth-Century England* (New York: Oxford University Press, 2006).

36. See Evelyn Kirkley, *Rational Mothers and Infidel Gentlemen: Gender and American Atheism, 1865–1915* (Syracuse, NY: Syracuse University Press, 2000); Paul Carter, *The Spiritual Crisis of the Gilded Age* (DeKalb, IL: Northern Illinois University Press, 1971); and James Turner, *Without God, Without Creed: The Origins of Unbelief in America* (Baltimore: Johns Hopkins University Press, 1985).

37. See, for example, Ford K. Brown, *Father of the Victorians: The Age of Wilberforce* (Cambridge: Cambridge University Press, 1961); Susan Budd, *Varieties of Unbelief: Atheists and Agnostics in English Society, 1850–1960* (London: Heinemann, 1977); and Edward Babinski, *Leaving the Fold: Testimonies of Former Fundamentalists* (Amherst, NY: Prometheus Books, 1995).

38. David Hempton, *Evangelical Disenchantment: Nine Portraits of Faith and Doubt* (New Haven, CT: Yale University Press, 2008), 12.

39. Hempton, *Evangelical Disenchantment*, 190. See, for example, D. Bruce Hindmarsh, *The Evangelical Conversion Narrative: Spiritual Autobiography in*

Early Modern England (Oxford: Oxford University Press, 2005); and David Bebbington, *Evangelicalism in Modern Britain: A History from the 1730s to the 1980s* (London: Routledge, 1996), 7.

40. Many of Hempton's subjects retained a love for evangelical hymns long after they abandoned the tradition's "propositional truth claims" (*Evangelical Disenchantment*, 194). As noted, this was the case for both Twain and Livy.

41. Hempton, *Evangelical Disenchantment*, 190–1, 193–4. See also Dominic Erdozain, *The Soul of Doubt: The Religious Roots of Unbelief from Luther to Marx* (New York: Oxford University Press, 2016).

42. Hempton, *Evangelical Disenchantment*, 191–3.

43. See, for example, Timothy Smith, *Revivalism and Social Reform: American Protestantism on the Eve of the Civil War* (Baltimore: Johns Hopkins University Press, 1980); Kathleen Heasman, *Evangelicals in Action: An Appraisal of Their Social Work* (London: Geoffrey Bles, 1962); and Norris Magnuson, *Salvation in the Slums: Evangelical Social Work, 1865–1920* (Grand Rapids, MI: Baker Book House, 1990).

44. Hempton, *Evangelical Disenchantment*, 196.

45. Hempton, *Evangelical Disenchantment*, 197.

46. Sloan, "Connecticut Yankee," 86.

47. "Clemens Is Dead but Mark Twain Lives," *Detroit Free Press*, April 23, 1910, https://twain.lib.virginia.edu/sc_as_mt/mtobit21.html; "Death of Mark Twain," *Presbyterian Banner* 96 (April 28, 1910), 3.

48. "Mark Twain Is Dead at 74," *New York Times*, April 22, 1910.

49. "Mark Twain," *Harper's Weekly*, April 30, 1910, https://twain.lib.virginia.edu/sc_as_mt/mtobit32.html.

50. Wilbur Nesbit, "Tributes to Mark Twain," *North American Review* 191 (June 1910), 832.

51. "Twain's Death This Time Not 'Exaggerated,'" *Cleveland News*, April 22, 1910; "Mark Twain," *Dial* 48 (May 1, 1910), https://twain.lib.virginia.edu/sc_as_mt/mtobit4.html.

52. Hamlin Garland, "Tributes to Twain," 833.

53. "Mark Twain—Philosopher of Democracy," *New York Times*, April 24, 1910; "Mark Twain," *Dial*; Sherman, "Mark Twain"; "The Death of Mark Twain," *Chautauquan* 59 (June 1910), https://twain.lib.virginia.edu/sc_as_mt/mtobit5.html.

54. Mark Twain, "Humanist," *Kansas City Star*, April 22, 1910, https://twain.lib.virginia.edu/sc_as_mt/mtobit28.html; "Mark Twain," *Dial*.

55. "America Mourns for Mark Twain," San Francisco *Call*, April 23, 1910, https://twain.lib.virginia.edu/sc_as_mt/mtobit30.html.

56. "Mark Twain," *Dial*.

57. "Mark Twain," *Washington Post*, April 22, 1910, https://twain.lib.virginia.edu/sc_as_mt/mtobit9.html; "A Great Author; A True American," *San Francisco Examiner*, April 22, 1910, https://twain.lib.virginia.edu/sc_as_mt/mtobit27.html.

58. "Clemens Is Dead"; "A Great Author"; "A Great Man Passes," *(Richmond) Times Dispatch*, April 22, 1910, https://twain.lib.virginia.edu/sc_as_mt/mtobit14.html; "Mark Twain," *Harper's Weekly*, April 30, 1910 (quotation), https://twain.lib.virginia.edu/sc_as_mt/mtobit32.html. Cf. "Mark Twain, World-Servant," *Atlanta Constitution*, April 23, 1910, https://twain.lib.virginia.edu/sc_as_mt/mtobit10.html; and *Outlook* 30 (April 1910), https://twain.lib.virginia.edu/sc_as_mt/mtobitm6.html.

59. Edith Wyatt, "An Inspired Critic," *North American Review* 205 (April 1917), 612, 613; quotations in that order; William Lyon Phelps, "Mark Twain, Chief of Sinners," *New York Times*, June 27, 1920, sec. 5, 1–2.

60. "Mark Twain 70th Birthday Supplement," *Harper's Weekly Magazine*, December 23, 1905, https://twain.lib.virginia.edu/sc_as_mt/70birthday/harpers02.html.

61. SLC to the author, March 12, 1910 letter, in Elizabeth Wallace, *Mark Twain and the Happy Island* (Chicago: A. C. McClurg, 1913), 138.

62. Aleksandr Solzhenitsyn, *The Gulag Archipelago*, vol. 1, trans. Thomas Whitney (New York: Harper & Row), 168.

63. MTSC, 9.

64. Eutsey, "Liberal Religion."

65. "Captain Simon Wheeler's Dream Visit to Heaven," in *The Bible According to Mark Twain*, ed. Howard Baetzbold and Joseph McCullough (Athens: University of Georgia Press, 1995), 191–4; first quotation from 193; others from 194.

66. Louis Budd, "Mark Twain on Joseph the Patriarch," *American Quarterly* 16 (Winter 1964), 182.

67. MTMW, 199, 216.

68. David Zahl, review of *Strange Rites: New Religions for a Godless World*, in *Christianity Today*, September 2020, 73. Zahl is discussing the benefits of Christianity, not Twain specifically.

69. Brodwin, "Theology of Mark Twain," 189.

70. RV, 185.

71. Frederick Douglass, "An Appeal to the British People," in *Selected Speeches and Writings*, ed. Philip Foner (Chicago: Lawrence Hill Books, 1999), 37; John Blassingame, *The Frederick Douglass Papers*, Series One: *Speeches, Debates, and Interviews*, Volume 1, *1841–1846* (New Haven, CT: Yale University Press, 1979), 328–9 (second quotation). See D. H. Dilbeck,

Frederick Douglass: American Prophet (Chapel Hill: University of North Carolina Press, 2018).

72. SLC to OLC, December 30, 1868, MTP.
73. Through the character of Roxy, Twain declares the orthodox position on salvation through God's grace. See PW, 26.
74. MTB, 1584.
75. Norman Cousins, "Anatomy of an Illness," *New England Journal of Medicine* 295 (1976), 1458–63.
76. E.g., Kavita Khajuria, "Laughter Is the Best Medicine," *Psychiatric Times*, August 17, 2018, https://www.psychiatrictimes.com/view/laughter-best-medicine.
77. WDH to SLC, March 22, 1880, https://www.marktwainproject.org/xtf/view?docId=letters/UCCL09197.xml;query=twichell%20god;searchAll=;sectionType1=;sectionType2=;sectionType3=;sectionType4=;sectionType5=;style=letter;brand=mtp#1.
78. MTSC, 284.
79. Reinhold Niebuhr, "Humor and Faith," in *Discerning the Signs of the Times: Sermons for Today and Tomorrow* (London: SCM Press, 1946), 112.
80. Reinhold Niebuhr, *Beyond Tragedy: Essays on the Christian Interpretation of History* (New York: Scribner's, 1937), 28.

Selected Bibliography

Primary Sources

Autobiography of Mark Twain. 3 vols. Berkeley: University of California Press: vol. 1, ed. Harriet Elinor Smith and Benjamin Griffin (2012); vol. 2, ed. Benjamin Griffin, Harriet Elinor Smith, Victor Fischer, and Michael Frank (2013); vol. 3, ed. Benjamin Griffin, Harriet Elinor Smith, and Grover Gardner (2015).

Bush, Harold, Steve Courtney, and Peter Messent, eds. *The Letters of Mark Twain and Joseph Hopkins Twichell*. Athens: University of Georgia Press, 2017.

DeVoto, Bernard, ed. *Mark Twain in Eruption*. New York: Harper, 1922.

Fatout, Paul, ed. *Mark Twain Speaking*. Iowa City: University of Iowa Press, 1976.

Frank, Michael and Harriet Elinor Smith, eds. *Mark Twain's Letters, 1876–80*. Berkeley: University of California Press, 2007.

Gibson, William, ed. *Mark Twain's Mysterious Stranger Manuscripts*. Berkeley: University of California Press, 1969.

Mark Twain Papers, The Mark Twain Collection, Bancroft Library, University of California, Berkeley.

Mark Twain's Letters. 6 vols. Berkeley: University of California Press: vol. 1: 1853–1866; vol. 2: 1867–1868; vol. 3: 1869; vol. 4: 1870–1871; 5: 1872–1873; vol. 6: 1874–1875.

Mark Twain's Letters. Electronic vols. 1–5: 1876–1880. Mark Twain Project.

Mark Twain's Notebook and Journals. 3 vols. Berkeley: University of California Press, 1975–1979: vol. 1: 1855–1873, ed. Frederick Anderson, Michael Frank, and Kenneth Sanderson; vol. 2: 1877–1883, ed. Frederick Anderson, Lin Salamo, and Bernard Stein; vol. 3: 1883–1891, ed. Robert Pack Browning, Michael Frank, and Lin Salamo.

Neider, Charles, ed. *Complete Short Stories of Mark Twain*. New York: Bantam Books, 1981.

Neider, Charles. *Outrageous Mark Twain: Some Lesser-Known but Extraordinary Works With "Reflections on Religion."* New York: Doubleday, 1987.

Paine, Albert Bigelow, ed. *Mark Twain's Autobiography*. 2 vols. New York: Harper, 1924.

Paine, Albert Bigelow, ed. *Mark Twain's Letters*. 2 vols. New York: Harper, 1917.

Paine, Albert Bigelow, ed. *Mark Twain's Notebook*. New York: Harper, 1935.

Paine, Albert Bigelow, ed. *Mark Twain's Speeches*. New York: Harper and Brothers, 1923.

Paine, Albert Bigelow, ed. *Writings of Mark Twain*. 35 vols. New York: Gabriel Wells, 1922–1925.

Scharnhorst, Gary, ed. *Mark Twain: The Complete Interviews*. Tuscaloosa: University of Alabama Press, 2006.

Smith, Henry Nash and William Gibson, eds. *Mark Twain-Howells Letters*. 2 vols. Cambridge, MA: Harvard University Press, 1960.

Smith, Janet, ed. *Mark Twain on the Damned Human Race*. New York: Hill and Wang, 1962.

Tuckey, John, Kenneth Sanderson, and Bernard Stein, eds. *Mark Twain's Fables of Man*. Berkeley: University of California Press, 2000.

Twain, Mark. *The Adventures of Huckleberry Finn*. Hartford, CT: American Publishing, 1885.

Twain, Mark. *The Adventures of Tom Sawyer*. Hartford, CT: American Publishing, 1876.

Twain, Mark. *Christian Science*. New York: Harper, 1907.

Twain, Mark. *Collected Tales, Sketches, Speeches, and Essays*, vol. 1: *1852–1890*, ed. Louis Budd. New York: Library of America, 1992.

Twain, Mark. *Collected Tales, Sketches, Speeches, and Essays*, vol. 2: *1891–1910*. New York: Library of America, 1992.

Twain, Mark. *A Connecticut Yankee in King's Arthur's Court*. New York: Charles L. Webster, 1889.

Twain, Mark. "The Czar's Soliloquy." *The North American Review* 180 (March 1905), 321–6.

Twain, Mark. *Early Tales & Sketches*, vol. 2: *1864–1869*, ed. Edgar Marquess Branch, Robert Hirst, and Harriet Elinor Smith. Berkeley: University of California Press, 1981.

Twain, Mark. *Europe and Elsewhere*. New York: Harper and Brothers, 1923.

Twain, Mark. *Following the Equator*. Hartford, CT: American Publishing, 1897.

Twain, Mark. *The Innocents Abroad: or the New Pilgrim's Progress Being Some Account of the Steamship Quaker City's Pleasure Excursion to Europe and the Holy Land*. Hartford, CT: American Publishing, 1869.

Twain, Mark. *King Leopold's Soliloquy: A Defence of His Congo Rule*. London: Unwin, 1907.

Twain, Mark. *Letters from Earth*, ed. Bernard DeVoto. New York: Harper & Row, 1962.

Twain, Mark. *Letters from the Sandwich Islands*. New York: Haskell House, 1866.

Twain, Mark. *The Man That Corrupted Hadleyburg and Other Essays and Stories*. New York: Harper and Brothers, 1900.

Twain, Mark. "To My Missionary Critics." *The North American Review* 172 (April 1901), 520–34.

Twain, Mark. "To the Person Sitting in Darkness." *The North American Review* 172 (February 1901), 161–76.

Twain, Mark. *Pudd'nhead Wilson*. Hartford, CT: Charles L. Webster, 1894.

Twain, Mark. *Roughing It*. Hartford, CT: American Publishing, 1872.

Twain, Mark. *A Tramp Abroad*. Hartford, CT: American Publishing, 1880.

Twain, Mark. "A True Story, Repeated Word for Word as I Heard It." *Atlantic Monthly* 34 (November 1874), 591–4.

Twain, Mark. "The Turning Point in My Life." *Harper's Bazaar* 44 (February 1910).

Twain, Mark. "The War Prayer." https://warprayer.org/.

Twain, Mark. *The Washoe Giant in San Francisco*, ed. Franklin Walker. San Francisco: Fields 1938.

Twain, Mark. *What Is Man? and Other Essays*. New York: Harper and Brothers, 1917.

Twain, Mark. *What Is Man? and Other Philosophical Writings*, ed. Paul Baender. Berkeley: University of California Press, 1973.

Twain, Mark and Charles Dudley Warner. *The Gilded Age*. Hartford, CT: American Publishing. 1873.

Wecter, Dixon, ed. *Love Letters of Mark Twain*. New York: Harper, 1949.

Wecter, Dixon, ed. *Mark Twain to Mrs. Fairbanks*. San Marino, CA: Huntington Library, 1949.

Zwick, Jim, ed. *Mark Twain's Weapons of Satire: Anti-Imperialist Writings on the Philippine-American War*. Syracuse, NY: Syracuse University Press, 1992.

Secondary Sources

Andrews, Kenneth. *Nook Farm: Mark Twain's Hartford Circle*. Cambridge, MA: Harvard University Press, 1950.

Baetzhold, Howard and Joseph McCullough, eds. *The Bible according to Mark Twain*. New York: Touchstone, 1995.

Berkove, Lawrence and Joseph Csicsila. *Heretical Fictions: Religion in the Literature of Mark Twain*. Iowa City: University of Iowa Press, 2010.

Bird, John. "Swinging the Pendulum: Mark Twain and Religion." *Papers on Language & Literature* 46 (Summer 2010), 342–6.

Boller, Paul. "Mark Twain's Credo." *Southwest Review* 63 (Spring 1978), 150–62.

Britton, Wesley. "Mark Twain: 'Cradle Skeptic.'" September 1997. http://www.twainweb.net/filelist/skeptic.html.

Brodwin, Stanley. "Mark Twain's Theology: The Gods of a Brevet Presbyterian." In *The Cambridge Companion to Mark Twain*, ed. Forrest Robinson, 220–48. New York: Cambridge University Press, 1995.

Brodwin, Stanley. "The Theology of Mark Twain: Banished Adam and the Bible." *Mississippi Quarterly* 29 (1976), 167–89.

Brooks, Van Wyck. *The Ordeal of Mark Twain*. New York: Dutton, 1920.

Bush, Jr., Harold. *Continuing Bonds with the Dead: Parental Grief and Nineteenth-Century American Authors*. Tuscaloosa: University Alabama Press, 2016.

Bush, Jr., Harold. *Mark Twain and the Spiritual Crisis of His Age*. Tuscaloosa: University of Alabama Press, 2007.

Camfield, Gregg. *The Oxford Companion to Mark Twain*. New York: Oxford University Press, 2003.

Carter, Paul. "Mark Twain and the American Labor Movement." *New England Quarterly* 30 (September 1957), 352–8.

Chadwick-Joshua, Jocelyn. *The Jim Dilemma: Reading Race in Huckleberry Finn.* Jackson: University Press of Mississippi, 1998.

Clemens, Clara. *My Father, Mark Twain.* New York: Harper, 1931.

Coplin, Keith. *John and Sam Clemens: A Father's Influence.* Kirkwood, MO: Mark Twain Memorial Association, 1970.

Cullen, Lynn. *Twain's End.* New York: Gallery Books, 2015.

Cummings, Sherwood. *Mark Twain and Science.* Baton Rouge: Louisiana State University Press, 1988.

De Voto, Bernard, ed. *Mark Twain in Eruption.* New York: Harper and Brothers, 1940.

Durocher, Aurele. "Mark Twain and the Roman Catholic Church." *Journal of the Central Mississippi Valley American Studies Association* 1 (Fall 1960), 32–43.

Ensor, Allison. *Mark Twain and the Bible.* Lexington: University of Kentucky Press, 1969.

Eutsey, Dwayne. "Be Never Afraid of Doubt": Mark Twain, Liberal Religion, and Huck Finn." October 7, 2018, http://uufeaston.org/services/never-afraid-doubt-mark-twain-liberal-religion-huck-finn/.

Eutsey, Dwayne. "God's 'Real' Message: 'No. 44, The Mysterious Stranger' and the Influence of Liberal Religion on Mark Twain." *Mark Twain Annual* 3 (September 2005), 53–66.

Eutsey, Dwayne. "The Influence of Liberal Religion on Mark Twain." https://www.meadville.edu/files/resources/v1-n2-eutsey-the-influence-of-liberal-religion-on-.pdf.

Eutsey, Dwayne. "Mark Twain's Attitudes toward Religion: Sympathy for the Devil or Radical Christianity?" *Religion & Literature* 31 (Summer 1999), 45–64.

Fatout, Paul. *Mark Twain in Virginia City.* Bloomington: Indiana University Press, 1964.

Fessenden, Tracy. *Culture and Redemption: Religion, the Secular and American Literature.* Princeton, NJ: Princeton University Press 2012.

Fishkin, Shelley Fisher. *Lighting Out for the Territory: Reflections on Mark Twain and American Culture.* New York: Oxford University Press, 1997.

Fishkin, Shelley Fisher. "Mark Twain and the Jews." *Arizona Quarterly* 61 (Spring 2005), 137–66.

Fishkin, Shelley Fisher. "Mark Twain and Race." In *A Historical Guide to Mark Twain,* ed. Shelley Fisher Fishkin, 127–62. New York: Oxford University Press, 2002.

Fishkin, Shelley Fisher. *Was Huck Black? Mark Twain and African-American Voices.* New York: Oxford University Press, 1993.

Foner, Philip. *Mark Twain: Social Critic.* New York: International Publishers, 1958.

Frear, Walter Francis. *Mark Twain and Hawaii.* Chicago: Lakeside Press, 1947.

Fulton, Joe. *Mark Twain Under Fire: Reception and Reputation, Criticism and Controversy, 1851–2015.* Rochester, NY: Camden House, 2016.

Fulton, Joe. *Reverend Mark Twain: Theological Burlesque, Form, and Content.* Columbus: Ohio State University Press, 2006.

Geismar, Maxwell. *Mark Twain: An American Prophet.* Boston: Houghton Mifflin, 1970.

Gribben, Alan. *Mark Twain's Library: A Reconstruction.* 2 vols. Boston: G. K. Hall, 1980.

Harnsberger, Caroline. *Mark Twain's Religion.* Evanston, IL: Schori Press, 1961.

Harris, Susan K. *The Courtship of Olivia Langdon and Mark Twain.* Cambridge: Cambridge University Press, 1996.

Harris, Susan K. "Mark Twain and Gender." In *A Historical Guide to Mark Twain,* ed. Shelley Fisher Fishkin, 163–94. New York: Oxford University Press, 2002.

Hawkins, Hunt. "Mark Twain's Involvement with the Congo Reform Movement: 'A Fury of Generous Indignation.'" *New England Quarterly* 51 (June 1978), 147–75.

Hays, John Q. *Mark Twain and Religion: A Mirror of American Eclecticism.* New York: Peter Lang, 1989.

Hoffman, Donald. *Mark Twain in Paradise: His Voyages to Bermuda.* Columbia: University of Missouri Press, 2006.

Holland, Jeffrey. "Soul-Butter and Hogwash: Mark Twain and Frontier Religion." March 8, 1977, https://speeches.byu.edu/talks/jeffrey-r-holland/soul-butter-hogwash-mark-twain-frontier-religion/.

Howells, William Dean. *My Mark Twain.* New York: Harper, 1910.

Howells, William Dean. "My Memoirs of Mark Twain." *Harper's Monthly* 121 (July 1910), 165–78.

Jones, Alexander. "Mark Twain and the Determinism of *What Is Man?*" *American Literature* 29 (March 1957), 1–17.

Kaplan, Fred. *The Singular Mark Twain.* New York: Anchor Books, 2003.

Kaplan, Justin. *Mr. Clemens and Mark Twain.* New York: Simon & Schuster, 1966.

Lawton, Mary. *A Lifetime with Mark Twain: Katy Leary, for Thirty Years His Faithful and Devoted Servant.* New York: Harcourt, Brace, 1925.

Leary, Lewis, ed. *Mark Twain's Correspondence with Henry Huttleston Rogers, 1893–1909.* Berkeley: University of California Press, 1969.

Leonard, James, Thomas Tenney, and Thadious Davis, eds. *Satire or Evasion? Black Perspectives on Huckleberry Finn.* Durham, NC: Duke University Press, 1992.

Loving, Jerome. *Mark Twain: The Adventures of Samuel L. Clemens.* Berkeley: University of California Press, 2011.

Lystra, Karen. *Dangerous Intimacy: The Untold Story of Mark Twain's Final Years.* Berkeley: University of California Press, 2004.

McCullough, Joseph and Janice McIntire-Strasburg, eds. *Mark Twain at the Buffalo Express.* Dekalb: Northern Illinois University Press, 1999.

McMahan, Elizabeth. "Finance and Fantasy as Destroyers in Twain's 'The $30,000 Bequest.'" *Mark Twain Journal* 21 (Summer 1982), 23–6.

Messent, Peter. *Mark Twain and Male Friendships: The Twichell, Howells, and Rogers Friendships*. New York: Oxford University Press, 2009.

Morris, Jr., Roy. *American Vandal: Mark Twain Abroad*. Cambridge, MA: Harvard University Press, 2015.

Nixon, Jude. "God." In *The Mark Twain Encyclopedia*, ed. J. R. LeMaster and Jim Wilson, 323–8. New York: Garland, 1993.

Paine, Albert Bigelow. *Mark Twain, a Biography*. New York: Harper, 1912.

Phipps, William. *Mark Twain's Religion*. Macon, GA: Mercer University Press, 2003.

Powers, Ron. *Dangerous Waters: A Biography of the Boy Who Became Mark Twain*. New York: Basic Books, 1999.

Powers, Ron. *Mark Twain: A Life*. New York: Free Press, 2005.

Quirk, Tom. *Mark Twain and Human Nature*. Columbia: University of Missouri Press, 2007.

Reesman, Jeanne Campbell. "Mark Twain vs. God: The Story of a Relationship." *Mark Twain Journal* 52 (Fall 2014), 112–35.

Robinson, Forrest. *In Bad Faith: The Dynamics of Deception in Mark Twain's America*. Cambridge, MA: Harvard University Press, 1986.

Schwartz, Thomas. "Mark Twain and Robert Ingersoll: The Freethought Connection." *American Literature* 48 (1976), 183–93.

Shelden, Michael. *Mark Twain: Man in White. The Grand Adventure of His Final Years*. New York: Random House, 2010.

Sloan, Gary. "Mark Twain's Secret Vendetta with the Almighty." May 2001, https://ffrf.org/faq/feeds/item/17327-mark-twains-secret-vendetta-with-the-almighty.

Smith, Henry Nash, ed. *Mark Twain of the "Enterprise."* Berkeley: University of California Press, 1957.

Strong, Leah. *Joseph Hopkins Twichell: Mark Twain's Friend and Pastor*. Athens: University of Georgia Press, 1966.

Townsend, James. "Grace in the Arts: Mark Twain: A Bitter Battle with God." *Journal of the Grace Evangelical Society* 17 (Autumn 2004).

Varble, Rachel. *Jane Clemens: The Story of Mark Twain's Mother*. Garden City, NY: Doubleday, 1964.

Wagenknecht, Edward. *Mark Twain: The Man and His Work*. Norman: University of Oklahoma Press, 1967.

Walker, Franklin and G. Ezra Dane, eds. *Mark Twain's Travels with Mr. Brown*. New York: Knopf, 1940.

Wecter, Dixon. *Sam Clemens of Hannibal*. Boston: Houghton Mifflin, 1961.

Weir, Robert. "Mark Twain and Social Class." In *A Historical Guide to Mark Twain*, ed. Shelley Fisher Fishkin, 195–225. New York: Oxford University Press, 2002.

Wilson, James. "In Quest of Redemptive Vision: Mark Twain's Joan of Arc." *Texas Studies in Literature and Language* 20 (Summer 1978), 181–98.

Wilson, James. "Religious and Esthetic Vision in Mark Twain's Early Career." *Canadian Review of American Studies* 17 (Summer 1986), 155–72.

Zwick, Jim. "Mark Twain and Imperialism." In *A Historical Guide to Mark Twain*, ed. Shelley Fisher Fishkin, 227–55. New York: Oxford University Press, 2002.

Zwick, Jim. "'Prodigally Endowed with Sympathy for the Cause': Mark Twain's Involvement with the Anti-Imperialist League." *Mark Twain Journal* 32 (Spring 1994), 3–25.

Index

For the benefit of digital users, indexed terms that span two pages (e.g., 52–53) may, on occasion, appear on only one of those pages.